By Maida Heatter

Maida Heatter's Book of Great Desserts (1974)

Maida Heatter's Book of Great Cookies (1977)

These are Borzoi Books, published by Alfred A. Knopf.

Maida Heatter's
Book of
Great Cookies

MAIDA HEATTER'S

BOOK
OF GREAT
COOKIES

Drawings by Toni Evins

ALFRED A. KNOPF   NEW YORK   1978

THIS IS A BORZOI BOOK
PUBLISHED BY ALFRED A. KNOPF, INC.

Copyright © 1977 by Maida Heatter

All rights reserved under International and Pan-American
Copyright Conventions. Published in the United States
by Alfred A. Knopf, Inc., New York, and simultaneously in
Canada by Random House of Canada Limited, Toronto.
Distributed by Random House, Inc., New York.

Library of Congress Cataloging in Publication Data

Heatter, Maida.
   Maida Heatter's Book of great cookies.

   Includes index.
   1. Cookies.   I. Title.   II. Title: Book of great cookies.
TX772.H4   1977   641.8′654   77–3337
ISBN 0–394–41021–1

Manufactured in the United States of America

Published September 8, 1977
Reprinted Three Times
Fifth Printing, December 1978

Contents

Introduction

Two women shared the same prison cell for twenty years. At the end of that time one of the women was released. The guards led her out through the front gates. As the gates closed behind her she ran back screaming, "Mary, Mary, I forgot to tell you something."

I felt like that woman when, after working for years on a dessert cookbook, I finally mailed the finished manuscript to the publisher. And then I suddenly remembered a whole batch of great cookie recipes that I had forgotten to include. They were the beginning of this collection.

Cookies are very special to me. All cooking and baking can be great fun and a wonderful escape, but cookies are in a class by themselves. I feel that one can be especially creative with cookies, actually handling the dough—kneading, shaping, building, designing.

I was talking to a friend who is an excellent cook and I was shocked when she said, "I haven't baked cookies since I was a little girl." Too bad—what fun she's been missing.

Another friend told me that she loves to bake cookies but not cakes. It is too frustrating for her not to be able to cut into a cake to see what it looks and tastes like before she serves it, but eating a few cookies does not affect the rest of them. She also said that she prefers cookies because, since you can usually stop at many stages along the way, she feels less pressure and finds it more relaxing.

My philosophy is that cookies are fun—pure, simple fun. You don't make cookies if you're hassled. It's not like pot roast—you don't *have* to make cookies.

Cookies are love, the love of making them and the love of sharing them. (It is so much looser and easier to bring someone a few cookies than a layer cake or chocolate mousse.)

One more word about this book—about any cookbook—before you get down to the serious (fun) business of making the cookies. A cookbook should be treated like a school textbook. When reading it, or cooking from it, keep a pencil handy for notations. Underline things you especially want to remember, make notes—just don't be afraid to write in it. Write your experiences with the recipes and any changes you make. (For instance, "bake 3 minutes longer," "use pecans instead of walnuts," "cut these thinner," or "these are the ones I made when S and G came to dinner." Or "divine" or "troublesome.") In the future you will find that your own notes have added to the book and made it more valuable to you.

Maida Heatter's
Book of
Great Cookies

Equipment

ALUMINUM FOIL

Many of these recipes call for placing the cookies on sheets of aluminum foil. (I have been accused of having some secret interest in South American tin mines.)

Most of these recipes specify placing the cookies on aluminum foil and then sliding a cookie sheet under the foil for baking. The foil is not called for in order to keep your cookie sheets clean (although it will, and if you do a lot of cookying you will be delighted with not having to wash and dry the sheets).

There are other reasons for using the foil. It will keep the cookies from sticking, and some of the really thin wafer-type cookies, which would be a problem without the foil, will be easy and fun if you use it. I also find that in many recipes the cookies hold their shape better on foil than they do on buttered sheets; often the butter makes them run too thin and become too brown on the edges. Another reason is mathematics—if you have only two sheets, and if you need four or five for a recipe, by using the foil you can prepare all of the cookies for baking, place them on the foil, and then just slide a sheet under the foil when you are ready to bake them. (You do not have to wait for the cookie sheet to cool.)

Therefore, the recipes say to cut the foil, place the cookies on it, slide a sheet under, and bake. I find this system works very well.

However, if you have as many cookie sheets as you might need for a recipe, and if you prefer to place the foil on the sheets before placing the cookies on the foil, by all means do so.

Either way, the foil may be wiped clean with a paper towel and re-used as often as you wish.

CELLOPHANE

I like to wrap bar cookies in clear cellophane (as you will see in reading the recipes). It gives them an attractive, professional look, keeps them fresh, easy to handle, easy to pack for the freezer or a lunch box or picnic, and it is quick and easy to slip a few of them into a little bag or a basket as a gift.

But clear cellophane is hard to find. It is available from wholesale paper companies, the kind that sells restaurant supplies. And in my experience most of them are agreeable about selling to individuals. The cellophane comes in rolls of different widths. It is easier to handle if the roll is not too wide. And it is easier to cut with a knife than with scissors. Cut off a long piece, fold it in half, cut through the fold with a long knife, fold again and cut again, and continue to fold and cut until you have the right-size pieces. If the size is close but a bit too large in one direction, do not cut them individually (it takes too long). Instead, place the whole pile in front of you, fold one side of the entire pile to the size you want, and hold the folded portion with one hand while, with the other hand, you cut through the fold with the knife.

Wrap one cookie as a sample to be sure that the cellophane is the right size.

Then, if you have room, spread out as many pieces of the cellophane as you will need, or as you have room for. Place a cookie in the center of each piece of cellophane (1). Bring the two long sides together up over the top (2). Fold over twice so that the second fold brings the paper tight against the cookie (3, 4). Now, instead of just tucking the ends underneath, fold in the corners of each end, making a triangular point (5) and then fold the triangle down under the cookie (6).

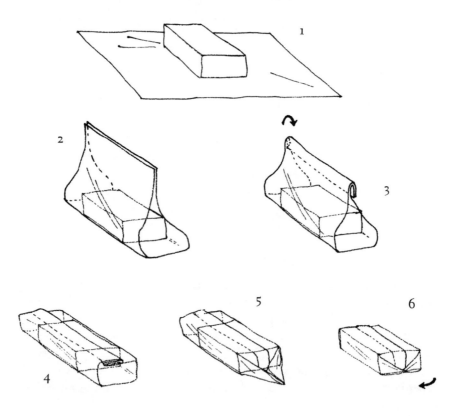

COOKIE CUTTERS

Obviously it is not necessary to use exactly the same size or shape cutter that the recipe calls for; that is just a guide. Cutters should be sharp with no rough edges. If the cutter sticks to the dough dip it into flour each time. Always start cutting at the edge of the dough and work toward the center, cutting the cookies as close to each other as possible.

COOKIE SHEETS

A cookie sheet should be flat, with only one raised side (that's for handling the sheet). The other three sides should not have a raised edge. Shiny, bright aluminum sheets are best. Cookie sheets should be at least 2 inches narrower and shorter than the oven so the heat will circulate around them and the cookies will bake evenly. Generally 12 by 15½ inches is the most practical size.

COOLING RACKS

You should have several cooling racks. Almost all cookies should be removed from the cookie sheet immediately after baking (unless the recipe specifies otherwise) and cooled with air circulating around them. Many racks are not raised enough for air to circulate underneath, which causes the bottoms of the cookies to be damp or soggy instead of dry and crisp (there should be ½ inch for thin, crisp wafers, 2 inches for large cookies). To raise the racks (especially if the cookies are large and/or thick), simply place the rack on a right-side-up cake pan or bowl.

DOUBLE BOILER

A double boiler is important, especially for melting chocolate, which should never come into direct contact with high heat or it will burn. (For melting chocolate with no other ingredients, make absolutely sure that the top of the double boiler is bone dry.) If necessary, you can create a double boiler by placing the ingredients in a heat-proof bowl over a saucepan containing an inch or so of hot water. The bowl should be wide enough so that the rim rests on the rim of the saucepan and the bowl is supported above the water.

ELECTRIC MIXER

An electric mixer is a time and labor saver, but almost all cookies may be made by creaming (or beating until soft) the butter in a bowl, using a wooden spoon or spatula, and then stirring in the remaining ingredients. I use an electric mixer on a stand, the type that comes with two different-size bowls. But I have made many cookies for which I creamed the butter with my bare hands and then, with my hands, worked in the remaining ingredients.

FLOUR SIFTER

With very few exceptions these recipes call for sifted flour. This means that you should sift it immediately before measuring it, even if the flour label says presifted. (If the flour is not sifted, or if it is sifted a long time before it is to be used, it packs down and 1 cup is liable to contain a few more spoonfuls than 1 cup of flour sifted immediately before measuring.)

Sift the flour onto a piece of wax paper. Make sure that there is no flour left in the sifter, and transfer the sifter to another piece of wax paper. Measure the amount you need of the sifted flour, place it in the sifter, add any other ingredients it is to be sifted together with, and sift onto the second piece of wax paper. Again, make sure that there is nothing left in the sifter.

If you don't have a sifter, flour can be sifted through a fine-mesh strainer.

GRATER

A few of these recipes call for grated lemon or orange rind. It is best to grate the fruit on a grater that has different-size and -shape openings. Use the side that has small round openings, rather than the diamond-shaped ones. And do not grate deeply. What you want is only the thinnest outer layer—the white part is bitter.

MEASURING CUPS

Glass or plastic measuring cups with the measurements marked on the sides and the 1-cup line below the top are only for measuring liquids. With the cup at eye level, fill carefully to measure exactly the amount needed.

To measure dry ingredients use the metal cups that come in sets of four: ¼ cup, ⅓ cup, ½ cup, and 1 cup. Fill to overflowing (if you are measuring flour do not pack it down) and then scrape off the extra with a metal spatula, a dough scraper, or the straight edge of a knife.

MEASURING SPOONS

Standard measuring spoons must be used for correct measurements. They come in sets of four: ¼ teaspoon, ½ teaspoon, 1 teaspoon, and 1 tablespoon. When measuring dry ingredients fill the spoon to overflowing and then scrape off the excess with a small metal spatula or the straight edge of a knife.

NUT GRINDER

When recipes call for ground nuts, that means they must be ground to a fine powder. A food processor or a blender does a good job but be careful that you do not overdo it and make nut butter. A nut grinder gives excellent results. I recommend the kind that screws onto the side of a table. The nuts go into the top and come out through the side when the handle is turned. They come in three sizes. I recommend the medium size. They are available at Paprikas Weiss, 1546 Second Avenue, New York, N.Y. 10028, or H. Roth and Son, 1577 First Avenue, New York, N.Y. 10028.

NUTMEG GRATER

Nutmeg is sold either ground (grated) or whole. Like peppercorns, it has better flavor if it is freshly grated. Nutmeg graters are available in specialty kitchen-equipment stores. Or you may use a regular four-sided grater. Use the smallest holes, either the round ones or the diamond-shaped; try both and see which you like best. Whole nutmegs are generally available in small jars in the spice section of food markets.

PASTRY BAG

A few of these cookies are shaped with a pastry bag. The best ones are made of soft canvas and are coated on the inside only with plastic. The small opening generally has to be cut a bit larger to allow a metal tube to fit into the bag. It is easier to work with a bag that is too large rather than one that is too small.

After using, the bag should be washed thoroughly in hot soapy water, rinsed well, and hung up or spread out on a towel to dry.

And it is easier to work with a pastry bag if you work on something table height instead of kitchen-counter height. The table is lower and you have better control of your work.

PASTRY BRUSH

Use a good one or the bristles will come out while you are using it. Sometimes I use a good-quality artist's watercolor brush in a large size; it is softer and does a very good job.

PASTRY CLOTH

A pastry cloth is most important for preventing cookie dough from sticking when you roll it out. Buy the largest and heaviest cloth you can find. Always wash it after using. The butter in the dough soaks into the cloth, and unless it is kept very clean it will smell rancid. It may be ironed or not. I've tried it both ways and it worked the same.

ROLLING PIN

A long, large, heavy rolling pin is better than one that is short, small, and lightweight because the extra length and weight give better and faster results. A French-type rolling pin, long and thin with tapered ends and no handles, works very well for cookies. Whichever you use, roll the dough evenly, being especially careful not to make it thinner on the edges.

Use a ruler for measuring the thickness of the rolled dough.

RUBBER SPATULAS

Rubber spatulas are almost indispensable (I prefer rubber to plastic). They are especially useful for scraping the bowl of an electric mixer while adding ingredients in order to keep everything well mixed. And for scraping all of the dough out of the bowl. And for folding, stirring, mixing, et cetera. I suggest that you have several. They are made in three sizes; medium is the one that you will have the most use for.

RULER

If you are baking a variety of cookies a ruler is an essential kitchen tool. Not only for measuring the thickness of rolled dough, and the thickness of icebox-cookie slices (place the ruler on top of the bar or roll of cookies, make small scoring lines with the tip of a knife, then remove the ruler and cut the cookies), but for measuring the diameter of cookie cutters, the size of cake pans, and especially for marking bar cookies in order to cut them evenly (measure with the ruler and mark by inserting a toothpick).

STOCKINETTE COVER
FOR A ROLLING PIN

These are often sold with pastry cloths. You might like them or you might prefer to work without them. Often they are too small. But try one and decide.

THERMOMETER

Correct oven temperature is of the utmost importance. Most gas and electric companies are helpful about checking your oven temperature for you. But, even better, buy a mercury oven thermometer and double-check the temperature before baking.

Most ovens take 10 to 15 minutes to preheat thoroughly. Place the thermometer in the middle of the oven, set the thermostat to the desired temperature, light the oven, and then after 10 or 15 minutes check your mercury thermometer. If it's not right, adjust the oven heat accordingly.

Ingredients

BUTTER

Use sweet butter, or if you use salted butter use less salt than the recipe calls for.

EGGS

Unless the recipe specifies otherwise, use eggs graded "extra-large."

Egg Whites

Some of these recipes (macaroons, meringues) call for egg whites and no yolks. Always save leftover whites to have them when you want them.

Leftover egg whites may be stored, covered, in the refrigerator for up to four days. Or they may be frozen. I suggest freezing them individually, since they will thaw faster that way. Place each white in an oven-proof glass custard cup; if there are many, place the cups in a small cake pan or tray for ease in handling, cover them all with plastic wrap or aluminum foil, and place in the freezer. When they are frozen, hold them, one at a time, upside down, under hot running water just until the frozen white may be removed from the cup. Then immediately package them individually in small freezer bags (plastic sandwich bags) or in small squares of plastic wrap, and return them to the freezer. To thaw, remove the number you want, place them in a cup or bowl, and let stand at room temperature for an hour or so, or place them in a barely warm oven.

Egg Yolks

If you have yolks left over you may store them as follows: Whole, unbroken yolks should be placed in a small cup of cold water deep enough to cover them. Cover airtight and refrigerate for up to three or four days. Carefully drain all the water before using the yolks. Yolks may be frozen (although I never do. I use them to make Swedish Fried Twists; Hungarian Butter Biscuits, from *Maida Heatter's Book of Great Desserts*; mayonnaise; or a custard sauce). To freeze yolks, they must first be beaten or stirred lightly with a bit of salt or sugar depending on how you will use them. (Of course the amount of salt or sugar depends on the number of yolks. But for each 4 yolks, a generous pinch of salt or a teaspoon of sugar is enough.) Place them in a small covered jar or freezer container; be sure to label them indicating the number of yolks and specifying salt or sugar. You will seldom have use for more than 4 yolks at a time; therefore, it is practical to freeze only 2 or 4 in each little jar. Thaw at room temperature for a few hours or in the refrigerator overnight.

FLAVORINGS

Naturally, for better flavor buy those labeled "pure extract" instead of "imitation." And make sure that the tops are always tightly closed. Flavorings contain both alcohol and water—the alcohol evaporates rapidly and then of course the water follows, taking some of the essential oils along with it.

FLOUR

Most of these recipes call for all-purpose flour. It may be either bleached or unbleached. Do not substitute cake flour.

FRUIT

Dried currants, raisins, dates, and figs must be soft and fresh; baking will not soften them. Currants and raisins may be softened by boiling in water for a few minutes; drain them in a strainer and dry between layers of paper towels.

NUTS

When you buy nuts smell them and taste them to be sure they're not rancid. Then store them in the refrigerator or freezer.

In most of the recipes that call for pecans, walnuts can be successfully substituted. However, if the recipe calls for that special pecan taste—as Praline Wafers (page 46) or the various pecan bars (pages 108–10)—you must use pecans.

OATMEAL

All cookie recipes that call for oatmeal mean uncooked. There are many varieties of oatmeal (oats) and they give different qualities to the cookies. Instant oatmeal should not be used in cookies; it is too fine, too absorbent, and does not give any of the crunchy quality you want. Oatmeal that cooks in 1 minute is passable but the kind that takes 3 to 5 minutes to cook is better. There are also rolled oats with cooking directions that call for a few minutes of boiling and then leaving them covered to stand for 12 to 15 minutes. These are fine for cookies; they will remain very crunchy. But, since they are less absorbent than the quicker-cooking ones, drop cookies made with them will spread out more in baking. Steel-cut oats (cooking directions are generally to simmer for 20 to 25 minutes) may be used for cookies but the oats will remain rather hard and will give an even crunchier texture.

SPICES

Spices must be stored airtight or they will lose their flavor; after using, always close the container carefully. Store them in a cool spot. They should not be stored in or near direct sunlight or heat; keep them away from the oven. (I keep mine in the refrigerator, but they may also be kept in the freezer; remember that cold inhibits deterioration.) Even tightly closed and refrigerated they do not last indefinitely. (I date the jar when I buy it, and if I still have some left after a year I replace it.) Even just-bought spices might be stale—you can get a good idea by unscrewing the cap and smelling the spice.

Cinnamon is one of the oldest spices known to man and it is one of the most popular spices used today. For many years we imported fine, pungent cinnamon from Vietnam. When we discontinued relations with Vietnam we lost our cinnamon source there. And much of the cinnamon today is weak and flavorless. However, I have recently received divine, flavorful, sweet (not weak or bitter as is sometimes the case) cinnamon from Paprikas Weiss. Mr. Edward Weiss, an expert on spices, tells me that this wonderful stuff comes from mainland China. You can buy it (by mail also) from Paprikas Weiss Importer, 1546 Second Avenue, New York, N.Y. 10028.

SUGAR

Brown sugar and confectioners sugar should be strained. Hard lumps in brown sugar will not disappear in mixing or baking. (For how to strain sugar, see page 13.)

Procedures

HOW TO PREPARE A PASTRY CLOTH AND/OR A STOCKINETTE COVER

Spread out the cloth, and slide the cover on the rolling pin. Then sprinkle flour generously over the cloth and the stockinette cover and, with your hand, rub it into the cloth and the cover very thoroughly. The fabric should hold as much flour as you can rub into it and there should be as little excess flour as possible. Keep additional flour handy for reflouring as necessary.

If you do not use the stockinette cover, just rub flour onto the rolling pin as necessary.

SIZES FOR CHOPPING AND CUTTING

All of the recipes that call for chopped, cut, or broken nuts specify a size: "Coarsely cut," "finely cut," or "cut into medium-size pieces." In most cases the size does not have to be exact and it may be a matter of your own taste.

However, "coarsely cut" means that each half of a walnut or pecan, or each whole almond, should be cut into two or three pieces depending on the size of the nuts. "Finely cut" does not mean ground or powdered—it means small pieces about the size of dried split peas or currants. "Medium" is somewhere between coarse and fine, or about the size of raisins.

For medium or finely cut nuts, I place them on a chopping board and cut them all together with a long, heavy French chef's knife. For coarse, I either break them, one at a time, with my fingers, or I cut them, one at a time, with a small paring knife.

ABOUT STRAINING SUGARS

Brown Sugar

Most of the recipes that call for brown sugar specify that it should be strained. The only reason for straining it is to get rid of any hard lumps in the sugar. It is difficult (almost impossible) to force it through a fine strainer—use a coarse strainer (the larger the better) placed over a large bowl. Place the sugar in the strainer and, with your fingertips, press the sugar through the strainer.

I strain several pounds at a time and it seems to last forever. I mean it does not get lumpy again no matter how long I keep it.

As for measuring the sugar, straining does not affect the measurement (as it does flour), since the sugar should always be pressed firmly (with your fingertips) into the measuring cup. And, of course, the cup should *not* be a glass cup meant for measuring liquids—it should be a metal cup, the same as you would use for flour.

After pressing the sugar into the cup, use your fingers to wipe off any excess sugar over the top of the cup and make a level measure. If the sugar has gotten really rock hard you can pulverize it back into usable condition in a blender.

Confectioners Sugar

Confectioners sugar is strained for two purposes: For eliminating lumps and for accuracy of measurement; it packs down on standing and the amount of sugar in a measuring cup will vary if the sugar has or has not been strained. But it is not necessary to strain confectioners sugar immediately before measuring as you do flour.

When using confectioners sugar for an icing or a glaze, the lumps might not show at first—however, when the sugar is mixed with a liquid, the resulting frosting will not be as smooth as if the sugar had been strained. Therefore, if you do much cookying, I suggest that you strain a pound (or several) at a time. This also does not seem to get lumpy again if it stands after being strained.

When measuring confectioners sugar, use the same metal cups as you use for measuring flour. Fill the cup lightly as though you were measuring flour—do not pack confectioners sugar firmly into the cup as you do brown sugar—and then cut excess sugar off the top of the cup.

If you plan to strain both brown sugar and confectioners sugar, do the confectioners first—then it will not be necessary to wash the strainer before doing the brown.

TIMING

It is important to time cookies carefully. Set a timer for a few minutes less than the recipe specifies, and check the cookies to be sure you aren't over-baking them.

When directions say to reverse the position of cookie sheets during baking, wait until the baking is at least half or three-quarters finished. Then work quickly—do not keep the oven door open any longer than necessary.

When you bake only one sheet at a time instead of two, cookies bake in a little less time.

ABOUT STORING COOKIES

With few exceptions these cookies are best when fresh. Even the ones that will last for weeks are best when fresh. So, unless I know that there will be people around to eat them, I freeze almost all cookies in plastic freezer boxes (after reserving at least a few for unexpected company and for my husband's usual daily cookie party). And even in the freezer they do not stay fresh forever—a few weeks, a month or two—but after that they lose their extra-special goodness. Although most charts say that cookies may be frozen for up to twelve months, as far as I'm concerned that only means that they will not spoil. I don't believe that they taste as good after many months in the freezer. (Thaw frozen cookies before removing them from their containers or they might sweat and become soggy or wet. Usually an hour or so at room temperature will do it, but it depends on the size of the container.)

For short-time storage at room temperature do not mix soft cookies with crisp cookies in the same container, or the crisp ones will soon become soft.

To add moisture to soft cookies that have begun to dry out (or that you might have baked too long), place half an apple, skin side down, or a whole lemon or orange, depending on the flavor you want, on top of the cookies in an airtight container (you may use a plastic bag). Let stand for a day or two and then remove the fruit.

But I'm putting the cart before the horse. Enough of what to do with the cookies once they're baked. Before baking, check on your equipment and ingredients, then go to it.

Drop Cookies

CHOCOLATE CHOCOLATE-CHIP
  COOKIES
SANTA FE CHOCOLATE WAFERS
"CHOCOLATE STREET" COOKIES
BIG OLD-FASHIONED CHOCOLATE
  COOKIES
KEY WEST CHOCOLATE TREASURES
CHOCOLATE APPLESAUCERS
COCONUT GROVE COOKIES
CHOCOLATE RAISIN COOKIES
CHOCOLATE BANANA COOKIES
CHOCOLATE AND PEANUT-BUTTER
  RIPPLES
CHOCOLATE PEANUT COOKIES
WHOLE-WHEAT AND HONEY HERMITS
CONNECTICUT NUTMEG HERMITS
MOUNTAIN-HONEY GINGERSNAPS
SOUR-CREAM GINGER COOKIES
GIANT GINGER COOKIES
SUNFLOWER COCONUT COOKIES
DATE-NUT WAFERS
LEMON WALNUT WAFERS
PRALINE WAFERS
THE FARMER'S WIFE'S PECAN COOKIES

ROUTE 7 RAISIN-NUT COOKIES

NUT-TREE WALNUT JUMBLES

24-KARAT COOKIES

INDIAN FIGLETS

HAWAIIAN PINEAPPLE COOKIES

PUMPKIN ROCKS

BANANA ROCKS

DATE-NUT ROCKS

BLIND DATE COOKIES

GERMAN OATMEAL COOKIES

NORMAN ROCKWELL'S OATMEAL
   WAFERS

OATMEAL SNICKERDOODLES

OATMEAL MOLASSES COOKIES

RAISIN OATMEAL COOKIES

BUTTERSCOTCH MOLASSES COOKIES

POPPY-SEED WAFERS

TIJUANA FIESTA COOKIES

VANILLA BUTTER WAFERS

Drop cookies are probably the easiest of all cookies to make. But the dough should not be dropped (or slopped) onto the cookie sheet. It should be placed carefully, gently, and neatly. The mounds should all be the same size and they should be as round and evenly shaped as possible. Use two spoons (not measuring spoons), one for picking up the dough and another for pushing it off.

Chocolate Chocolate- Chip Cookies

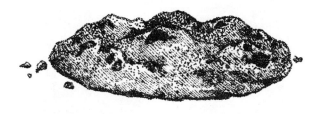

These are thin, dark, and brittle-crisp.

54 COOKIES

1¾ cups sifted all-purpose flour
¼ teaspoon baking soda
½ pound (2 sticks) butter
1 teaspoon vanilla extract
1 cup granulated sugar
½ cup dark brown sugar, firmly packed
⅓ cup unsweetened cocoa
2 tablespoons light cream
3½ ounces (1 cup) pecans, cut or broken
    into medium-size pieces
6 ounces (1 cup) semisweet chocolate morsels

Adjust two racks to divide the oven into thirds and preheat to 350 degrees. Cut aluminum foil to fit cookie sheets.

Sift together the flour and baking soda and set aside. In the large bowl of an electric mixer cream the butter. Add the vanilla and both sugars and beat to mix well. On low speed add the cocoa and beat to mix. Then mix in the cream and, on low speed, gradually add the sifted dry ingredients, scraping the bowl with a rubber spatula and beating only until mixed.

Remove the bowl from the mixer and, with a wooden spatula, stir in the pecans and chocolate morsels.

Use a rounded (less than heaping) teaspoonful of the dough for each cookie. Place them about 1½ inches apart (the cookies will spread during baking) on the cut aluminum foil. Slide cookie sheets under the foil.

Bake for 12 to 13 minutes, reversing the sheets top to bottom and front to back once to insure even baking. The cookies will still feel soft and not done but don't overbake them or they will become too hard.

Slide the foil off the sheets and let the cookies stand for a minute or two. (After baking, the cookies will flatten into thin, bumpy, uneven wafers.) With a wide metal spatula transfer the cookies to racks to cool.

Santa Fe Chocolate Wafers

36 WAFERS

These dark, thin, c.   :ookies are easily mixed in a saucepan. They are very fragile and not suitable for picnics.

1 cup sifted all-purpose flour
½ teaspoon baking soda
⅛ teaspoon salt
¼ pound (1 stick) butter
6 ounces (1 cup) semisweet chocolate morsels
⅓ cup granulated sugar
¼ cup light corn syrup
1 teaspoon vanilla extract
1 extra-large or jumbo egg

Adjust two racks to divide the oven into thirds and preheat to 350 degrees. Cut aluminum foil to fit cookie sheets.

Sift together the flour, baking soda, and salt and set aside. Cut the butter into ½-inch slices and place in a heavy 2½- to 3-quart saucepan. Add the chocolate morsels, sugar, and corn syrup. Stir over low heat until melted and smooth. If the mixture is not smooth (some morsels do not melt completely) stir or beat it briefly with a small wire whisk. Remove from the heat and let cool for 5 minutes.

Then stir in the vanilla and the egg. When smooth, add the sifted dry ingredients and stir and mix vigorously until smooth. Transfer to a small bowl for ease in handling.

Use a rounded teaspoonful of dough for each cookie. Place them at least 2 inches apart (these spread) on the cut aluminum foil, keeping the shapes as round as possible.

Slide cookie sheets under the foil and bake for 10 to 15 minutes (see Note), reversing the position of the sheets top to bottom and front to back once to insure even baking. If you bake only one sheet at a time use the higher rack, and with only one sheet in the oven the cookies will take less time to bake. The cookies will puff up in the oven and then they will flatten—they are not done until they have flattened. These will crisp as they cool and they should be very crisp, but be careful not to overbake or the chocolate will taste burnt.

Let the cookies stand on the sheet for a minute or so to firm, and then slide the foil off the sheet and transfer the cookies with a wide metal spatula to racks to cool. Store airtight.

NOTE: If, after the cookies have cooled, they are not crisp, you may re-place them in the oven briefly to bake a bit longer.

"Chocolate Street" Cookies

42 COOKIES

Sometimes called Brownie Drops, these are small, rather thin, semisoft, and very chocolaty.

¼ cup <u>un</u>sifted all-purpose flour
¼ teaspoon double-acting baking powder
Scant ¼ teaspoon cinnamon
⅛ teaspoon salt
8 ounces German's sweet chocolate
1 tablespoon butter
2 eggs
¾ cup granulated sugar
½ teaspoon vanilla extract
2½ ounces (¾ cup) walnuts, finely chopped

Adjust two racks to divide the oven into thirds and preheat to 350 degrees. Cut aluminum foil to fit cookie sheets.

Sift together the flour, baking powder, cinnamon, and salt and set aside.

Break up the chocolate and place it in the top of a small double boiler over hot water. Add the butter, and place over moderate heat. Cover and cook until melted. Stir until smooth. Remove from hot water and set aside to cool.

In the small bowl of an electric mixer beat the eggs at high speed for a minute or two until they are light in color. Gradually add the sugar and continue to beat for 4 or 5 minutes until the mixture is almost white in color and forms a ribbon when beaters are raised. Beat in the vanilla.

Add the cooled, melted chocolate and beat on low speed, scraping the bowl with a rubber spatula and beating only until smooth. Add the sifted dry ingredients and beat only enough to blend. Stir in the nuts. Transfer to a small shallow bowl for ease in handling.

Use a slightly rounded teaspoonful of dough for each cookie and place them 1½ inches apart on the prepared foil. Keep the shape of the cookies as round and even as possible.

Slide the cookie sheets under the foil and bake about 12 minutes, reversing position of sheets top to bottom and front to back during baking to insure even baking. When done, the tops of the cookies will be cracked and will feel semifirm when lightly touched with a fingertip. Do not overbake—the centers of these cookies should be moist and chewy.

Let cool on the foil on cookie sheets for about a minute. Then, with a wide metal spatula, transfer to racks to finish cooling.

NOTE: An interesting variation, almost the same recipe, is made with 8 ounces (8 squares) semisweet chocolate (instead of sweet) and ¾ cup dark brown sugar, firmly packed (instead of granulated).

Big Old-Fashioned Chocolate Cookies

18 COOKIES

Dark, thick, and soft, covered with a thin, dark chocolate glaze. These are easily mixed in a saucepan.

2 cups sifted all-purpose flour
½ teaspoon baking soda
Pinch of salt
2 ounces (2 squares) unsweetened chocolate
¼ pound (1 stick) butter
1 cup dark brown sugar, firmly packed
1 egg
1 teaspoon vanilla extract
½ cup milk

Adjust two racks to divide the oven into thirds and preheat to 375 degrees. Cut aluminum foil to fit cookie sheets.

Sift together the flour, baking soda, and salt and set aside. Cut the butter into ½-inch slices and place in a heavy 3-quart saucepan. Add the chocolate and cook over low heat until melted. Remove from heat and, with a heavy wooden spatula, stir in the sugar. (The mixture will look curdled—O.K.) Add the egg and the vanilla to the warm chocolate mixture and stir until smooth. Stir in half of the sifted dry ingredients. Then, very gradually, just a few drops at a time at first, stir in the milk. Add the remaining dry ingredients and stir briskly until completely smooth.

Use a heaping tablespoonful of dough for each cookie. Place them in even mounds 2 to 3 inches apart on the prepared foil.

Slide cookie sheets under the foil and bake for 12 to 15 minutes, reversing sheets top to bottom and front to back to insure even baking. The cookies are done when the tops spring back firmly if lightly touched with a fingertip.

Slide the foil off the sheets. Let stand for about a minute or so and then, with a wide metal spatula, transfer the cookies to racks to cool.

Prepare glaze.

CHOCOLATE GLAZE

1 ounce (1 square) unsweetened chocolate
1 tablespoon butter
1½ tablespoons hot water
2 tablespoons heavy cream
1 cup strained confectioners sugar
　　(see page 14)

Over hot water, in the top of a small double boiler melt the chocolate with the butter on moderate heat. Remove top of double boiler and stir in the 1½ tablespoons hot water and the heavy cream. Add the confectioners sugar and stir until smooth. If necessary, adjust with a bit more water or sugar to make the consistency similar to a heavy cream sauce.

With a small metal spatula, smooth the glaze over the tops of the cookies, staying about ½ inch away from the edges.

Let stand for a few hours to dry.

Key West Chocolate Treasures

These are large semisoft chocolate-coconut cookies with chocolate icing.

2 cups sifted all-purpose flour
¼ teaspoon salt
½ teaspoon baking soda
1 teaspoon instant coffee
½ cup boiling water
3 ounces (3 squares) unsweetened chocolate
¼ pound (1 stick) butter
1 teaspoon vanilla extract
1 cup dark brown sugar, firmly packed
1 egg
⅔ cup sour cream
2 ounces (generous ½ cup, firmly packed) shredded coconut

Adjust two racks to divide the oven into thirds and preheat to 375 degrees. Cut aluminum foil to fit cookie sheets.

Sift together the flour, salt, and baking soda and set aside. Dissolve the instant coffee in the boiling water.

Melt the chocolate with the prepared coffee in the top of a small double boiler over hot water on moderate heat. Stir until smooth. Remove the top of the double boiler and set aside.

In the large bowl of an electric mixer cream the butter. Add the vanilla and sugar and beat to mix well. Beat in the egg. Add the chocolate mixture (which may still be slightly warm) and beat until smooth. On low speed gradually add half of the sifted dry ingredients, then all of the sour cream, and then the remaining dry ingredients, scraping the bowl with a rubber spatula and beating only until smooth after each addition.

Remove the bowl from the mixer and stir in the coconut.

Use a heaping tablespoonful of dough for each cookie—make these large—place them 2 inches apart on the cut aluminum foil.

Slide cookie sheets under the foil and bake the cookies for 12 to 15 minutes, reversing the sheets top to bottom and front to back once to insure even baking. The cookies are done when the tops spring back firmly if lightly pressed with a fingertip. (If you bake only one sheet at a time use the higher rack.)

Slide the foil off the cookie sheets and with a wide metal spatula transfer the cookies to racks to cool.

Prepare the following icing.

KEY WEST CHOCOLATE ICING

1½ ounces (1½ squares) unsweetened
    chocolate
1 tablespoon butter
¼ cup sour cream
½ teaspoon vanilla extract
1½ cups strained confectioners sugar
    (see page 14)

Melt the chocolate with the butter and sour cream in the top of a small double boiler over hot water on moderate heat. Stir until the mixture is smooth. Remove the top of the double boiler and off the heat stir in the vanilla and then, gradually, stir in the sugar.

Use the icing quickly as it thickens while it stands. With a small metal spatula, a table knife, or the back of a teaspoon, spread the icing over the top of each cookie but do not spread it all the way to the edges; leave a small margin.

Let the cookies stand for about an hour or more until the icing is firm and dry.

NOTE: If you store these in a box, place wax paper between the layers.

Chocolate Applesaucers

22 EXTRA-LARGE
COOKIES

These soft, moist, spicy, extra-large cookies were created and perfected in the kitchen of an apple farm in Pennsylvania.

2½ cups sifted all-purpose flour
1 teaspoon baking soda
½ teaspoon salt
1½ teaspoons cinnamon
½ teaspoon powdered cloves
1 teaspoon instant coffee
2 tablespoons boiling water
¼ pound (1 stick) butter
1 cup granulated sugar
1 egg
¼ cup unsweetened cocoa
15 ounces (1½ cups) smooth (not chunky) applesauce
5 ounces (1 cup) raisins
½ cup walnuts, cut into medium-size pieces

Adjust two racks to divide the oven into thirds and preheat to 350 degrees. Cut aluminum foil to fit cookie sheets.

Sift together the flour, baking soda, salt, cinnamon, and cloves and set aside. Dissolve the instant coffee in the boiling water and set aside. In the large bowl of an electric mixer cream the butter. Add the sugar and beat to mix well. Add the egg and beat to mix well. On low speed beat in the cocoa, then the prepared coffee, and then the applesauce (the mixture will look curdled—it's O.K.). On low speed add the sifted dry ingredients, scraping the bowl with a rubber spatula and beating only until thoroughly mixed. Stir in the raisins and nuts.

These are very large cookies—use a ¼-cup measuring cup (4 level tablespoons) of the dough for each cookie, and place only 5 mounds on each piece of foil.

Slide cookie sheets under the foil. Bake for 25 minutes, reversing the sheets top to bottom and front to back as necessary to insure even baking. If you bake only one sheet at a time use the higher rack.

With a wide metal spatula transfer the cookies to racks to cool (see Notes).

While the cookies are cooling prepare the following icing.

CHOCOLATE ICING

1½ cups strained confectioners sugar
½ cup unsweetened cocoa
Pinch of salt
2⅔ ounces (5⅓ tablespoons) butter
About 3 tablespoons boiling water

Place the sugar, cocoa, and salt in the small bowl of an electric mixer. Melt the butter and pour the hot butter and 3 tablespoons of boiling water into the bowl. Beat until smooth. The icing should be semifluid, but not thin enough to run off the cookies. It might be necessary to add a little more hot water, but add it very gradually, only a few drops at a time. Or, if the icing is too thin, add a little more sugar. Transfer to a small shallow bowl for ease in handling.

With a teaspoon, spoon the icing onto a cookie and then, with the back of the spoon, spread it over the center of the cookie, keeping it ½ to ¾ inch away from the edges. Ice all of the cookies and then let them stand for a few hours to set.

NOTES: Since these are very large cookies, the cooling racks should be raised sufficiently from the counter top for air to circulate under the cookies; place the racks on right-side-up cake pans or bowls.

These do not freeze well after they are iced; the icing may become sticky when thawed.

Coconut Grove Cookies

These are chocolate cookies with hidden chunks of chocolate and a baked-on coconut meringue topping.

44 COOKIES

CHOCOLATE DOUGH

2½ cups sifted cake flour (see Notes)
1½ teaspoons double-acting baking powder
¼ teaspoon salt
8 ounces sweet, bittersweet, or semisweet
    chocolate (see Notes)
¼ pound (1 stick) butter
1 teaspoon vanilla extract
2 teaspoons instant coffee
½ cup granulated sugar
¼ cup dark brown sugar, firmly packed
2 egg yolks (reserve the whites for the
    meringue topping)
⅓ cup milk

Adjust two racks to divide the oven into thirds and preheat to 375 degrees.

Sift together the flour, baking powder, and salt and set aside. Place 4 ounces (reserve remaining 4 ounces) of the chocolate in the top of a small double boiler over hot water on moderate heat. Stir occasionally until melted and smooth, then remove from the heat and set aside to cool.

To cut the remaining 4 ounces of chocolate, use a heavy knife, work on a cutting board, and cut the chocolate into pieces measuring ¼ to ½ inch across. Set aside.

In the large bowl of an electric mixer cream the butter. Add the vanilla and the instant coffee and then both sugars, and beat well. Beat in the egg yolks, scraping the bowl with a rubber spatula. Beat in the melted chocolate. On low speed gradually add half of the sifted dry ingredients, continuing to scrape the bowl with the spatula. Now gradually add the milk and then the remaining dry ingredients and beat only until smooth. Remove the bowl from the mixer and stir in the cut chocolate pieces.

Set the chocolate dough aside at room temperature and prepare the meringue topping.

MERINGUE TOPPING

2 egg whites
Pinch of salt
½ cup granulated sugar
Scant ¼ teaspoon almond extract
2 tablespoons sifted cake flour (see Notes)
7 ounces (2 cups, packed) finely shredded
  coconut

In the small bowl of an electric mixer, with clean beaters, beat the egg whites together with the salt until the whites hold soft peaks. Gradually add the sugar, 1 to 2 spoonfuls at a time, and then beat at high speed for 3 to 5 minutes until the meringue is very stiff. Toward the end of the beating, beat in the almond extract.

Remove the bowl from the mixer and fold in the flour and then the coconut.

To form the cookies: Use a rounded teaspoonful of the chocolate dough for each cookie and place them 2 inches apart on unbuttered cookie sheets. Then top each cookie with a slightly rounded teaspoonful of the meringue topping. In order to wind up even, use a tiny bit less of the meringue topping than you use of the chocolate dough for each cookie. Try to place the topping carefully so that it won't all run off the chocolate cookie while it is baking. A little of it will probably run down the side of the cookie, no matter what, but that's O.K.; it looks nice anyhow.

Bake for 12 to 13 minutes, until the topping is lightly browned. Reverse the cookie sheets top to bottom and front to back once during baking to insure even browning.

With a wide metal spatula transfer the cookies to racks to cool.

NOTES: Lindt Excellence, Tobler Tradition, Lindt or Tobler extra-bittersweet, and Baker's German Sweet are all good chocolates to use for these cookies. Or you could use semisweet morsels, in which case you would use them whole (⅔ cup) in place of the cut-up 4 ounces of another chocolate.

Cake flour (not cake mix and not self-rising) is more finely ground than all-purpose flour and comes in a box. One cup sifted cake flour equals 1 cup minus 2 tablespoons sifted all-purpose flour, so in the dough recipe you could substitute 2¼ cups minus 1 tablespoon all-purpose flour if cake flour is unobtainable.

Chocolate Raisin Cookies

These are large, rather thin cookies that are both soft-chewy and crisp-crunchy. They are old-fashioned cookie-jar cookies from Rhode Island.

42 COOKIES

1¾ cups sifted all-purpose flour
1 teaspoon double-acting baking powder
½ teaspoon baking soda
¼ teaspoon salt
2 ounces (2 squares) unsweetened chocolate
5 ounces (1 cup) raisins
Boiling water
5⅓ ounces (10⅔ tablespoons) butter
1 teaspoon vanilla extract
1⅔ cups granulated sugar
1 egg
½ cup sour cream

Adjust two racks to divide the oven into thirds and preheat to 375 degrees. Cut the aluminum foil to fit cookie sheets.

Sift together the flour, baking powder, baking soda, and salt and set aside. In the top of a small double boiler over hot water on moderate heat, melt the chocolate. Remove the top of double boiler and set aside to cool slightly.

Pour boiling water over the raisins to cover, let stand for 5 to 10 minutes, and then drain them in a strainer.

In the large bowl of an electric mixer, cream the butter. Add the vanilla and sugar and beat well. Add the egg and beat well again. Beat in the chocolate, and then add the sour cream and beat to mix. On low speed, gradually add the sifted dry ingredients, scraping the bowl with a rubber spatula and beating only until mixed. Stir in the raisins. Transfer to a small bowl for ease in handling.

Use a heaping teaspoonful of dough for each cookie. Place them 2 to 3 inches apart on the cut foil. (These spread.) Slide cookie sheets under the foil.

Bake for 18 to 20 minutes, reversing the sheets top to bottom and front to back once to insure even baking. These are done when the tops spring back if lightly pressed with a fingertip. Do not overbake—these cookies should remain slightly soft and chewy in the centers (with crisp edges). Overbaking will make them too hard.

If you are baking only one sheet at a time bake it on the upper rack and be extra-careful about not overbaking.

VARIATION: To make Chocolate Rum-Raisin Cookies follow above directions with the following change. Prepare the raisins ahead of time as follows: Place them in a small saucepan and over them pour ½ cup dark rum. Place over moderate heat and bring to a low boil. Remove from the heat, cover, and let stand for several hours or overnight. Drain the raisins in a strainer set over a bowl and use any leftover rum for something else. I pour it (and a little more) into a Coke.

Chocolate Banana Cookies

55 LARGE COOKIES

These are large, thick, and soft.

6 ounces (1 cup) semisweet chocolate morsels
2¼ cups sifted all-purpose flour
2 teaspoons double-acting baking powder
¼ teaspoon baking soda
Scant ½ teaspoon salt
3 small or 2 large ripe bananas (to make
*   1 cup, mashed)*
5⅓ ounces (10⅔ tablespoons) butter
½ teaspoon vanilla extract
1 cup granulated sugar
2 eggs
6 ounces (generous 1½ cups) walnuts, cut
*   or broken into medium-size pieces*

Adjust two racks to divide the oven into thirds and preheat to 400 degrees. Cut aluminum foil to fit cookie sheets.

Place the chocolate morsels in the top of a small double boiler over hot water on moderate heat. Cover and cook until partially melted. Then uncover and stir until completely melted and smooth. Remove from the heat and set aside to cool.

Sift together the flour, baking powder, baking soda, and salt and set aside. In the small bowl of an electric mixer beat the bananas at low speed to mash them and make 1 cup of pulp. Set aside. In the large bowl of the electric mixer (without washing the beaters) cream the butter. Add the vanilla and sugar and beat well. Add the eggs one at a time and beat well. On low speed gradually add half the sifted dry ingredients, scraping the bowl with a rubber spatula and beating only until mixed. Add the cooled chocolate and the bananas and beat until smooth. Add the remaining half of the dry ingredients and beat only until smooth. Stir in the nuts.

Use a heaping teaspoonful (make these rather large) of the dough for each cookie. Place them 2 inches apart on the cut aluminum foil. Slide cookie sheets under the foil.

Bake the cookies for 12 to 14 minutes, reversing the position of the sheets top to bottom and front to back once or twice to insure even baking. The cookies are done when the tops spring back firmly if lightly pressed with a fingertip.

Slide the foil off the cookie sheet. Let the cookies stand for a moment and then, with your fingers (or a spatula if you prefer), transfer the cookies to racks to cool.

Chocolate and Peanut- Butter Ripples

ABOUT 30 COOKIES

A chocolate dough and a peanut-butter dough baked together to make a rather thin, crisp, candylike cookie.

CHOCOLATE DOUGH

2 ounces (2 squares) unsweetened chocolate
¼ pound (1 stick) butter
1 teaspoon vanilla extract
¼ teaspoon salt
¾ cup granulated sugar
1 egg
1 cup sifted all-purpose flour

Adjust two racks to divide the oven into thirds and preheat to 325 degrees.

Melt the chocolate in the top of a small double boiler over hot water on moderate heat. Remove the top of the double boiler and set aside.

In the large bowl of an electric mixer cream the butter. Add the vanilla, salt, and sugar and beat well. Beat in the egg and then the melted chocolate, scraping the bowl as necessary with a rubber spatula. On low speed gradually add the flour and mix only until smooth.

Transfer the dough to a small shallow bowl for ease in handling. Set it aside and prepare the peanut-butter dough.

PEANUT-BUTTER DOUGH

2 tablespoons butter
¼ cup smooth (not chunky) peanut butter
½ cup light brown sugar, firmly packed
2 tablespoons sifted all-purpose flour

In the small bowl of an electric mixer cream the butter with the peanut butter. Beat in the sugar until well mixed. Add the flour and beat to mix.

Transfer to a small shallow bowl for ease in handling.

To shape the cookies: Divide the chocolate dough in half and set one-half aside. By level or barely rounded teaspoonfuls, drop the remaining half on unbuttered cookie sheets, placing the mounds 2 inches apart. You will need 2 or 3 cookie sheets and will end up with about 30 mounds of the dough. Top each chocolate mound with a scant teaspoonful of the peanut-butter dough. And then top each cookie with another teaspoonful of the set-aside chocolate dough. Don't worry about the doughs being exactly on top of each other.

Flatten the cookies slightly with a fork, dipping the fork in granulated sugar as necessary to keep it from sticking.

Bake for 15 minutes, reversing the cookie sheets top to bottom and front to back once to insure even baking. If you bake only one sheet at a time use the higher rack. Do not overbake. These cookies will become crisp as they cool.

Let the cookies cool briefly on the sheets only until they are firm enough to transfer with a wide metal spatula to racks. When cool, handle with care—these are fragile.

Chocolate Peanut Cookies

45 COOKIES

These dark chocolate cookies have whole salted peanuts throughout and a chocolate glaze. They are dense, rich, and candylike.

3 ounces (3 squares) unsweetened chocolate
¼ pound (1 stick) butter
1½ cups granulated sugar
3 eggs
1½ cups sifted all-purpose flour
4 ounces (1 cup) whole salted peanuts
    (preferably dry roasted)

Adjust two racks to divide the oven into thirds and preheat to 350 degrees. Cut aluminum foil to fit cookie sheets.

In a small, heavy saucepan over low heat, or in the top of a small double boiler over hot water on moderate heat, melt the chocolate together with the butter. Then transfer it to the large bowl of an electric mixer and let stand for 2 to 3 minutes to cool briefly. Beat in the sugar and then the eggs, one at a time. On low speed add the flour, scraping the bowl with a rubber spatula and beating only until thoroughly mixed. Stir in the peanuts. Transfer to a small bowl for ease in handling.

Place the dough by well-rounded teaspoonfuls 1 inch apart on the cut foil. Slide cookie sheets under the foil.

Bake for about 15 minutes, reversing the cookie sheets top to bottom and front to back once to insure even baking. The cookies are done when the tops barely spring back if lightly pressed with a fingertip.

With a wide metal spatula transfer the cookies to racks to cool.

CHOCOLATE GLAZE

¼ cup milk
2 ounces (4 tablespoons) butter
2 ounces (2 squares) unsweetened chocolate
Pinch of salt
1 teaspoon vanilla extract
2½ cups plus about 1 tablespoon strained
    confectioners sugar (see page 14)

Place the milk, butter, chocolate, and salt in a heavy saucepan over low heat, or in the top of a double boiler over hot water on moderate heat.

Stir frequently until the butter and chocolate are melted and the mixture is smooth (if it appears cu dled don't worry). Remove from the heat and stir in the vanilla and 2½ cups of the sugar—if necessary transfer the mixture to a larger bowl in order to have room to stir well. If it is not completely smooth stir it vigorously with a wire whisk.

The glaze should be thick enough so that it does not run off the cookies, but it should be thin enough so that it will spread out by itself to form a smooth layer about ⅛ inch thick. It might be necessary to add about 1 more tablespoon of the sugar.

Transfer the glaze to a small bowl for easier handling. Work quickly —the glaze thickens as it stands. If it becomes too thick add a bit of hot water, but be careful and add only a drop at a time.

Place about a teaspoonful of the glaze on the top of each cookie, flattening it slightly with the back of the spoon, but do not spread it. As noted above, if it is the right consistency, it will run slightly by itself and almost cover the tops of the cookies. If just a bit runs off the edges in places, it is to be expected.

Place the glazed cookies on racks set over wax paper and let them stand for a few hours until the glaze is set.

Whole-Wheat and Honey Hermits

48 TO 60 COOKIES

Recipes for Hermits go back hundreds of years. Some were made as bar cookies. But they all have fruit, nuts, and spices.

2½ cups strained all-purpose whole-wheat flour (see Note)
1 teaspoon baking soda
1 teaspoon cinnamon
½ teaspoon allspice
¼ teaspoon nutmeg
¼ teaspoon salt
¼ pound (1 stick) butter
½ cup raw sugar, or light or dark brown sugar, firmly packed
1 cup honey
2 eggs
3 tablespoons milk
5 ounces (1 cup) currants
5 ounces (1 cup) raisins
8 ounces (1 cup) pitted dates, coarsely cut
8 ounces (2¼ cups) walnuts, cut or broken into medium-size pieces

Adjust two racks to divide the oven into thirds and preheat to 400 degrees. Cut aluminum foil to fit cookie sheets.

Strain together (see Note) the flour, baking soda, cinnamon, allspice, nutmeg, and salt and set aside. In the large bowl of an electric mixer cream the butter. Add the sugar and beat well. Beat in the honey, then the eggs and the milk. On low speed gradually add the strained dry ingredients, scraping the bowl with a rubber spatula and beating only until mixed. Stir in the currants, raisins, dates, and nuts.

Use a heaping teaspoonful of the dough for each cookie. Place them 2 inches apart on the cut aluminum foil. Slide cookie sheets under the foil.

Bake for 12 to 15 minutes, until the cookies barely spring back when lightly touched with a fingertip. Reverse the cookie sheets top to bottom and front to back once to insure even baking.

Slide the foil off the cookie sheet and with a wide metal spatula transfer the cookies to racks to cool.

NOTE: Since whole-wheat flour is generally too coarse to be sifted, it is better to strain it. With your fingertips, press it through a large strainer set over a large bowl. Any pieces that are too coarse to go through the strainer should be stirred into the strained flour.

Connecticut Nutmeg Hermits

36 COOKIES

2 cups sifted all-purpose flour
½ teaspoon baking soda
¼ teaspoon salt
¾ teaspoon nutmeg
¼ pound (1 stick) butter
1 cup light brown sugar, firmly packed
2 eggs
2 tablespoons water
5 ounces (1 cup) raisins
2½ ounces (¾ cup) walnuts, cut or broken
    into medium-size pieces

Adjust two racks to divide the oven into thirds and preheat to 375 degrees. Cut aluminum foil to fit cookie sheets.

Sift together the flour, baking soda, salt, and nutmeg and set aside. In the large bowl of an electric mixer cream the butter. Add the sugar and beat well, then the eggs one at a time, beating well after each addition. On low speed gradually add the sifted dry ingredients, scraping the bowl with a rubber spatula and beating only until thoroughly blended. Mix in the water and then the raisins and nuts.

Use a rounded teaspoonful of dough for each cookie, and place them 2 inches apart on the cut aluminum foil. Slide cookie sheets under the foil.

Bake for 12 to 15 minutes, until the cookies are well browned and semifirm to the touch. Reverse the sheets top to bottom and front to back as necessary to insure even browning. If you are baking only one sheet at a time use the higher rack.

With a wide metal spatula transfer the cookies to racks to cool.

Mountain-Honey Ginger-snaps

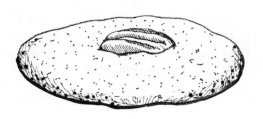

36 LARGE COOKIES

These come from Chamonix in the French Alps. They are crisp, crunchy, chewy, and mildly spiced.

2¼ cups sifted all-purpose flour
1½ teaspoons baking soda
½ teaspoon salt
1 teaspoon ginger
½ teaspoon cinnamon
¼ teaspoon powdered cloves
6 ounces (1½ sticks) butter
1 cup light brown sugar, firmly packed
1 egg
¼ cup honey
36 pecan halves

Adjust two racks to divide the oven into thirds and preheat to 350 degrees. Cut aluminum foil to fit cookie sheets.

Sift together the flour, baking soda, salt, ginger, cinnamon, and cloves and set aside. In the large bowl of an electric mixer cream the butter. Beat in the sugar to mix. Beat in the egg and then the honey. On low speed gradually add the sifted dry ingredients, scraping the bowl with a rubber spatula and beating only until thoroughly mixed. Transfer the mixture to a small bowl for ease in handling.

Place the dough by well-rounded teaspoonfuls on the cut aluminum foil. Shape the cookies carefully in even mounds and place them 3 to 4 inches apart (these spread; place only 6 to 8 cookies on a 12-by-15½-inch cookie sheet).

Place a pecan half on the top of each cookie, pressing it slightly into the cookie in order to keep it centered and to keep it from sliding off to one side. Slide cookie sheets under the cut foil.

Bake for 13 to 15 minutes, until the cookies are richly browned all over. Reverse the cookie sheets top to bottom and front to back as necessary during baking to insure even browning. The cookies will still feel soft to the touch but they will harden as they cool—do not overbake. These cookies will rise during baking and then flatten while cooling.

Slide the foil off the sheets and with a wide metal spatula transfer the cookies to racks to cool.

These must be stored airtight or they become soft and limp. (This has to do with the humidity. In the French Alps they stay crisp, but in Miami they do not.) They may be recrisped by placing them on cookie sheets in a moderate oven for a few minutes until they are very hot. Then cool again on racks.

Sour-Cream Ginger Cookies

42 COOKIES

These are light-colored cookies—thick, soft, and gingery—with a thin, dry, white glaze.

2½ cups sifted all-purpose flour
½ teaspoon baking soda
⅛ teaspoon salt
2 teaspoons ginger
1 teaspoon cinnamon
6 ounces (1½ sticks) butter
1 cup light brown sugar, firmly packed
2 tablespoons light molasses
1 egg
½ cup sour cream

Adjust two racks to divide the oven into thirds and preheat to 375 degrees. Cut aluminum foil to fit cookie sheets.

Sift together the flour, baking soda, salt, ginger, and cinnamon and set aside. In the large bowl of an electric mixer cream the butter. Add the sugar and beat well. Beat in the molasses. Add the egg and beat well. On low speed add the dry ingredients in three additions, alternating with the sour cream in two additions. Scrape the bowl with a rubber spatula and beat only until smooth.

Use a rounded teaspoonful of the dough for each cookie. Shape the mounds carefully and place them 1½ to 2 inches apart on the cut aluminum foil.

Slide cookie sheets under the foil. Bake for 12 to 14 minutes, reversing the sheets top to bottom and front to back once during baking to insure even browning. When the tops of the cookies are lightly pressed with a fingertip and spring back, the cookies are done.

With a wide metal spatula transfer the cookies to racks to cool.

Prepare the following glaze.

WHITE GLAZE

1 egg white
1½ cups strained confectioners sugar
  (see page 14)
⅛ teaspoon salt
1 tablespoon butter, melted
1 teaspoon vanilla extract

In the small bowl of an electric mixer beat the egg white briefly only until it is foamy. Add the sugar, salt, butter, and vanilla and beat well for 2 or 3 minutes. The mixture should be runny enough to make a smooth glaze, but not so thin that much of it runs off the sides (a little bit will)—if necessary add more sugar. Transfer to a small bowl for ease in handling.

Place the racks of cookies over wax paper.

With a pastry brush, brush the glaze over the cookies and then let stand on the racks until the glaze is completely hard and dry.

Giant Ginger Cookies

28 EXTRA-LARGE
COOKIES

These won first prize in a New England county fair. They are huge, soft, and spicy—and enough for filling a large cookie jar (or two).

4¾ cups sifted all-purpose flour
3 teaspoons baking soda
½ teaspoon salt
2 teaspoons cinnamon
2 teaspoons ginger
1 teaspoon powdered cloves
1 teaspoon mustard powder

½ pound (2 sticks) butter
1 tablespoon instant coffee
1 cup granulated sugar
1 cup molasses
1 extra-large or jumbo egg
¾ cup milk
6¼ ounces (1¼ cups) currants (see Note)

Adjust two racks to divide the oven into thirds and preheat to 350 degrees. Cut aluminum foil to fit cookie sheets.

Sift together the flour, baking soda, salt, cinnamon, ginger, cloves, and mustard and set aside. In the large bowl of an electric mixer cream the butter. Add the instant coffee and beat well. Then beat in the sugar. Add the molasses and beat until smooth. Add the egg and beat well; the mixture will look curdled—it's O.K. On low speed add the sifted dry ingredients in three additions alternately with the milk in two additions, scraping the bowl as necessary with a rubber spatula and beating only until smooth after each addition. Stir in the currants.

Use a heaping tablespoonful of the dough for each cookie. Make these extra-large—use as much dough as you can reasonably pile on the spoon. Place the cookies 2½ to 3 inches apart on the cut aluminum foil, keeping the cookies as round and as even as possible. Slide cookie sheets under the foil.

Bake for 20 to 22 minutes, reversing the sheets top to bottom and front to back a few times to insure even baking. Be careful that the bottoms of the cookies on the lower sheet do not burn; if the bottoms of the cookies seem to be turning too dark, change the position of the sheets often, or raise the rack, or slide an extra cookie sheet under the lower one. If you bake only one sheet at a time use the higher rack. Bake until the tops of the cookies spring back sharply when lightly pressed with a fingertip.

Slide the foil off the sheet. With a wide metal spatula transfer the cookies to racks to cool. Because these are such large cookies they will form steam as they cool and the steam will make the bottoms moist. To prevent that, raise the cooling racks by placing them on any right-side-up cake pans or mixing bowls.

NOTE: If the currants are not especially soft and fresh they should be softened before using. Do this before starting with the rest of the recipe. Cover the currants with boiling water, let stand for a few minutes, drain them in a strainer, and then spread them out on several layers of paper towels and pat the top with paper towels. Let the currants stand on the paper until you are ready for them.

Sunflower Coconut Cookies

36 LARGE COOKIES

2½ cups sifted all-purpose flour
1 teaspoon double-acting baking powder
½ teaspoon baking soda
½ teaspoon salt
6 ounces (1½ sticks) butter
1 cup light brown sugar, firmly packed
½ cup honey
1 egg
1 tablespoon orange juice (grate and reserve the rind before squeezing the juice)
¾ cup sour cream
Finely grated rind of 1 large orange
Finely grated rind of 1 large lemon
1 cup old-fashioned or quick-cooking (not "instant") oatmeal
3½ ounces (1 cup, packed) shredded coconut
5 ounces (1 cup) raisins
4 ounces (1 cup) sunflower kernels (see Note)
Optional: additional shredded coconut or coarsely chopped walnuts or pecans (for topping the cookies)

Adjust two racks to divide the oven into thirds and preheat to 375 degrees. Cut aluminum foil to fit cookie sheets.

Sift together the flour, baking powder, baking soda, and salt and set aside. In the large bowl of an electric mixer cream the butter. Beat in the brown sugar, then the honey, egg, and orange juice. On low speed gradually add half of the sifted dry ingredients, then the sour cream, and then the remaining dry ingredients, scraping the bowl with a rubber spatula and beating only until thoroughly mixed.

Remove the bowl from the mixer. Add the orange and lemon rinds and stir to mix well. Then stir in the oatmeal, coconut, raisins, and the sunflower kernels.

Use a heaping teaspoonful, or a rounded tablespoonful, of the dough for each cookie—make them rather large. Place the mounds evenly 2½ to 3 inches apart on the cut aluminum foil.

If you wish, sprinkle the tops of the cookies with the optional coconut or chopped nuts.

Slide cookie sheets under the foil and bake the cookies for 18 to 20 minutes, until the tops spring back when lightly pressed with a fingertip and the cookies are golden brown. Reverse the position of the sheets top to bottom and front to back as necessary to insure even browning. These cookies have a tendency to burn on the bottom, so be prepared to slide extra cookie sheets under the sheets holding the cookies—at least under the one on the lower rack. If you bake only one sheet at a time use the higher rack.

With a wide metal spatula transfer the cookies to racks to cool.

NOTE: Do not use toasted or salted sunflower kernels (seeds). Use the raw, natural, unprocessed ones that are available at health-food stores.

Date-Nut Wafers

These are large, thin, crisp-chewy, old-fashioned wafers.

35 LARGE WAFERS

8 ounces (1 cup, firmly packed) pitted dates,
  cut into medium-size pieces (each date
  should be cut into 4 or 5 pieces)
2 cups sifted all-purpose flour
1 teaspoon baking soda
1 teaspoon cream of tartar
½ teaspoon cinnamon
½ pound (2 sticks) butter
1 teaspoon vanilla extract
½ cup granulated sugar
1 cup dark brown sugar, firmly packed
2 eggs
3½ ounces (1 cup) walnuts, cut or broken
  into medium-size pieces

Adjust two racks to divide the oven into thirds and preheat to 350 degrees. Cut aluminum foil to fit cookie sheets.

Place the cut dates in a medium-size mixing bowl. Add about 2 tablespoons of the sifted flour. With your fingers, toss the dates to separate them thoroughly and coat each piece with flour. Set aside.

Sift together the remaining flour, baking soda, cream of tartar, and cinnamon and set aside. In the large bowl of an electric mixer cream the butter. Beat in the vanilla and then add both sugars and beat well. Add the eggs one at a time, beating well after each addition. On low speed gradually add the sifted dry ingredients, scraping the bowl with a rubber spatula and beating only until thoroughly mixed.

Remove the bowl from the mixer. With a rubber or wooden spatula, stir in the dates (including any leftover flour) and the nuts.

Use a heaping teaspoonful of the dough for each cookie—make these rather large. Place the mounds of dough 3 inches apart, placing only 5 on each piece of foil (these spread during baking). With the back of the spoon, flatten the cookies slightly in order to distribute the dates and nuts and keep them from piling up in the centers of the cookies. Slide cookie sheets under the foil.

Bake for about 15 minutes, until the cookies are well browned all over, including the centers. Do not underbake. Reverse the sheets top to bottom and front to back as necessary to insure even browning. When done, the cookies will flatten into thin, bumpy wafers. (If you bake only one sheet at a time, use the upper rack.)

Slide the foil off the sheet. Let stand for a few seconds until the cookies are firm enough to be moved (no longer). Then, with a wide metal spatula, transfer the cookies to racks to cool.

As soon as the cookies have cooled they should be placed in an air-tight container in order to keep the edges crisp and crunchy.

Lemon Walnut Wafers

36 COOKIES

These are semisoft with a tart lemon flavor—an old-fashioned cookie from Florida.

1½ cups sifted all-purpose flour
½ teaspoon double-acting baking powder
¼ teaspoon salt
Generous pinch of ginger
Finely grated rind of 1 large lemon
3 tablespoons lemon juice
¼ pound (1 stick) butter
1 cup granulated sugar
1 egg plus 2 egg yolks
2 ounces (generous ½ cup) walnuts, cut or
  broken into medium-size pieces

Adjust two racks to divide the oven into thirds and preheat to 350 degrees. Cut aluminum foil to fit cookie sheets.

Sift together the flour, baking powder, salt, and ginger and set aside. In a small cup mix the lemon rind and juice and set aside. In the small bowl of an electric mixer cream the butter. Add the sugar and beat well. Add the egg and the yolks, scraping the bowl with a rubber spatula and beating until the mixture is light and fluffy. On low speed gradually add the sifted dry ingredients, scraping the bowl with the spatula and beating only until the mixture is smooth.

Remove the bowl from the mixer and stir in the lemon rind and juice and then the nuts.

Use a well-rounded teaspoonful of the dough for each cookie. Place them 2 inches apart on the cut aluminum foil. Slide cookie sheets under the foil.

Bake for 18 to 20 minutes, reversing the sheets top to bottom and front to back once to insure even baking. These cookies will not brown on the tops, but there will be a thin brown edge. They are done when the tops spring back if lightly pressed with a fingertip. (If you bake one sheet at a time, use the upper rack.)

Slide the foil off the sheets and with a wide metal spatula transfer the cookies to racks to cool.

Praline Wafers

This is an old recipe from New Orleans. They are fragile wafers similar to praline candy—made without a mixer.

28 WAFERS

1½ ounces (3 tablespoons) butter
1 cup light brown sugar, firmly packed
1 tablespoon vanilla extract
1 egg
2 tablespoons (must be exact) sifted all-purpose flour
3½ ounces (1 cup) pecans, cut medium fine (see page 13)

Adjust two racks to divide the oven into thirds and preheat to 350 degrees. Cut aluminum foil to fit cookie sheets.

Melt the butter in a 1½- to 2-quart saucepan. Remove from the heat and stir in the sugar. Add the vanilla and the egg and stir until smooth. Then stir in the flour and finally the nuts.

Place well-rounded teaspoonfuls of the dough 2½ to 3 inches apart (no closer, these spread) on the cut aluminum foil. With the back of the spoon move the nuts around gently so they are spread out all over the cookie and not piled on top of each other. Slide cookie sheets under the foil.

Bake for 7 to 10 minutes, reversing the cookie sheets top to bottom and front to back as necessary to insure even browning. The cookies are done when they are completely colored, including the centers—the nuts will remain light. If you bake only one sheet at a time place the rack in the center of the oven.

Slide the foil off the cookie sheet. Let the cookies stand on the foil until they are completely cool and the foil may be easily (but gently) peeled away. If the foil does not peel away easily, the cookies have not baked long enough.

As soon as these are removed from the foil they must be stored airtight in order to remain crisp. If they are not to be served soon they may be frozen.

The Farmer's Wife's Pecan Cookies

36 THREE-INCH COOKIES

An old Southern recipe, mixed in a saucepan, for thin cookies that are both crisp and chewy.

1¼ cups sifted all-purpose flour
¼ teaspoon baking soda
⅛ teaspoon salt
¼ pound (1 stick) butter
1¼ cups light brown sugar, firmly packed
½ teaspoon vanilla extract
1 egg
2¼ ounces (⅔ cup) pecans, cut medium fine (see page 13)
36 pecan halves

Adjust two racks to divide the oven into thirds and preheat to 350 degrees. Cut aluminum foil to fit cookie sheets.

Sift together the flour, baking soda, and salt and set aside. Cut the butter into 1-inch pieces and place in a heavy 2- to 3-quart saucepan. Melt slowly over low heat, stirring occasionally. Off the heat, with a heavy wooden spatula stir in the sugar, then the vanilla and the egg. Add the sifted dry ingredients, stirring until smooth. Mix in the cut pecans. Transfer to a small bowl for ease in handling.

Use a rounded teaspoonful of dough for each cookie. Place them 2 inches apart on the cut aluminum foil. Place a pecan half on each cookie, pressing it gently and lightly into the dough.

Slide cookie sheets under the foil and bake for 12 to 14 minutes, reversing the position of the sheets top to bottom and front to back to insure even browning. When baking only one sheet at a time use the higher rack.

These will rise during baking and then will settle down. They should be medium-brown—do not underbake.

Slide the foil off the sheet and, with a wide metal spatula, slide the cookies off the foil and place on racks to cool.

Route 7 Raisin-Nut Cookies

36 LARGE COOKIES

This recipe comes from New England. The cookies are thick and crunchy, a traditional cookie-jar cookie.

1¾ cups sifted all-purpose flour
½ teaspoon salt
½ teaspoon baking soda
1 teaspoon double-acting baking powder
1 teaspoon cinnamon
1 teaspoon nutmeg
¼ teaspoon powdered cloves
¼ pound (1 stick) butter
1 teaspoon vanilla extract
1 cup granulated sugar
2 eggs
5 ounces (1 cup) raisins
6 ounces (generous 1½ cups) walnuts, cut or broken into medium-size pieces

Adjust two racks to divide the oven into thirds and preheat to 400 degrees. Cut aluminum foil to fit cookie sheets.

Sift together the flour, salt, baking soda, baking powder, cinnamon, nutmeg, and cloves and set aside.

In the large bowl of an electric mixer cream the butter. Add the vanilla and sugar and beat well. Add the eggs one at a time and beat until smooth. On lowest speed gradually add the sifted dry ingredients and beat only until they are thoroughly incorporated. Stir in the raisins and nuts.

Place well-rounded teaspoonfuls of the dough 2 inches apart on the cut aluminum foil. Slide cookie sheets under the foil.

Bake for 12 to 15 minutes, reversing the cookie sheets top to bottom and front to back as necessary to insure even browning. The cookies are done when they are browned and spring back if lightly pressed with a fingertip. If you bake only one sheet at a time use the higher rack.

Slide the foil off the cookie sheet. With a wide metal spatula transfer the cookies to a rack to cool.

Nut-Tree Walnut Jumbles

These are large, semisoft, sour-cream cookies.

24 LARGE COOKIES

1¾ cups sifted all-purpose flour
¾ teaspoon baking soda
Scant ½ teaspoon salt
¼ pound (1 stick) butter
1 teaspoon vanilla extract
1 cup dark brown sugar, firmly packed
1 egg
½ cup sour cream
4 ounces (generous 1 cup) walnuts, cut or
    broken into medium-size pieces
24 walnut halves

Adjust two racks to divide the oven into thirds and preheat to 375 degrees. Cut aluminum foil to fit cookie sheets.

Sift together the flour, baking soda, and salt and set aside. In the large bowl of an electric mixer cream the butter. Add the vanilla and sugar and beat well. Add the egg and beat well. On lowest speed gradually add half of the sifted dry ingredients, then all of the sour cream, and finally the remaining dry ingredients, scraping the bowl with a rubber spatula and beating only until thoroughly mixed. Stir in the cut or broken walnuts.

Use a rounded tablespoonful (make these large) of the dough for each cookie. Place them 2 inches apart on the cut aluminum foil. Top each cookie with a walnut half.

Slide cookie sheets under the foil. Bake for 12 to 13 minutes, reversing the cookie sheets top to bottom and front to back as necessary during baking to insure even browning. The cookies are done when they spring back if lightly pressed with a fingertip.

Slide the foil off the cookie sheet and with a wide metal spatula transfer the cookies to racks to cool.

24-Karat Cookies

These are made with grated raw carrots. Probably no one will recognize the taste, but the carrots will keep the cookies soft and moist.

32 COOKIES

1 cup sifted all-purpose flour
1 teaspoon double-acting baking powder
1 teaspoon baking soda
¼ teaspoon salt
¼ pound (1 stick) butter
1 egg
½ cup honey
¾ cup grated raw carrots, firmly packed
    (see Note)
½ cup old-fashioned or quick-cooking (not
    "instant") oatmeal
½ cup raisins
2½ ounces (¾ cup) walnuts, cut or broken
    into medium-size pieces

Adjust two racks to divide the oven into thirds and preheat to 350 degrees. Cut aluminum foil to fit cookie sheets.

Sift together the flour, baking powder, baking soda, and salt and set aside. In the large bowl of an electric mixer cream the butter. Add the egg and beat to mix. Beat in the honey and then the carrots. On low speed add the sifted dry ingredients and then the oatmeal, scraping the bowl with a rubber spatula and beating only until thoroughly mixed. Stir in the raisins and the walnuts.

Place the dough by rounded teaspoonfuls about 2 inches apart on the cut aluminum foil. Slide cookie sheets under the foil.

Bake for about 15 minutes, reversing the position of the cookie sheets top to bottom and front to back as necessary to insure even browning. The cookies are done when they are golden-colored and the tops spring back if lightly pressed with a fingertip.

With a wide metal spatula transfer the cookies to racks to cool.

NOTE: It is not necessary to peel the carrots, just clean them with a brush under running water. Grate them on the medium-fine side of a grater. Two medium-large carrots will make ¾ cup when grated.

Indian Figlets

The inspiration for this recipe came to me from an Indian woman in Taos, New Mexico, in exchange for some Florida seashells. The cookies are soft, plain, not too sweet.

44 COOKIES

8 ounces (1 cup, packed) dried brown figs
½ cup water
2½ cups sifted all-purpose flour
1 teaspoon baking soda
½ teaspoon salt
1 teaspoon cinnamon
¼ teaspoon ginger
¼ teaspoon nutmeg
5⅓ ounces (10⅔ tablespoons) butter
½ cup light brown sugar, firmly packed
½ cup dark corn syrup
1 teaspoon vanilla extract
1 egg
Finely grated rind of 2 lemons

Adjust two racks to divide the oven into thirds and preheat to 375 degrees. Cut aluminum foil to fit cookie sheets.

Remove the hard stems from the figs and cut the figs into medium-small pieces (see page 13). Place them in a small saucepan with the water. Bring to a boil over moderate heat. Cook, stirring occasionally, for about 5 minutes until the water is absorbed. Set aside to cool.

Sift together the flour, baking soda, salt, cinnamon, ginger, and nutmeg and set aside. In the large bowl of an electric mixer cream the butter. Add the sugar and beat well. Beat in the corn syrup and then the vanilla and the egg. On low speed gradually add the sifted dry ingredients, scraping the bowl with a rubber spatula and beating only until mixed. Remove the bowl from the mixer and stir in the lemon rind and then the cooled figs.

Using a rounded teaspoonful of the dough for each cookie, place them 2 inches apart on the cut aluminum foil. Slide cookie sheets under the foil.

Bake for 12 to 15 minutes, reversing the sheets top to bottom and front to back once to insure even browning. The cookies are done when the tops spring back firmly if they are lightly pressed with a fingertip.

With a wide metal spatula transfer the cookies to racks to cool.

Hawaiian Pineapple Cookies

30 COOKIES

1 eight-ounce can crushed pineapple
2 cups sifted all-purpose flour
1 teaspoon double-acting baking powder
½ teaspoon baking soda
¼ teaspoon salt
¼ pound (1 stick) butter
½ cup granulated sugar
½ cup dark brown sugar, firmly packed
1 egg
4 ounces (generous 1 cup) pecans, cut or
   broken into medium-size pieces
Finely grated rind of 2 lemons
30 pecan halves

Adjust two racks to divide the oven into thirds and preheat to 375 degrees. Cut aluminum foil to fit cookie sheets.

Drain the pineapple in a strainer set over a bowl. Press gently on the pineapple to extract most of the juice, but do not squeeze it so hard that the pineapple actually becomes dry. Set aside both the pineapple (you should have ⅔ cup) and the juice.

Sift together the flour, baking powder, baking soda, and salt and set aside. In the large bowl of an electric mixer cream the butter. Add both sugars and beat well, scraping the bowl as necessary with a rubber spatula. Add the egg and beat well. Beat in 1 tablespoon of the reserved pineapple juice (you will not need the remainder of it), the drained pineapple, and the cup of cut pecans. On lowest speed gradually add the sifted dry ingredients, continuing to scrape the bowl with the rubber spatula, and beating only until thoroughly incorporated. Remove the bowl from the mixer and stir in the lemon rind.

Use a rounded tablespoonful (make these large) of the dough for each cookie. Place them 2 inches apart on the cut aluminum foil. Place a pecan half, rounded side up, on each cookie and press it down very slightly. Slide cookie sheets under the foil.

Bake the cookies for 15 to 17 minutes, reversing the position of the cookie sheets top to bottom and front to back once to insure even browning. The cookies are done when they are golden brown and spring back if lightly pressed with a fingertip. If you bake only one sheet at a time use the higher rack.

Slide the foil off the cookie sheet. With a wide metal spatula transfer the cookies to racks to cool.

Pumpkin Rocks

Many old cookie recipes are called "rocks," not because they're as hard as, but because of their shape. These are thick, soft, spicy, and old-fashioned.

48 LARGE COOKIES

2½ cups sifted all-purpose flour
2 teaspoons double-acting baking powder
½ teaspoon baking soda
½ teaspoon salt
1 teaspoon cinnamon
¾ teaspoon nutmeg
½ teaspoon ginger
¼ teaspoon powdered cloves
¼ teaspoon allspice
¼ pound (1 stick) butter
1 cup granulated sugar
½ cup dark brown sugar, firmly packed
2 eggs
1 pound (about 1¾ cups) canned pumpkin
   (not pumpkin pie filling)
5 ounces (1 cup) raisins
7 ounces (2 cups) walnuts, cut or broken into
   medium-size pieces

Adjust two racks to divide the oven into thirds and preheat to 375 degrees. Cut aluminum foil to fit cookie sheets.

Sift together the flour, baking powder, baking soda, salt, cinnamon, nutmeg, ginger, cloves, and allspice and set aside. In the large bowl of an electric mixer cream the butter. Beat in both sugars. Add the eggs one at a time and beat well, then beat in the pumpkin. (The mixture might look curdled—it's O.K.) On low speed gradually add the sifted dry ingredients, scraping the bowl with a rubber spatula and beating only until thoroughly mixed. Stir in the raisins and walnuts.

Use a rounded tablespoonful of the dough (make these large) for each cookie, and place them 1 to 1½ inches apart (these do not run or change shape in baking) on the cut aluminum foil. Slide cookie sheets under the foil.

Bake the cookies for about 18 minutes, reversing the sheets top to bottom and front to back as necessary to insure even browning. The cookies are done when they are lightly browned and spring back if gently pressed with a fingertip.

While the cookies are baking, prepare the following glaze.

GLAZE

2 tablespoons soft butter
1½ cups confectioners sugar
Pinch of salt
2 tablespoons lemon juice
1 tablespoon milk

Place all of the glaze ingredients in the small bowl of an electric mixer and beat until completely smooth. The mixture should have the consistency of soft whipped cream—it might be necessary to add more liquid (either lemon juice or milk) or more sugar. Cover the glaze airtight when you are not using it.

As you remove the baked cookies from the oven, slide the foil off the cookie sheet and immediately, while the cookies are very hot, brush the glaze generously over the tops. It should be a rather heavy coating, which should run unevenly down the sides.

With a wide metal spatula transfer the cookies to racks to cool. The glaze will dry completely.

Banana Rocks

48 LARGE COOKIES

These thick, soft oatmeal cookies contain raisins, dates, prunes, nuts, and bananas.

1½ cups sifted all-purpose flour
½ teaspoon baking soda
½ teaspoon salt
1 teaspoon cinnamon
¼ teaspoon nutmeg
¼ teaspoon ginger
3½ ounces (¾ cup) raisins

6 ounces (¾ cup) pitted dates, coarsely cut
    (see Note)
6 ounces (¾ cup) pitted prunes (not stewed),
    coarsely cut (see Note)
6 ounces (1½ cups) walnuts, cut or broken
    into medium-size pieces
3 small or 2 large ripe bananas (to
    make 1 cup, mashed)
6 ounces (1½ sticks) butter
1 cup dark brown sugar, firmly packed
1 egg
1¾ cups old-fashioned or quick-cooking
    (not "instant") oatmeal
Finely grated rind of 2 lemons

Adjust two racks to divide the oven into thirds and preheat to 375 degrees. Cut aluminum foil to fit cookie sheets.

Sift together the flour, baking soda, salt, cinnamon, nutmeg, and ginger and set aside.

Place the raisins, dates, and prunes in a medium-size mixing bowl. Add a large spoonful of the sifted dry ingredients and, with your fingertips, toss the fruit until the pieces are all separated and coated with the dry ingredients. Add the nuts, toss again, and set aside.

In the small bowl of an electric mixer beat the bananas to mash them. Measure out 1 cup of pulp and set aside.

In the large bowl of the electric mixer cream the butter. Add the sugar and beat well, then beat in the egg. Add the mashed banana and beat, scraping the bowl with a rubber spatula, until well mixed. Beat in the oatmeal, then on lowest speed add the sifted dry ingredients, scraping the bowl with the rubber spatula and beating only until incorporated.

Remove the bowl from the mixer. With a large wooden spatula or spoon stir in the lemon rind and then the floured fruit-nut mixture.

Use a heaping teaspoonful of the dough (make these rather large) for each cookie. Place them 1½ to 2 inches apart on the cut aluminum foil, mounding the dough high. Do not flatten. Slide cookie sheets under the foil.

Bake the cookies 17 to 18 minutes, reversing the sheets top to bottom and front to back once to insure even browning. The cookies are done when they are lightly browned and spring back firmly if gently pressed with a fingertip. Do not overbake—these should remain semisoft.

While the cookies are baking prepare the following glaze.

GLAZE

3 tablespoons soft butter
1½ cups confectioners sugar
Pinch of salt
3 tablespoons milk

In the small bowl of the electric mixer beat all of the glaze ingredients together until the mixture is completely smooth. The mixture should have the consistency of very heavy cream sauce; if necessary add a bit more milk or sugar—do not make the glaze too thin.

As you remove the baked cookies from the oven, slide the foil off the cookie sheet and immediately, while the cookies are very hot, use a pastry brush and brush the glaze over the tops of the cookies. Work quickly— the heat of the cookies will melt the glaze and it will run down the sides unevenly.

With a wide metal spatula transfer the cookies to racks to cool and let the glaze dry completely.

NOTE: The dates and prunes should not be cut into very small pieces— cutting them into thirds or quarters is about right.

Date-Nut Rocks

These are large, thick, and soft—cookie-jar or lunch-box cookies. In the western part of the country these are called Billy Goats.

36 LARGE COOKIES

2 cups sifted all-purpose flour
2 teaspoons double-acting baking powder
½ teaspoon baking soda
Pinch of salt
1 teaspoon allspice
¼ pound (1 stick) butter
1 teaspoon vanilla extract
1 cup light brown sugar, firmly packed
2 eggs
½ cup sour cream
1 pound (2 cups, firmly packed) pitted dates, coarsely cut (see page 13)
7 ounces (2 cups) pecans or walnuts, coarsely cut or broken (see page 13)

Adjust two racks to divide the oven into thirds and preheat to 350 degrees. Cut aluminum foil to fit cookie sheets.

Sift together the flour, baking powder, baking soda, salt, and allspice and set aside. In the large bowl of an electric mixer cream the butter. Beat in the vanilla and then add the sugar and beat well. Add the eggs one at a time, beating well after each addition. On low speed add half of the sifted dry ingredients, then the sour cream, and finally the remaining dry ingredients, scraping the bowl with a rubber spatula and beating only until mixed.

Remove from the mixer. Add the dates and, with a rubber or wooden spatula, stir until they are evenly distributed through the dough. Then stir in the nuts.

Use a heaping teaspoonful (make these rather large) of the dough for each cookie, and place them 2 to 2½ inches apart on the cut foil. Slide cookie sheets under the foil.

Bake for 18 to 20 minutes, reversing the sheets top to bottom and front to back as necessary to insure even browning. Bake only until the cookies are lightly colored all over and the tops spring back when lightly pressed with a fingertip—do not overbake. If you bake only one sheet at a time, use the upper rack.

With a wide metal spatula transfer the cookies to racks to cool.

Blind Date Cookies

30 COOKIES

Although these came to me from a friend in New York, I am told that the recipe originated over 100 years ago with a famous pastry shop in Milwaukee. They are semisoft drop cookies with a surprise date and nut hidden inside. Technically these cookies are dropped onto the cookie sheet but, since each cookie contains a stuffed date, the procedure is slightly different from that of the usual drop cookie.

30 large (about 10 ounces) pitted dates
30 large (1¼ ounces) walnut halves, or about
　　⅓ cup large pieces
1¼ cups sifted all-purpose flour
¼ teaspoon salt
¼ teaspoon double-acting baking powder
½ teaspoon baking soda
2 ounces (4 tablespoons) butter
½ teaspoon vanilla extract
¾ cup light brown sugar, firmly packed
1 egg
½ cup sour cream

Adjust a rack to the top position in the oven and preheat to 400 degrees. Cut aluminum foil to fit cookie sheets.

Slit one long side of each date, stuff with one walnut half or a few pieces of walnut, close the dates around the nuts, and set aside.

Sift together the flour, salt, baking powder, and baking soda and set aside. In the small bowl of an electric mixer cream the butter. Add the vanilla and the sugar and beat to mix well. Add the egg and beat thoroughly. On lowest speed gradually add half of the sifted dry ingredients, then all of the sour cream, and then the remaining half of the dry ingredients, scraping the bowl with a rubber spatula and beating only until smooth after each addition. Remove the dough from the mixer and transfer it to a shallow bowl for easy handling.

Using two forks, drop each stuffed date into the dough and roll it around until the date is completely coated. There will be enough dough to cover each date with a generous coating but don't overdo it or you will not have enough dough to go around. Using the forks, place the dough-coated dates 2 to 3 inches apart on the cut aluminum foil. Slide cookie sheets under the foil.

Bake one sheet at a time for about 10 minutes until lightly browned, reversing the position of the sheet once during baking to insure even browning.

While the first sheet of cookies is baking, prepare the following glaze.

GLAZE

2 ounces (4 tablespoons) butter
1 cup confectioners sugar
½ teaspoon vanilla extract
2 to 3 tablespoons milk

Melt the butter and mix it well with the remaining ingredients, using only enough milk to make a mixture the consistency of soft mayonnaise. Keep the glaze covered when you are not using it.

Remove the baked cookies from the oven. Slide the foil off the cookie sheet. With a pastry brush, immediately brush the tops of the hot cookies with a generous coating of the glaze. Then, with a wide metal spatula, transfer the cookies to a rack to cool.

Bake and glaze the remaining cookies. Let them stand until the glaze is dry.

German Oatmeal Cookies

48 COOKIES

These are thick, soft cookies full of fruit, nuts, and chocolate bits. They are real old-fashioned cookie-jar cookies.

5 ounces (1 cup) raisins
Boiling water
2 cups sifted all-purpose flour
½ teaspoon salt
½ teaspoon baking soda
1 teaspoon cinnamon
½ teaspoon powdered cloves
½ teaspoon allspice
½ pound (2 sticks) butter
1 cup granulated sugar
3 eggs
4 ounces (½ cup) pitted dates, coarsely cut
    (see page 13)
2 cups old-fashioned or quick-cooking
    (not "instant") oatmeal
⅓ cup water (in which the raisins were boiled)
4 ounces (generous 1 cup) pecans, coarsely
    cut or broken (see page 13)
6 ounces (1 cup) semisweet chocolate morsels
Optional: 48 pecan halves

Adjust two racks to divide the oven into thirds and preheat to 400 degrees. Cut aluminum foil to fit cookie sheets.

Place the raisins in a small saucepan. Cover with boiling water and let simmer for 5 minutes. Then drain the raisins in a strainer set over a small bowl (reserve ⅓ cup of the water).

Sift together the flour, salt, baking soda, cinnamon, cloves, and all-spice and set aside.

In the large bowl of an electric mixer cream the butter. Add the sugar and beat well. Add the eggs one at a time and beat until smooth after each addition. Add the dates and drained raisins and beat just to mix. Beat in the oatmeal. Gradually beat in the reserved ⅓ cup water that the raisins cooked in. Then, on low speed, slowly add the sifted dry ingredients, scraping the bowl with a rubber spatula and beating only until mixed. Stir in the cut pecans and the chocolate morsels.

Place the dough by heaping teaspoonfuls (make these rather large) 2 inches apart on the cut aluminum foil. Place an optional pecan half on each cookie.

Slide cookie sheets under the foil. Bake for 12 to 14 minutes, reversing the sheets top to bottom and front to back as necessary to insure even browning. (If you bake only one sheet at a time use the higher rack.) Bake until the cookies are golden brown and the tops spring back if lightly pressed with a fingertip. Slide the foil off the sheets.

With a wide metal spatula transfer the cookies to racks to cool.

Norman Rockwell's Oatmeal Wafers

18 LARGE WAFERS

These are large, thin wafers that are crisp, crunchy, and fragile. They are a favorite of Norman Rockwell, the great illustrator of Americana.

½ cup sifted all-purpose flour
¼ teaspoon salt
¼ teaspoon baking soda
¼ pound (1 stick) butter
¼ cup granulated sugar
½ cup light brown sugar, firmly packed
½ teaspoon vanilla extract
2 tablespoons water (measure carefully)
1 egg
1 cup old-fashioned or quick-cooking (not "instant") oatmeal
2½ ounces (¾ cup) walnuts, cut medium fine (see page 13)

Adjust two racks to divide the oven into thirds and preheat to 350 degrees. Cut aluminum foil to fit cookie sheets.

Sift together the flour, salt, and baking soda, and then set aside.

In the small bowl of an electric mixer cream the butter. Gradually add both sugars and beat for 2 to 3 minutes. Add the vanilla, water, and egg and beat well. On low speed gradually add the sifted dry ingredients, scraping the bowl with a rubber spatula and beating only until smooth. Stir in the oatmeal and then the nuts.

Use a rounded tablespoonful of dough for each cookie. Place them 3½ to 4 inches apart (these spread a lot) on the cut aluminum foil. With the back of a wet spoon, flatten each cookie until it is ¼ to ⅓ inch thick. Slide cookie sheets under the foil.

Bake for 13 to 15 minutes, reversing the position of the cookie sheets top to bottom and front to back as necessary to insure even browning. Bake until the cookies are completely golden brown. These must be timed carefully; if they are underbaked the bottoms will be wet and sticky and it will be difficult to remove the cookies from the aluminum foil; if overbaked they will taste burnt and bitter.

If you bake only one sheet at a time use the higher rack.

Slide the aluminum foil off the cookie sheet and let the cookies stand until they are completely cool. Then, carefully and gently, peel the foil away from the backs of the cookies. (If you have any trouble, use a wide metal spatula to remove the cookies.) Turn the cookies upside down and let them stand for 5 to 10 minutes on the foil to allow the bottoms to dry a bit.

These must be stored airtight.

Oatmeal Snicker-doodles

54 COOKIES

Snickerdoodles are Early American; there are many different versions. These from Connecticut are plain old-fashioned—thin, crisp, and crunchy.

2 cups sifted all-purpose flour
1 teaspoon baking soda
½ teaspoon salt
1 teaspoon cinnamon
½ pound (2 sticks) butter
1 teaspoon vanilla extract
¾ cup granulated sugar
¾ cup light brown sugar, firmly packed
2 eggs
1½ cups old-fashioned or quick-cooking (not "instant") oatmeal

Adjust two racks to divide the oven into thirds and preheat to 400 degrees. Cut aluminum foil to fit cookie sheets.

Sift together the flour, baking soda, salt, and cinnamon and set aside. In the large bowl of an electric mixer cream the butter. Add the vanilla and both sugars and beat well. Add the eggs one at a time and beat well. On low speed gradually add the sifted dry ingredients, scraping the bowl with a rubber spatula and beating only until mixed. Stir in the oatmeal.

Place by rounded teaspoonfuls 2 inches apart on the cut foil.

TOPPING

2 tablespoons granulated sugar
2 teaspoons cinnamon

Stir the sugar and cinnamon together well and, with a teaspoon, sprinkle it generously over the cookies.

Slide cookie sheets under the foil. Bake the cookies for 10 to 12 minutes, reversing sheets top to bottom and front to back as necessary to insure even browning. Bake until the cookies are browned all over, including the centers.

Let cookies stand on the sheets for a few seconds until they are firm enough to transfer. Slide the foil off the sheets and with a wide metal spatula transfer to racks to cool.

Store airtight.

Oatmeal Molasses Cookies

72 COOKIES

These are crunchy and chewy, with a molasses flavor.

3 cups sifted all-purpose flour
2 teaspoons baking soda
1 teaspoon salt
½ pound (2 sticks) butter
1½ teaspoons vanilla extract
2 cups granulated sugar
½ cup molasses (see Note)
2 eggs
2 cups old-fashioned or quick-cooking
(not "instant") oatmeal
3½ ounces (1 cup, firmly packed) shredded
coconut
4 ounces (generous 1 cup) walnuts or pecans,
cut or broken into medium-size pieces

Adjust two racks to divide the oven into thirds and preheat to 375 degrees. Cut aluminum foil to fit cookie sheets.

Sift together the flour, baking soda, and salt and set aside. In the large bowl of an electric mixer cream the butter. Beat in the vanilla and then add the sugar and beat well. Add the molasses and beat to mix. Add the eggs one at a time, scraping the bowl with a rubber spatula and beating well after each addition. On low speed gradually add the sifted dry ingredients, continuing to scrape the bowl and beating only until incorporated. Then add the oatmeal, coconut, and nuts, stirring only until mixed.

Use a well-rounded (but not heaping) teaspoonful of dough for each cookie. Place them 2 inches apart on the cut foil. Slide cookie sheets under the foil.

Bake two sheets at a time for about 15 minutes, reversing the sheets top to bottom and front to back once to insure even browning, until the cookies are lightly colored. The cookies will still feel slightly soft and underdone, but do not overbake. If you bake only one sheet at a time, use the upper rack (it will take less time to bake than two sheets).

Remove from the oven and let the cookies stand on the sheets for a minute or so and then, with a wide metal spatula, transfer them to racks to cool.

NOTE: You will definitely taste the molasses in these. Unless you love the flavor of strong, dark molasses, use a light, mild-flavored kind.

Raisin Oatmeal Cookies

24 LARGE COOKIES

These are rather thin, very chewy, and crunchy.

½ cup <u>un</u>sifted all-purpose flour
¼ teaspoon baking soda
¼ teaspoon salt
2 tablespoons butter
1 tablespoon salad oil (not olive oil)
½ cup dark brown sugar, firmly packed
¼ cup honey
1 egg
1 tablespoon water
1½ cups old-fashioned or quick-cooking
      (not "instant") oatmeal
2½ ounces (½ cup) currants
2½ ounces (½ cup) raisins

Adjust two racks to divide the oven into thirds and preheat to 350 degrees. Cut aluminum foil to fit cookie sheets.

Sift together the flour, baking soda, and salt and set aside. In the small bowl of an electric mixer cream the butter together with the oil. Add the sugar, honey, egg, and the water and beat until smooth. Add the sifted dry ingredients and beat until smooth, scraping the bowl as necessary with a rubber spatula. Remove from the mixer. With a wooden spoon or spatula stir in the oats and then the currants and raisins.

Use a heaping teaspoonful of dough for each cookie. Place them 2 to 2½ inches apart on the cut aluminum foil—these will spread and flatten in baking. Slide cookie sheets under the foil.

Bake for 17 to 20 minutes, reversing the cookie sheets top to bottom and front to back as necessary to insure even browning. The cookies are done when they are lightly colored and spring back if gently pressed with a fingertip. If you bake only one sheet at a time use the higher rack.

The cookies will still feel soft when they are done, but they will crisp as they cool. Slide the foil off the cookie sheet. With a wide metal spatula transfer the cookies to racks to cool.

Butter-scotch Molasses Cookies

36 COOKIES

These are crisp and chewy cookie-jar cookies, easily mixed in a saucepan.

5 ounces (1¼ sticks) butter
1 cup light brown sugar, firmly packed
¼ cup molasses
2½ cups sifted all-purpose flour
1 teaspoon baking soda
¼ teaspoon mace
⅛ teaspoon salt
1 egg
½ teaspoon vanilla extract

Melt the butter in a heavy 3-quart saucepan over moderate heat. Still on heat, add the sugar and molasses and stir until the sugar is melted. Bring the mixture to a rolling boil and then remove it from the heat and set it aside to cool to room temperature.

Adjust two racks to divide the oven into thirds and preheat to 375 degrees. Cut aluminum foil to fit cookie sheets.

Sift together the flour, baking soda, mace, and salt and set aside.

Add the egg and the vanilla to the cooled butter mixture and beat with a wooden spatula until smooth. Gradually add the sifted dry ingredients and beat with the wooden spatula until smooth. Transfer to a small bowl for ease in handling.

Using a rounded teaspoonful of dough for each cookie, place the mounds 1 to 1½ inches apart on the cut aluminum foil. Slide cookie sheets under the foil.

Bake for 10 minutes, reversing the sheets top to bottom and front to back once to insure even baking. The cookies will still feel slightly soft, or barely set, but they will crisp as they cool. (If you bake only one sheet at a time use the higher rack.)

With a wide metal spatula transfer the cookies to racks to cool.

Poppy-Seed Wafers

(*Mohn Cookies*)

42 COOKIES

These Hungarian cookies are thin, crisp, and crunchy. The poppy seeds have a mild nutlike flavor. Incidentally, poppy seeds do come from a poppy plant (so does opium). The seeds are usually slate blue and they are so tiny that it is said there are more than 900,000 to the pound.

½ cup milk
5 ounces (1 cup) poppy seeds (see Notes)
1 cup sifted all-purpose flour
1 teaspoon double-acting baking powder
Pinch of salt
¼ teaspoon nutmeg
2½ ounces (½ cup) raisins (see Notes)
¼ pound (1 stick) butter
½ teaspoon almond extract
½ cup granuated sugar

Adjust two racks to divide the oven into thirds and preheat to 350 degrees. Cut aluminum foil to fit cookie sheets.

In a small saucepan heat the milk until it is very hot but not boiling. Stir in the poppy seeds and set aside.

Sift together the flour, baking powder, salt, and nutmeg and set aside.

Place the raisins on a board. With a long, heavy knife chop them into medium-small pieces and set aside.

In the small bowl of an electric mixer cream the butter. Add the almond extract and the sugar and beat well. On low speed gradually add the sifted dry ingredients, scraping the bowl with a rubber spatula and beating only until incorporated. Mix in the chopped raisins and the poppy-seed-and-milk mixture.

Using a slightly rounded teaspoonful of the dough for each cookie, place them 2 inches apart on the cut aluminum foil.

Slide cookie sheets under the foil and bake the cookies for 18 to 20 minutes, reversing the sheets top to bottom and front to back to insure even browning. The cookies are done when they are lightly browned on the rims and semifirm to the touch in the centers. They will crisp as they cool.

Slide the foil off the sheets. With a wide metal spatula (or with your fingers) transfer the cookies to racks to cool.

NOTES: Poppy seeds are available in small jars in the spice departments of food stores.

The raisins have to be chopped. If they are frozen when you chop them they will be less sticky and easier to cut. Incidentally, I always store raisins (and currants) in the freezer anyhow—they keep better.

Tijuana Fiesta Cookies

36 COOKIES

These are from Mexico. They are soft cookies with an exotic flavor and white vanilla icing.

2¼ cups sifted all-purpose flour
2 teaspoons baking soda
2 teaspoons ginger
1 teaspoon cinnamon
¼ teaspoon powdered cloves
¼ teaspoon salt
2 teaspoons instant coffee
⅓ cup boiling water
¼ pound (1 stick) butter
½ cup granulated sugar
1 egg
½ cup molasses
1 tablespoon whole aniseed
1 teaspoon coriander seeds, crushed (see Note)

Adjust two racks to divide the oven into thirds and preheat to 350 degrees. Cut aluminum foil to fit cookie sheets.

Sift together the flour, baking soda, ginger, cinnamon, cloves, and salt and set aside. Dissolve the instant coffee in the boiling water and set aside.

In the large bowl of an electric mixer cream the butter. Beat in the sugar and then the egg. Gradually beat in the molasses, scraping the bowl as necessary with a rubber spatula. On low speed gradually add half of the sifted dry ingredients, continuing to scrape the bowl and beating only until mixed. Beat in the prepared coffee and then the remaining dry ingredients, beating only until smooth. Stir in the aniseed and coriander seeds.

Place heaping teaspoonfuls of the dough 2 inches apart on the cut aluminum foil. Slide cookie sheets under the foil.

Bake the cookies for 12 to 13 minutes, reversing the sheets top to bottom and front to back once to insure even browning. (If you bake only one sheet at a time, place the rack in the center of the oven.) The cookies are done when the tops spring back if lightly pressed with a fingertip.

With a wide metal spatula transfer the cookies to racks to cool.

ICING

3 cups strained confectioners sugar
  (see page 14)
1½ teaspoons vanilla extract
About 5 tablespoons milk
36 pecan halves

In a small bowl, with a rubber spatula, mix the sugar, vanilla, and milk. Stir well until smooth. The icing should be about the consistency of soft mayonnaise. Add more sugar or milk as necessary to make it soft enough to form a smooth layer. It should not be so thin that it will run off the sides.

Place a teaspoonful of icing on the top of a cookie and spread it with the back of the spoon, leaving a ½- to ¾-inch un-iced margin. Place a pecan half on top of each cookie and let the cookies cool on racks until the icing is set.

NOTE: The coriander seeds may be crushed in a blender or with a mortar and pestle—they do not have to be powdered.

Vanilla Butter Wafers

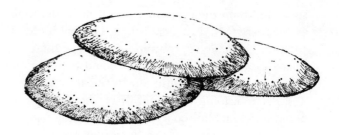

24 SMALL COOKIES

These thin, buttery rounds will be brown and crisp on the edges, light and slightly soft on the tops. They are simple, easy cookies to make, but are extremely delicate and fragile. This recipe makes only 24—double it if you wish.

¼ pound (1 stick) butter
1 teaspoon vanilla extract
⅓ cup granulated sugar
1 egg
⅓ cup sifted all-purpose flour

Adjust two racks to divide the oven into thirds and preheat to 350 degrees. Cut aluminum foil to fit cookie sheets.

In the small bowl of an electric mixer cream the butter. Add the vanilla and the sugar and beat very well for 2 to 3 minutes. Add the egg and beat well again for 2 to 3 minutes more. On low speed add the flour, scraping the bowl with a rubber spatula and beating only until smooth.

Transfer the dough to a shallow bowl for ease in handling.

Use a slightly rounded teaspoonful of the dough for each cookie (keep these small). If you place the dough neatly and carefully the cookies will bake into perfect rounds, which is the way they should be. Place the mounds of dough 3 inches apart on the cut aluminum foil. Slide cookie sheets under the foil.

Bake for 12 to 15 minutes, until the edges are well browned. Reverse the sheets top to bottom and front to back once to insure even browning.

With a wide metal spatula transfer the cookies to racks to cool.

NOTE: If these are dropped too large or too close to each other they will run together.

Bar Cookies

PETITES TRIANONS

ALL-AMERICAN BROWNIES

GREENWICH VILLAGE BROWNIES

CREAM-CHEESE BROWNIES

FUDGE BROWNIES

CHOCOLATE MINT STICKS

DUTCH CHOCOLATE BARS

VIENNESE CHOCOLATE-WALNUT BARS

SUPREMES

DARK ROCKY ROADS

LIGHT ROCKY ROADS

BUTTERSCOTCH BROWNIES

FLORIDA CREAM-CHEESE SQUARES

FLORIDA LEMON SQUARES

PALM BEACH PINEAPPLE SQUARES

CHRISTMAS FRUITCAKE BARS

HERMIT BARS

BRITTLE PEANUT BARS

HUNGARIAN WALNUT BARS

BUTTERSCOTCH WALNUT BARS

CINNAMON ALMOND COOKIES

GEORGIA PECAN BARS

PECAN FESTIVAL BARS

PECAN CHEWS

ASPEN OATMEAL BARS

TEXAS COWBOY BARS

HONEY DATE-NUT BARS

ASPEN DATE-NUT FINGERS

VIENNESE LINZER COOKIES

POLISH WEDDING CAKES

VIENNESE MARZIPAN BARS

These are made in a shallow pan and then cut into bars after baking.

Some of the recipes in this section call for dusting the pan with either flour or breadcrumbs after it has been buttered. This is done as a further precaution against the cake's sticking. I have tried both flour and breadcrumbs for each recipe and whichever I have specified is the one that seemed to me to work better. When flour is used, it is always in addition to the amount listed in the ingredients.

Petites Trianons

A French recipe for small, plain, fudgelike squares similar to Brownies without nuts. These are quick and easy to make; they are mixed in a saucepan.

16 SQUARES OR 12 TO 24 BARS

¼ pound (1 stick) butter, cut into
    1-inch slices
2 ounces (2 squares) unsweetened chocolate
1 cup granulated sugar
½ teaspoon vanilla extract
2 extra-large or jumbo eggs
1 cup sifted all-purpose flour
Pinch of salt

Adjust a rack one-third up from the bottom of the oven and preheat to 350 degrees. Prepare an 8-inch-square cake pan as follows: Turn pan upside down. Cut a 12-inch square of aluminum foil. Center it over the inverted pan. Fold down the sides and the corners and then remove the foil and turn the pan right side up. Place the foil in the pan. In order not to tear the foil use a pot holder or a folded towel and, pressing gently with the pot holder or towel, smooth the foil into place. Lightly butter the bottom and halfway up the sides, using soft or melted butter and a pastry brush or crumpled wax paper. Set aside.

Place the butter and chocolate in a heavy 2- to 3-quart saucepan over low heat. Stir occasionally with a rubber or wooden spatula until melted and smooth. Set aside to cool for about 3 minutes.

Stir in the sugar and the vanilla and then the eggs one at a time, stirring until smooth after each addition. Add the flour and the salt and stir until smooth.

Pour the mixture into the prepared pan and spread evenly.

Bake for exactly 28 minutes. Do not overbake; this should remain moist in the center. Cool in the pan for 5 minutes.

Cover with a rack and invert. Remove the pan and aluminum foil. The bottom of the cake will be slightly moist in the center. Cover with another rack and invert again to cool right side up. (The cake will be about ¾ inch thick.)

When the cake is cool transfer it to a cutting board. With a long, thin, sharp knife cut the cake into squares or oblongs.

These may be arranged on a tray and covered with plastic wrap until serving time. Or they may be wrapped individually in clear cellophane or wax paper. Either way, do not allow them to dry out. They may be frozen and may be served either at room temperature or about 5 minutes after being removed from the freezer—they're awfully good still frozen.

All-American Brownies

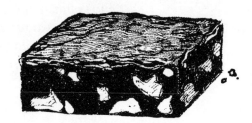

This recipe is almost the same as the Petites Trianons above. There are a few minor changes.

Use only ½ cup sifted all-purpose flour and, at the end, stir in 2 ounces (generous ½ cup) walnuts, cut or broken into medium-size pieces (see page 13).

Bake for 20 to 25 minutes. To test, insert a toothpick into the center of the cake. When it just barely comes out clean but not dry, the Brownies are done. Do not overbake. These should be soft and moist to be at their best.

Since this dough is moister than the Petites Trianons (less flour), let the Brownies cool to room temperature in the pan before inverting and removing.

These may be served frozen, directly from the freezer (delicious), or at room temperature.

Greenwich Village Brownies

These are a specialty of a New York City pastry shop. It is a recipe with a large yield. The Brownies are moist, fudgy, and extra-chewy—almost like chocolate caramels.

2 cups <u>unsifted</u> all-purpose flour
¼ teaspoon salt
6 ounces (6 squares) unsweetened chocolate
½ pound (2 sticks) butter
1 teaspoon vanilla extract
2 cups granulated sugar
1 cup light brown sugar, firmly packed
⅔ cup light corn syrup
6 eggs
10 ounces (3 cups) pecan halves or large pieces

Adjust a rack one-third up from the bottom of the oven and preheat to 350 degrees. Grease a 15½-by-10½-by-1-inch jelly-roll pan. Line it with a large piece of wax paper, butter the paper, and dust it lightly all over with flour. Invert the pan to shake out excess flour.

Measure the flour before sifting, then sift it together with the salt and set aside. Melt the chocolate in the top of a small double boiler over hot water on moderate heat. Stir until smooth, remove the top of the double boiler, and set aside.

In the large bowl of an electric mixer cream the butter. Add the vanilla and the granulated and brown sugars. Beat to mix well. Add the corn syrup and beat until smooth. Add the eggs one at a time, beating until smooth after each addition. Beat in the melted chocolate. On low speed, gradually add the flour, scraping the bowl as necessary with a rubber spatula and beating until smoothly mixed. Stir in 2 cups (reserve 1 cup) of the pecans.

Turn the mixture into the prepared pan and spread to make a smooth layer. (The pan will be filled to the top.) Sprinkle the reserved 1 cup pecans over the top.

Bake for 40 to 45 minutes until a toothpick inserted in the center of the cake comes out clean but not dry.

Cool in the pan for 30 minutes. Then cover with a large rack or cookie sheet and invert. Remove the pan and the wax paper. Cover with a large rack and invert again, leaving the cake right side up to cool completely.

The cake will be easier to cut if it is chilled first; place it in the freezer or refrigerator until it is quite firm. Or cover the cake with aluminum foil or plastic wrap and let it stand overnight at room temperature.

Slide the cake onto a cutting board. Use a long, thin, sharp knife or a finely serrated one to cut it into bars. (See Note.)

Wrap the Brownies individually in clear cellophane or wax paper, or store them in an airtight freezer box.

NOTE: If there are any burnt edges on the cake they should be cut off. Cut the cake into quarters and place the quarters upside down on the board to trim the edges. Then turn the cake right side up again for cutting into bars.

Cream-Cheese Brownies

24 BROWNIES

Part Brownies, part cheesecake—layered and marbled together. These must be stored in the refrigerator or they may be frozen. And they may be eaten directly from the freezer or thawed.

CHOCOLATE MIXTURE

½ cup <u>unsifted</u> all-purpose flour
½ teaspoon double-acting baking powder
¼ teaspoon salt
4 ounces (4 squares) semisweet chocolate
3 tablespoons butter
2 eggs
¾ cup granulated sugar

1 teaspoon vanilla extract
2½ ounces (¾ cup) walnuts, cut into
medium-size pieces (see page 13)

Adjust a rack one-third up from bottom of oven and preheat to 350 degrees. Butter a 9-inch-square pan.

Sift together the flour, baking powder, and salt and set aside. Melt the chocolate and the butter in the top of a small double boiler over hot water on moderate heat. Stir until smooth, remove from heat, and set aside to cool slightly.

In the small bowl of an electric mixer beat the eggs until foamy. Add the sugar and vanilla and beat at high speed for 3 to 4 minutes, until the mixture is light lemon-colored and forms a ribbon when beaters are lifted. On low speed beat in the chocolate mixture and then the sifted dry ingredients, scraping the bowl with a rubber spatula and beating only until the dry ingredients are incorporated.

Remove and set aside ¾ cup of the mixture. To the remaining batter add ½ cup of the nuts (reserve ¼ cup for topping) and stir to mix. Spread the chocolate mixture evenly in the buttered pan; it will be a very thin layer.

CHEESE MIXTURE

4 ounces cream cheese
2 tablespoons butter
½ teaspoon vanilla extract
¼ cup granulated sugar
1 egg

In the small bowl of an electric mixer beat the cream cheese with the butter until soft and smooth. Add the vanilla and sugar and beat well. Then add the egg and beat again until very smooth.

Spread the cheese mixture evenly over the chocolate layer. Place the reserved ¾ cup of the chocolate mixture by heaping tablespoonfuls onto the cheese layer, letting the cheese show through between mounds—you should have about 8 or 9 chocolate mounds. With a small metal spatula or a table knife cut through the chocolate mounds and the cheese layer. It is best if you don't cut down into the bottom layer. Zigzag the knife to marbleize the batters slightly; don't overdo it. Sprinkle with reserved ¼ cup nuts.

Bake for 35 minutes.

Cool completely in the pan and then let stand at room temperature for a few hours. Do not cut too soon or the cake will be too sticky to cut neatly.

With a small, sharp knife cut around the sides to release and cut the cake into bars or squares. If you find it is still a bit sticky, cut the cake into quarters; use a wide metal spatula to transfer the quarters to a small board or cookie sheet and chill in the freezer or refrigerator until firm enough to cut neatly. Cut each quarter into 6 bars.

Transfer the bars to a serving plate, cover airtight with plastic wrap, and refrigerate. Or pack them in a freezer box and freeze. Or they may be wrapped individually in clear cellophane or wax paper and then placed in the refrigerator or freezer.

Fudge Brownies

24 BROWNIES

On the theory that there can't be too much of a good thing, here is still another Brownie—another fudgy, moist, candylike, dark chocolate bar cookie.

> *4 ounces (4 squares) unsweetened chocolate*
> *¼ pound (1 stick) butter, cut into large pieces*
> *3 eggs*
> *1½ cups granulated sugar*
> *1 teaspoon vanilla extract*
> *Pinch of salt*

¾ cup sifted all-purpose flour
Optional: 2½ ounces (¾ cup) walnuts, cut or
broken into medium-size pieces (these
cookies are equally good with or without
the nuts)

Adjust an oven rack one-third up from the bottom and preheat to 350 degrees. Butter a 9-inch-square cake pan and dust the bottom with fine dry breadcrumbs, shake out excess crumbs, and set aside.

Place the chocolate and the butter in the top of a small double boiler over hot water on moderate heat. Cover and cook until almost melted. Remove the cover and stir until completely melted and smooth. Then remove the top of the double boiler and set it aside to cool slightly.

In the small bowl of an electric mixer beat the eggs at high speed for only about half a minute until foamy and slightly increased in volume. On low speed gradually add the sugar and beat for only a few seconds to mix. Add the vanilla, salt, and the chocolate mixture, scraping the bowl with a rubber spatula and beating only until barely mixed. Do not overbeat (see Note). Now add the flour, still scraping the bowl and beating only until mixed.

Remove the bowl from the mixer and, if you are using the walnuts, fold them in.

Turn the mixture into the prepared pan and smooth the top.

Bake for 35 minutes or a few minutes longer until a toothpick inserted in the center of the cake comes out barely clean. The inside should still be soft. Do not overbake.

Remove the pan from the oven, place it on a rack, and let it stand for 45 minutes to 1 hour until the bottom of the pan is only slightly warm. With a small, sharp knife cut around the sides of the cake carefully to release.

Cover the cake with a rack and invert, remove the cake pan, cover the cake again with a rack or a small cookie sheet, and invert again.

In order to cut the cake neatly it is best to chill it first in the freezer or refrigerator. If you partially freeze it, it will cut perfectly.

Slide the chilled cake onto a cutting board and with a long, sharp knife or a finely serrated one, cut it into bars.

The bars may be placed on a tray and covered airtight with plastic wrap, or they may be stored airtight in a plastic freezer box—or, preferably, wrap them individually in clear cellophane or wax paper.

NOTE: If you overbeat the eggs or the eggs and sugar, it will make the Brownies cakelike, spongy, and dry instead of moist.

Chocolate Mint Sticks

32 SMALL BARS

These are similar to Brownies, covered with a layer of mint-flavored icing and a thin bitter-chocolate glaze.

2 ounces (2 squares) unsweetened chocolate
¼ pound (1 stick) butter
2 eggs
Pinch of salt
½ teaspoon vanilla extract
1 cup granulated sugar
½ cup sifted all-purpose flour
2 ounces (generous ½ cup) walnuts, cut or
    broken into medium-size pieces
    (see page 13)

Adjust a rack one-third up from the bottom of the oven and preheat to 350 degrees. Butter a 9-inch-square cake pan and dust it all over with fine dry breadcrumbs; invert the pan to shake out excess. (This cake has a tendency to stick to the pan; using the crumbs will prevent that.)

Melt the chocolate and the butter in the top of a small double boiler over hot water on moderate heat. Stir until smooth. Remove the top of the double boiler and set aside to cool slightly.

In the small bowl of an electric mixer beat the eggs until they are foamy. Beat in the salt, vanilla, and sugar. Add the chocolate mixture (which may still be warm) and beat to mix. On low speed add the flour, scraping the bowl with a rubber spatula and beating only until mixed. Stir in the nuts.

Pour the mixture into the prepared pan and spread it to make a smooth layer.

Bake for 28 minutes, or until a toothpick inserted in the center of the cake comes out clean.

Remove the cake from the oven and let it stand, in the pan, at room temperature until completely cool.

Prepare the following Mint Icing.

MINT ICING

2 tablespoons butter, at room temperature
1 cup strained or sifted confectioners sugar

1 tablespoon (or a few drops more)
heavy cream
½ teaspoon peppermint extract

Place all of the icing ingredients in the small bowl of an electric mixer and beat until smooth. It might be necessary to add a few drops more of the heavy cream, but it should be a thick mixture, not runny.

Spread the icing evenly over the cake still in the pan. It will be a very thin layer. Place the cake in the refrigerator for 5 minutes, no longer.
Prepare the following glaze.

BITTER-CHOCOLATE GLAZE

1 ounce (1 square) unsweetened chocolate
1 tablespoon butter

Melt the chocolate and the butter in the top of a small double boiler over hot water on moderate heat. Stir until completely smooth.

Pour the hot glaze onto the chilled icing and quickly tilt the pan in all directions, to cover the icing completely with the glaze. It will be a very, very thin layer of glaze, just barely enough to cover all of the icing. (But, if the icing does show through in a few small spots, don't worry—it will be all right.)
Refrigerate the cake for about half an hour or until the glaze starts to look dull.
With a small, sharp knife cut around the sides of the cake to release it. Wipe the knife blade as necessary to keep it clean, and cut the cake into quarters.
With a wide metal spatula transfer the quarters to a cutting board. With a long, sharp knife cut each quarter in half and then cut each half into four small bars, wiping the knife blade as necessary.
Transfer the bars to a tray or cake plate and let stand at room temperature for several hours at least before serving to allow the glaze to dry.
These may be frozen and are especially good when served directly from the freezer.

Dutch Chocolate Bars

These have a crisp, crunchy base with a thick, moist, baked-on chocolate topping. They are made without a mixer.

16 OR 18 BARS

BOTTOM LAYER

⅓ cup sifted all-purpose flour
¼ teaspoon baking soda
⅛ teaspoon salt
½ cup light brown sugar, firmly packed
1 cup old-fashioned or quick-cooking
    (not "instant") oatmeal
2 ounces (generous ½ cup) pecans, finely
    chopped (see page 13)
2⅔ ounces (5⅓ tablespoons) butter, melted

Adjust a rack to the center of the oven and preheat to 350 degrees.

Into a mixing bowl sift together the flour, baking soda, and salt. Add the sugar and stir to mix thoroughly. Stir in the oatmeal and nuts and then the butter. The mixture will be crumbly and it will not hold together.

Turn the dough into an unbuttered 8-inch-square cake pan. With your fingertips, press the dough to form a smooth, compact layer.

Bake for 10 minutes.

Meanwhile, prepare the topping.

TOPPING

⅔ cup sifted all-purpose flour
¼ teaspoon baking soda
¼ teaspoon salt
1 ounce (1 square) unsweetened chocolate
2 ounces (4 tablespoons) butter
¾ cup granulated sugar
1 egg
1 teaspoon vanilla extract
2 tablespoons milk

Sift together the flour, baking soda, and salt and set aside. Melt the chocolate and the butter in the top of a large double boiler over hot water on moderate heat (or in a heavy saucepan over very low heat). Stir the chocolate and butter until smooth and remove from the heat. Mix in the sugar and then the egg, stirring until thoroughly mixed. Stir in the vanilla and milk. Add the sifted dry ingredients and stir until smooth.

Pour the chocolate topping over the hot bottom layer and spread smoothly.

Bake for about 35 minutes or until a toothpick inserted in the center of the cake barely comes out clean and dry. Do not overbake; the chocolate should remain moist.

Cool the cake completely in the pan.

With a small, sharp knife cut the cooled cake ino squares or bars.

These are best when very fresh. Wrap them individually in clear cellophane or wax paper or place them on a tray and cover airtight. Or leave them in the baking pan and cover airtight. Or pack them in an airtight freezer box. Just don't let them dry out.

Viennese Chocolate-Walnut Bars

32 SMALL BARS

These are soft, rich, and fudgy. There is a buttery crust, a walnut filling, and a dark chocolate icing.

CRUST

¼ pound (1 stick) butter
¼ cup dark brown sugar, firmly packed
1¼ cups sifted all-purpose flour

Adjust a rack one-third up from the bottom of the oven and preheat to 375 degrees.

In the small bowl of an electric mixer cream the butter. Beat in the sugar. On low speed gradually add the flour and beat only until the mixture holds together.

Place the dough by large spoonfuls over the bottom of an unbuttered 9-inch-square cake pan. With your fingertips press the dough to make a smooth layer over the bottom of the pan.

Bake for 10 minutes.

Meanwhile prepare the filling.

CHOCOLATE WALNUT FILLING

¼ cup apricot preserves
6 ounces (generous 1½ cups) walnuts
2 eggs
¼ teaspoon salt
½ teaspoon vanilla extract
¾ cup dark brown sugar, firmly packed
2 tablespoons unsweetened cocoa

In a small bowl stir the preserves just to soften them and set aside.

Grind the walnuts to a fine powder in a blender or a nut grinder and set aside.

In the small bowl of an electric mixer beat the eggs at high speed for 2 or 3 minutes until they are slightly thickened. Add the salt and vanilla, and then, on low speed, add the sugar and cocoa. Increase the speed to high again and beat for 2 to 3 minutes more. On low speed mix in the ground walnuts, beating only until the nuts are incorporated.

Spread the preserves over the hot crust, leaving a ½-inch border. It will be a very thin layer but it is really enough.

Pour the filling over the preserves and tilt the pan to level the filling.

Bake at 375 degrees for 25 minutes.

Let the cake cool completely and then prepare the icing.

CHOCOLATE ICING

6 ounces (1 cup) semisweet chocolate morsels
2 tablespoons light corn syrup
2 teaspoons rum or strong prepared coffee
2 teaspoons boiling water
2 ounces (generous ½ cup) walnuts, cut
    medium fine (see page 13)

In the top of a small double boiler, covered, over hot water on moderate heat, cook the chocolate until it is partially melted. Still on the heat stir the chocolate with a rubber spatula until it is completely melted and smooth. Add the corn syrup, rum or coffee, and the boiling water, and stir until smooth.

Spread the icing evenly over the cake. Sprinkle with the nuts and press down gently with a wide metal spatula to press the nuts slightly into the icing.

Let stand at room temperature until the icing is firm; it will probably take a few hours.

With a small, sharp knife cut around the sides of the cake to release it and then cut the cake into quarters. With a wide metal spatula transfer the quarters to a cutting board and cut each quarter into small bars.

Place the bars on a serving dish, cover with plastic wrap, and let stand at room temperature for a few hours (or overnight) before serving.

Supremes

32 OR 48 LARGE BARS, OR 64 SMALL

These are rich walnut-oatmeal bars with a baked-in sweet chocolate filling. The recipe gives a large yield and the cookies are generally best stored in the refrigerator and served cold.

2½ cups sifted all-purpose flour
1 teaspoon baking soda
½ teaspoon salt
½ pound (2 sticks) butter
1 teaspoon instant coffee
1 teaspoon vanilla extract
2 cups light brown sugar, firmly packed
2 eggs
3 cups old-fashioned or quick-cooking
(not "instant") oatmeal
7 ounces (2 cups) walnuts, cut or broken into
medium-size pieces

Adjust a rack one-third up from the bottom of the oven and preheat to 350 degrees. Butter a 15½-by-10½-by-1-inch jelly-roll pan.

Sift together the flour, baking soda, and salt and set aside. In the large bowl of an electric mixer cream the butter. Add the coffee, vanilla, and sugar and beat well. Add the eggs and beat well. On low speed gradually beat in the sifted dry ingredients and then the oatmeal, scraping the bowl with a rubber spatula as necessary. Finally mix in 1 cup of the walnuts (reserve the remaining cup for the topping).

Remove and reserve 2 cups of the dough. Place the remainder by large spoonfuls over the bottom of the buttered pan. With well-floured fingertips press all over to make a smooth, even layer. Set aside and prepare the following filling.

CHOCOLATE FILLING

1 fourteen- or fifteen-ounce can
sweetened condensed milk
12 ounces (2 cups) semisweet chocolate
morsels
2 tablespoons butter
Pinch of salt
1 teaspoon vanilla extract

Place the condensed milk, chocolate morsels, butter, and salt in the top of a large double boiler over hot water on moderate heat. Stir occasionally until the chocolate and butter are melted and the mixture is smooth.

Remove the top of the double boiler from the heat and stir in the vanilla. Pour the warm chocolate mixture over the bottom oatmeal layer and spread evenly. Place the reserved oatmeal mixture by small spoonfuls over the chocolate, letting the chocolate show through between spoonfuls. Do not spread smooth. Sprinkle the reserved cup of walnuts evenly over the top.

Bake for 25 minutes or until the top is golden brown. Reverse the pan front to back once toward the end of baking to insure even browning. The top mounds of dough will flatten slightly but they will not run together to cover the chocolate.

Cool completely in the pan at room temperature, not in the refrigerator, for several hours or overnight.

To cut the cookies: Cut around the sides to release the cake. Then cut the panful into eighths and with a wide metal spatula transfer the sections to a cutting board. Cut each eighth into 4 or 6 pieces. If the cookies are soft and do not cut neatly and evenly (if they squash), chill the pieces on wax paper on a tray or cookie sheet in the freezer or refrigerator only until they are firm enough to cut neatly.

The cookies may be placed on a tray and covered with plastic wrap or packed in a freezer box or wrapped individually in clear cellophane or wax paper.

If the filling is too soft these should be stored in the refrigerator.

Dark Rocky Roads

24 BARS

Made without a mixer, these chocolate, Brownie-like bars are topped with marshmallows, pecans, and a thick, dark chocolate glaze. It is best to make these the night before, or early in the day of the night they are to be served, because they must stand before being cut into bars.

CHOCOLATE LAYER

¾ cup sifted all-purpose flour
½ teaspoon double-acting baking powder
¼ teaspoon salt
1 ounce (1 square) unsweetened chocolate
3 ounces (6 tablespoons) butter
½ teaspoon vanilla extract
1 cup granulated sugar
2 eggs
2 ounces (generous ½ cup) pecans, coarsely
    cut or broken (see page 13)

Adjust a rack to the center of the oven and preheat to 350 degrees. Butter an 11-by-7½-by-1¾-inch baking pan and set aside.

Sift together the flour, baking powder, and salt and set aside.

Place the chocolate and the butter in a 2- to 3-quart saucepan over moderately low heat. Stir constantly until they are melted. Remove from the heat. Add the vanilla and sugar and stir to mix well. Add the eggs one at a time, stirring until thoroughly incorporated after each addition. Stir in the sifted dry ingredients until thoroughly mixed, then stir in the nuts.

Pour into the prepared pan and spread into an even layer.

Bake for 23 to 25 minutes or until a toothpick inserted in the middle of the cake barely comes out dry. Do not overbake.

While the cake is baking prepare the topping and start to prepare the glaze.

TOPPING

23 regular-size marshmallows
2½ ounces (¾ cup) pecan halves or large
   pieces

Cut the marshmallows in half crossways. This may be done with a knife or with scissors (try both and see which you prefer). If the marshmallows stick, dip the knife blade or the scissors into cold water to eliminate this problem. Set the cut marshmallows aside on wax paper, placing them cut side up. Also have the pecans ready.

A few minutes before the chocolate layer is done, start to prepare the glaze.

GLAZE

1 ounce (1 square) unsweetened chocolate
1 tablespoon butter
1 cup strained confectioners sugar
¼ teaspoon vanilla extract
About 2 tablespoons boiling water

Melt the chocolate and butter in the top of a small double boiler over hot water on moderate heat. Remove from the heat but do not mix in the remaining ingredients until you are ready to use the glaze.

When the chocolate layer is done, remove it from the oven, but do not turn off the oven heat. Quickly place the cut marshmallow halves in even rows over the top of the cake—cut side down, five in each short row and nine in each long row. They should just touch each other (there will be one half left over).

Immediately return the pan to the oven and bake for exactly 1 minute —no longer; the marshmallows should only soften slightly; they should not bake long enough to melt. Remove the pan from the oven and finish the glaze as follows: Add the sugar, vanilla, and 2 tablespoons of boiling water to the melted chocolate-butter mixture. Stir until smooth. The mixture should be thick, but thin enough to drizzle over the marshmallows. It will probably be necessary to add a bit more water but add it very gradually and be sure that you do not add too much.

Quickly sprinkle the pecans over the marshmallows and then immediately (while the cake is still hot and before the glaze thickens), drizzle the glaze unevenly over the marshmallows and nuts. Some of the marshmallows should show through in a few spots but the nuts should all be at least partly covered in order to keep them from falling off.

Let stand uncovered overnight or for at least 5 or 6 hours if possible; if you try to cut these any sooner the marshmallows might be sticky and difficult to handle. (See Note.) Cut around the sides with a small, sharp knife to release the cake. Then cut the cake into eighths. Keep dipping the knife into cold water to prevent it from sticking.

Dip a wide metal spatula into cold water (every time) and transfer the eighths to a cutting board. Then, with a wet knife, cut each eighth into 3 bars.

NOTE: Cutting these into bars is liable to be a little messy and frustrating even after letting them stand. Just be brave and remember that you're the boss. The cookies are well worth a little trouble.

Light Rocky Roads

18 BARS

These candylike bars have a thin brown-sugar layer that is topped with marshmallows, nuts, and chocolate.

¼ cup sifted all-purpose flour
¼ teaspoon double-acting baking powder
Pinch of salt
1 egg
⅓ cup dark or light brown sugar, firmly packed
½ teaspoon vanilla extract
1 tablespoon butter, melted
½ cup walnuts or pecans, finely cut
 (see page 13)

Adjust a rack one-third up from the bottom of the oven and preheat to 350 degrees. Butter an 8-inch-square cake pan.

Sift together the flour, baking powder, and salt and set aside. In a small bowl beat the egg lightly only until it is foamy. Add the brown sugar and vanilla and beat just to mix. Mix in the butter and then the sifted dry ingredients. Stir in the nuts.

Turn the dough into the prepared pan and spread it evenly. It will be a very thin layer.

Bake for 15 minutes or until the top of the cake springs back when lightly pressed with a fingertip.

Meanwhile line up the ingredients for the topping.

ROCKY ROAD TOPPING

1 cup miniature marshmallows
2 ounces (½ cup) walnuts or pecans, coarsely
 cut or broken
6 ounces (1 cup) semisweet chocolate morsels

Remove the cake from the oven and immediately cover it with a layer of the marshmallows, then with the nuts, and then place the chocolate morsels on top.

Raise the oven rack to the top position in the oven. Bake the cake for only 2 to 3 minutes, no longer, just until the chocolate is softened but not long enough to melt the marshmallows. Immediately, with the back of a spoon, spread the chocolate lightly and unevenly over the marshmallows and nuts, letting some of the marshmallows show through in a few places.

Cool the cake to room temperature and then chill it briefly to barely set the chocolate.

With a small, sharp knife cut the cake in half in one direction and in thirds in the opposite direction. Cut around the sides to release. With a wide metal spatula transfer the pieces to a cutting board and then cut each piece into 3 bars.

NOTE: If the chocolate becomes spotty after the cookies have cooled, sprinkle the top with confectioners sugar, pressing the sugar through a fine strainer held over the cookies.

Butter-scotch Brownies

24 BARS

All Brownies are not chocolate; these are brown-sugar bars with a butterscotch flavor, especially moist and chewy.

¼ pound (1 stick) butter
1 teaspoon vanilla extract
1 tablespoon light molasses
1¼ cups dark brown sugar, firmly packed
2 eggs
1 cup sifted all-purpose flour
2½ ounces (¾ cup) pecans, coarsely
     cut or broken

Adjust a rack one-third up from the bottom of the oven and preheat to 350 degrees. Butter a 9-inch-square baking pan.

In the large bowl of an electric mixer cream the butter. Beat in the vanilla and molasses. Add the brown sugar and beat well. Add the eggs one at a time, beating well after each addition, and then beat at moderately high speed for a minute or two, scraping the bowl occasionally with a rubber spatula, until the mixture is very smooth and light in color. On low speed add the flour, continuing to scrape the bowl with the spatula, and beating only until thoroughly mixed.

Remove the bowl from the mixer and stir in the nuts.

Transfer the dough to the buttered pan. Spread the top to make it an even layer.

Bake for 32 to 35 minutes until a toothpick inserted in the center just barely comes out dry.

Let the cake cool completely in the pan.

With a small, sharp knife cut around the sides to release and then cut the cake into quarters. With a wide metal spatula transfer the quarters to a cutting board. Cut each quarter in half and then cut each piece into 3 bars.

The bars may be wrapped individually in clear cellophane or wax paper. Or they may be placed on a tray and covered with plastic wrap, or stored in a covered freezer box. Or, for a picnic, leave the cake in the pan but cut it into 24 bars. Cover the pan with plastic wrap or aluminum foil and take a metal spatula along with you and remove the bars from the pan at the picnic.

Florida Cream-Cheese Squares

These are layered squares with a baked-in cream-cheese filling. They should be refrigerated until serving time.

16 SQUARES

2⅔ ounces (5⅓ tablespoons) butter
⅓ cup dark brown sugar, firmly packed
1 cup sifted all-purpose flour
½ cup walnuts, chopped medium fine
Finely grated rind of 1 lemon
1 tablespoon lemon juice
8 ounces cream cheese, preferably at room temperature
¼ cup granulated sugar
½ teaspoon vanilla extract
1 egg

Adjust a rack one-third up from the bottom of the oven and preheat to 350 degrees. Butter an 8-inch-square cake pan.

In the small bowl of an electric mixer cream the butter. Add the brown sugar and beat well. On low speed gradually add the flour and then the walnuts, scraping the bowl with a rubber spatula and beating until well mixed. The mixture will be crumbly and won't hold together. Remove and set aside 1 cup of the mixture.

Distribute the remainder evenly over the bottom of the prepared pan. Then, with your fingertips, press it firmly to make a smooth, compact layer.

Bake for 15 minutes.

Meanwhile, mix the lemon rind with the lemon juice and set aside. In the small bowl of an electric mixer cream the cheese. Add the granulated sugar and beat well. Add the vanilla and the egg and beat to mix well. Remove the bowl from the mixer and stir in the lemon rind and juice mixture.

Pour the cream-cheese mixture over the hot baked crust. Tilt the pan gently to level the filling. Carefully sprinkle the reserved crumb mixture evenly over the filling.

Bake for 25 minutes.

Cool the cake in its pan to room temperature. Then refrigerate it for 1 hour or more.

With a small, sharp knife cut around the sides to release. Then cut the cake into quarters. With a wide metal spatula transfer the quarters to a cutting board. If you have trouble releasing the first piece, cut it into quarters and remove the pieces individually. If necessary, use a fork to ease the first few pieces out of the pan. Use a long knife to cut each quarter into four squares, wiping the blade with a damp cloth after each cut.

Place the squares on a tray or serving dish. Cover with plastic wrap and refrigerate until serving time. Or pack the squares in a freezer box and freeze them. These may be served frozen, directly from the freezer.

Florida Lemon Squares

24 OR 32 SQUARES

These are rich layered bars with a baked-in tart lemon filling. They should be refrigerated until serving time.

1½ cups sifted all-purpose flour
1 teaspoon double-acting baking powder
½ teaspoon salt
1 fourteen- or fifteen-ounce can
    sweetened condensed milk
Finely grated rind of 1 large lemon
½ cup lemon juice
5⅓ ounces (10⅔ tablespoons) butter
1 cup dark brown sugar, firmly packed
1 cup old-fashioned or quick-cooking
    (not "instant") oatmeal

Adjust a rack one-third up from the bottom of the oven and preheat to 350 degrees. Butter a 9-by-13-by-2-inch pan.

Sift together the flour, baking powder, and salt and set aside. Pour the condensed milk into a medium-size mixing bowl. Add the grated lemon rind and then, gradually, add the lemon juice, stirring with a small wire whisk to keep the mixture smooth. (The lemon will thicken the milk.) Set the mixture aside.

In the large bowl of an electric mixer cream the butter. Add the sugar and beat well. On lowest speed gradually add the sifted dry ingredients, scraping the bowl with a rubber spatula and beating only until thoroughly mixed. Mix in the oatmeal. The mixture will be crumbly—it will not hold together.

Sprinkle a bit more than half of the oatmeal mixture (2 generous cups) evenly over the bottom of the prepared pan. Pat the crumbs firmly with your fingertips to make a smooth, compact layer. Drizzle or spoon the lemon mixture evenly over the crumb layer and spread it to make a thin, smooth layer. Sprinkle the remaining crumbly oatmeal mixture evenly over the lemon layer. Pat the crumbs gently with the palm of your hand to smooth them—it is O.K. if a bit of the lemon layer shows through in small spots.

Bake for 30 to 35 minutes until the cake is lightly colored.

Cool the cake completely in the pan. Then refrigerate it for about 1 hour (or more).

With a small, sharp knife cut around the sides of the cake to release it. Cut it into small squares. With a wide metal spatula remove the squares from the pan; transfer them to a serving plate, cover with plastic wrap, and refrigerate.

OPTIONAL: Just before serving, the cookies may be topped with confectioners sugar. Use your fingertips to press the sugar through a fine strainer held over the cookies. (It is best to have the cookies on wax paper while coating them with sugar.)

Palm Beach Pineapple Squares

These have a soft cakelike chocolate bottom and a pineapple topping.

24 TO 36 SQUARES
OR BARS

1½ cups sifted all-purpose flour
1½ teaspoons double-acting baking powder
¼ teaspoon salt
2 ounces (2 squares) unsweetened chocolate
1 eight-ounce can (1 cup) crushed pineapple
6 ounces (1½ sticks) butter
1 teaspoon vanilla extract
1½ cups granulated sugar
3 eggs
Finely grated rind of 1 lemon
4 ounces (generous 1 cup) walnuts, cut into
    medium-size pieces

Adjust a rack one-third up from the bottom of the oven and preheat to 375 degrees. Butter a 13-by-9-by-2-inch pan and then dust it all over lightly with fine dry breadcrumbs; invert the pan to shake out excess.

Sift together the flour, baking powder, and salt and set aside. Melt the chocolate in the top of a small double boiler over hot water on moderate heat and then set aside to cool.

Place the pineapple in a strainer set over a bowl and let stand to drain.

In the large bowl of an electric mixer cream the butter. Add the vanilla and sugar and beat well. Add the eggs one at a time, beating well after each addition. On low speed add the dry ingredients, scraping the bowl with a rubber spatula and beating only until thoroughly mixed.

Remove 1 cup of the mixture and place it in a medium-size bowl. Stir the lemon rind and the drained pineapple into this cup of batter. Set aside.

Add the melted chocolate to the mixture remaining in the large bowl and beat until thoroughly mixed. Stir in the nuts.

Spread the chocolate mixture in an even layer in the prepared pan. Place the pineapple mixture by small spoonfuls evenly over the chocolate layer. With the back of a small spoon spread the pineapple mixture to make a smooth thin layer—it is all right if a bit of the chocolate shows through in places.

Bake for 40 to 45 minutes, reversing the position of the pan once to insure even browning. The cake is done when the top springs back if lightly pressed with a fingertip and the cake begins to come away from the sides of the pan.

Let the cake cool in the pan for about 15 minutes. Then cover it with a cookie sheet and invert. Remove the pan and cover the cake with a large rack. Invert again to cool completely right side up.

When completely cool transfer the cake to a cutting board. With a long, thin, sharp knife cut into squares or bars.

Christmas Fruitcake Bars

32 BARS

These are traditional for the holidays—and they're good for mailing.

6 ounces (generous 1½ cups) walnuts, coarsely cut or broken
5 ounces (1 cup) raisins
8 ounces (1 cup, packed) pitted dates, cut in large pieces
8 to 10 ounces (generous 1 cup) candied fruit (see Note)
1 cup sifted all-purpose flour
4 eggs
½ teaspoon salt
1 cup light brown sugar, firmly packed
1 teaspoon vanilla extract
Finely grated rind of 1 large, deep-colored orange
Confectioners sugar

Adjust a rack to the center of the oven and preheat to 325 degrees. Butter a 10½-by-15½-by-1-inch jelly-roll pan.

Place the walnuts, raisins, dates, and candied fruit in a large mixing bowl. Add ¼ cup of the flour (reserve remaining ¾ cup). With your fingers, toss the fruit and nuts with the flour to separate and coat all the pieces thoroughly. Set aside.

In the small bowl of an electric mixer beat the eggs just to mix. Add the salt, sugar, and vanilla and beat just to mix. On low speed add the reserved ¾ cup flour, scraping the bowl with a rubber spatula and beating only until mixed. Remove from the mixer and stir in the orange rind.

The batter will be thin. Pour it over the floured fruit and nuts. Stir to mix thoroughly.

Turn the mixture into the buttered pan and spread evenly.

Bake for 30 to 35 minutes, until the top is golden brown. Reverse the pan front to back once during baking to insure even browning.

Cool completely in the pan.

With a small, sharp knife cut around the edges to release, and cut the cake into bars—they will be only a scant ½ inch thick.

With a wide metal spatula transfer the bars to a large piece of wax paper. Dust the tops generously with confectioners sugar by pressing the sugar with your fingertips through a fine strainer held over the cookies.

These may be wrapped individually in cellophane (clear, red, or green) or wax paper, or they may be stored with wax paper between the layers in an airtight box.

NOTE: The candied fruit may be a mixture of either red and/or green cherries and candied pineapple or cherries alone, or it may be the prepared mixed fruit. The cherries and pineapple should be cut into medium-size pieces (not small); the mixed fruit should be used as is.

Hermit Bars

24 BARS

An Early American classic; every woman had her own version—the fruits and spices varied, and some were made as drop cookies. The ladies on Cape Cod packed Hermits for their men who went to sea because the cookies kept well.

2 cups sifted all-purpose flour
¾ teaspoon baking soda
¾ teaspoon double-acting baking powder
½ teaspoon salt
1 teaspoon cinnamon
½ teaspoon powdered cloves
¼ teaspoon nutmeg
¼ teaspoon mace
⅛ teaspoon allspice
5 ounces (1 cup) currants or raisins
Boiling water
¼ pound (1 stick) butter
½ cup granulated sugar
2 eggs
½ cup molasses
4 ounces (generous 1 cup) pecans, coarsely cut
    or broken (see page 13)

Adjust a rack to the center of the oven and preheat to 350 degrees. Butter a 13-by-9-by-2-inch baking pan.

Sift together the flour, baking soda, baking powder, salt, cinnamon, cloves, nutmeg, mace, and allspice and set aside.

Place the currants or raisins in a small bowl and pour boiling water over them to cover. Let stand for a few minutes. Drain in a strainer and then spread the fruit out on paper towels to dry slightly.

In the large bowl of an electric mixer cream the butter. Add the sugar and beat well. Add the eggs one at a time and beat until smooth. Beat in the molasses; the mixture will look curdled—it's O.K. On low speed gradually add the sifted dry ingredients, scraping the bowl with a rubber spatula and beating only until mixed. Mix in the currants or raisins and the nuts.

Spread the dough smoothly in the buttered pan.

Bake for about 30 minutes until the top of the cake springs back when lightly pressed with a fingertip.

Remove the pan from the oven and prepare the glaze immediately.

GLAZE

1½ cups confectioners sugar
2 tablespoons butter, melted
½ teaspoon vanilla extract
3 to 4 tablespoons boiling water

Place the sugar in the small bowl of an electric mixer (see Note). Add the butter and vanilla. Beat on low speed while gradually adding the boiling water. Use only enough water to make a mixture the consistency of medium-thick cream sauce.

Pour the glaze over the hot cake and brush it with a pastry brush to make it cover the cake. Let the cake stand until the glaze is dry.

With a small, sharp knife cut the cake into bars.

The bars may be left in the pan and covered airtight so they remain moist and fresh, or they may be wrapped individually in clear cellophane or wax paper.

NOTE: The glaze may be mixed without the electric mixer: Follow the above directions using a medium-size mixing bowl and stirring well with a rubber spatula. But it must be smooth with no lumps.

Brittle Peanut Bars

32 BARS

These are hard, chewy, and crunchy like brittle candy.

½ pound (2 sticks) butter
1 cup granulated sugar
2 cups sifted all-purpose flour
4 ounces (1 cup) salted peanuts, chopped into
    medium-size pieces

Adjust a rack to the center of the oven and preheat to 375 degrees.

In the large bowl of an electric mixer cream the butter. Add the sugar and beat to mix well. On low speed gradually add the flour, scraping the bowl with a rubber spatula and beating only until the dough holds together. Mix in one-half of the nuts (reserve the remaining nuts for topping).

Turn the dough into an unbuttered 15½-by-10½-by-1-inch jelly-roll pan. Dip your fingertips in flour and use them to press the dough into a thin layer. Don't worry about smoothing the layer now, that will come soon.

Sprinkle the reserved nuts evenly over the dough.

Place a large piece of wax paper over the nuts. With a small rolling pin or a straight-sided glass, roll over the paper to press the nuts firmly into the top of the dough and to smooth the dough at the same time.

Bake for 23 to 25 minutes until golden brown. Reverse the pan once during baking to insure even browning. The cake will puff up during baking and then sink, leaving the edges higher and the surface slightly wrinkled.

Cool in the pan for about 5 minutes and then, while the cake is still warm, cut into bars. (When cool, it will become too hard and brittle to cut.)

With a wide metal spatula remove the bars from the pan and finish cooling them on racks.

Hungarian Walnut Bars

18 BARS

This is a classic recipe—two layers of rolled-out pastry with a rich, baked-in walnut filling.

PASTRY

1½ cups sifted all-purpose flour
1 teaspoon double-acting baking powder
¼ teaspoon salt
⅓ cup granulated sugar
6 ounces (1½ sticks) cold butter, cut into
   ½- to 1-inch slices
1 egg yolk (reserve the white for the filling)
1 tablespoon milk
Finely grated rind of 1 large lemon

Adjust a rack one-third up from the bottom of the oven and preheat to 375 degrees. Prepare a 9-inch-square cake pan as follows: Turn it upside down and place a 12-inch square of aluminum foil over the inverted pan. Turn down the sides and corners of the foil just to shape. Remove the foil and turn the pan right side up. Place the foil in the pan. In order not to tear the foil place a folded towel or a pot holder in the pan and, pressing against the towel or pot holder, press the foil gently into place. Coat the foil with soft or melted butter, spreading it thin with crumpled wax paper or a pastry brush. Dust the pan thoroughly with fine dry breadcrumbs and then invert to shake out excess.

Sift together into a mixing bowl the flour, baking powder, and salt. Stir in the sugar. With a pastry blender cut in the butter until the particles are fine and the mixture resembles coarse meal.

In a small cup stir the egg yolk with the milk just to mix, then stir it into the dry ingredients. Add the lemon rind.

Either in the bowl or on a smooth work surface, work the dough with your hands only until it is smooth and holds together.

Divide the dough into halves. Place each half between 2 large pieces of wax paper. Roll over the wax paper with a rolling pin, rolling each piece of dough into a 9-inch square. To make perfect squares: Use the baking pan as a pattern and place it on the top of the wax paper. Use the back (or dull side) of a small knife to trace around the pan, pressing just enough to mark the dough without cutting through the wax paper. Then remove the pan and the top layer of paper and cut away excess dough, using it to fill in the corners or wherever needed. Replace the wax paper and with the rolling pin roll very gently only to smooth the top.

Slide a cookie sheet under both squares of dough (still in wax paper) and transfer them to the freezer or refrigerator to chill briefly. (At this stage the dough will be sticky and will stick to the wax paper. It should be chilled until it is almost firm and the wax paper comes away neatly.)

WALNUT FILLING

6 ounces (generous 1½ cups) walnuts, finely
   chopped (not ground, see Note)
1¼ cups strained or sifted confectioners sugar
   (see page 14)
Pinch of salt
2 tablespoons rum or water
1 egg white

Place the walnuts, sugar, and salt in a bowl and stir to mix well.

In a small bowl beat the rum or water with the egg white only until it increases in volume and starts to thicken. Then stir it into the nut mixture and set aside.

Remove the dough squares from the freezer or refrigerator and remove the top piece of wax paper from each square. Invert one dough square into the prepared pan and remove the remaining piece of wax paper.

Place the filling by spoonfuls on the dough and spread to make an even layer. Invert the second square of dough over the filling and remove the remaining wax paper.

With a fork pierce the top layer of dough all over at ½-inch intervals.

Bake for 30 minutes or until the top is lightly browned.

Let cool in the pan for 30 minutes. Cover with a rack or a small cookie sheet and invert. Remove the pan and the aluminum foil. Cover with a rack and invert again, leaving the cake right side up to cool.

It will be easier to cut the cake neatly if it is cold; chill it briefly in the freezer or refrigerator. Then transfer it to a cutting board. Cut with a long, thin, sharp knife, cutting with the full length of the blade. To make 18 bars, first cut the cake in one direction into thirds, and then cut each strip into 6 bars.

If you wish, strain confectioners sugar generously over the tops.

With a wide metal spatula transfer the bars to a serving plate and cover with plastic wrap.

NOTE: I place the walnuts on a large cutting board and chop them with a long, heavy French chef's knife. They should be cut into small pieces, but if a few larger pieces are left, that's O.K.

Butterscotch Walnut Bars

These have a crisp, buttery layer with a chewy, candylike, caramel-nut topping. They are made without a mixer.

32 BARS

CRUST

1½ cups sifted all-purpose flour

Scant ¼ teaspoon salt

¾ cup light brown sugar, firmly packed (If the sugar is at all lumpy it must be strained. With your fingertips press it through a large strainer set over a large bowl.)

¼ pound (1 stick) butter, cut into ½- to 1-inch slices

Adjust a rack one-third up from the bottom of the oven and preheat to 375 degrees.

Place the flour, salt, and sugar in a mixing bowl and stir to mix well. Add the pieces of butter to the flour mixture, and with a pastry blender cut in the butter until the particles are very fine and the mixture resembles coarse meal. (It will be dry and powdery but will hold together when pressed into the pan.)

Place the mixture in an unbuttered 9-by-13-by-2-inch pan. With your fingertips, distribute it evenly over the bottom of the pan. Then, with your fingertips and the palm of your hand, press firmly to make a smooth, compact layer.

Bake the crust for about 12 minutes until it is lightly browned. Remove it from the oven but do not turn off the oven. Let the crust stand while you prepare the topping.

BUTTERSCOTCH WALNUT TOPPING

¼ cup light corn syrup

6 ounces (1 cup) butterscotch morsels

Pinch of salt

2 tablespoons butter

1 tablespoon water

7 ounces (2 cups) walnuts, cut medium fine (see page 13)

Place the corn syrup, butterscotch morsels, salt, butter, and water in the top of a large double boiler over hot water on moderate heat. Stir constantly with a rubber spatula, pressing against the morsels, until they are melted and the mixture is smooth. (A few tiny pieces of unmelted morsels are O.K.)

Now work quickly because the mixture will harden if it is left standing. Stir in the nuts, remove from the heat, and place the mixture by large spoonfuls over the baked crust (which will still be warm). Then with the back of the spoon, spread the butterscotch around on the crust, leaving a ½- to ¾-inch border. (During baking, the topping will run toward the edges.)

Return to the oven and bake for 10 minutes—no more, no less.

Let the cake cool in the pan for 30 to 40 minutes, until it is only slightly warm. Then, with a small, sharp knife, cut around the edges to release and then cut into 16 oblongs. The bars in the center of the pan will appear too soft but they will become firmer as they cool (it might be necessary to wait a little longer before removing them).

With a wide metal spatula transfer the bars to a cutting board. Let them stand until they are completely cool and firm. Then cut each one in half, making small bars.

Place the bars in a covered freezer box, or on a tray, and cover with plastic wrap. Or wrap them individually in clear cellophane or wax paper.

Cinnamon Almond Cookies

In a small tearoom near London these are called "toffee." They are served there with tea and also packaged in little brown bags to take out. They are rather thin, buttery, crisp cinnamon cookies with a lemon glaze.

32 COOKIES

6 ounces (1¾ cups) thinly sliced blanched
    almonds
½ pound (2 sticks) butter
2 teaspoons cinnamon
1 cup granulated sugar
1 egg, separated
2 cups sifted all-purpose flour

Adjust a rack to the center of the oven and preheat to 300 degrees. Butter a 10½-by-15½-by-1-inch jelly-roll pan.

The almonds must be crumbled and broken into coarse pieces. If they have been stored in the freezer it is easiest to do this while they are still frozen. It may be done by squeezing the nuts between your hands in a bowl or over paper. Or place the almonds in a plastic bag and squeeze and press on the bag to break the nuts. Set aside.

In the large bowl of an electric mixer cream the butter. Add the cinnamon and sugar and beat to mix well. Beat in the egg yolk (reserve the white) and then on low speed gradually add the flour, scraping the bowl with a rubber spatula and beating only until thoroughly mixed.

Place the dough by large spoonfuls in the buttered pan. With the back of the spoon spread the dough to cover the bottom of the pan. Cover the dough with a large piece of wax paper and press down on the paper with your hands to make a smooth, even layer. Or use a straight-sided glass as a rolling pin and roll over the paper. Remove the wax paper.

In a small bowl beat the egg white only until it is foamy and slightly thickened. Pour it over the layer of dough, and with a pastry brush spread it to cover the top of the dough.

With your fingertips sprinkle the crushed almonds evenly over the egg white. Cover again with wax paper. With the straight-sided glass roll over the paper to press the almonds into the dough and then remove the wax paper.

Bake for 45 minutes until golden brown.

A minute or so before removing the pan from the oven prepare the following glaze.

GLAZE

1 cup strained confectioners sugar (see Note)
1 tablespoon butter, melted
1 tablespoon boiling water
1 tablespoon lemon juice

Place the sugar, butter, water, and lemon juice in a small bowl and mix with a rubber spatula until completely smooth. The glaze should be the consistency of heavy cream.

When you remove the pan from the oven drizzle the glaze unevenly in a thin stream over the top of the cake. It will form a shiny, transparent glaze.

Let the cake cool in the pan for 10 to 15 minutes; the cake will still be warm. With a small, sharp knife cut around the sides to release and then cut the cake into eighths. With a wide metal spatula transfer each piece to a cutting board and cut each eighth into quarters. Transfer to a rack to finish cooling.

NOTE: The confectioners sugar should be strained before measuring. With your fingertips press the sugar through a strainer set over a bowl.

Georgia Pecan Bars

32 BARS

The taste and texture of these will remind you of pecan pie.

CRUST

1⅓ cups sifted all-purpose flour
½ teaspoon double-acting baking powder
½ cup dark brown sugar, firmly packed
¼ pound (1 stick) butter, cut into ½- to
    1-inch slices

Adjust a rack one-third up from the bottom of the oven and preheat to 350 degrees. Butter a 13-by-9-by-2-inch pan. Line the bottom with aluminum foil. Butter the foil and dust it with fine dry breadcrumbs.

Sift the flour and baking powder together into a bowl. Stir in the sugar. Add the pieces of butter to the bowl with the dry ingredients. With a pastry blender cut in the butter until the mixture resembles fine meal.

Turn the crust mixture into the buttered pan. With your fingertips and with the palm of your hand press down on the crust to make a smooth, firm layer. Set aside and prepare the topping.

TOPPING

2 eggs
1 teaspoon vanilla extract
¼ cup dark brown sugar, firmly packed
¾ cup dark corn syrup
3 tablespoons sifted all-purpose flour
7 ounces (2 cups) pecan halves or large pieces

In a bowl beat the eggs lightly just to mix. Add the vanilla, sugar, corn syrup, and flour and beat until smooth.

Pour the topping over the crust and tilt the pan gently to form an even layer. If the pecan halves are large they may be placed evenly, rounded side up, to cover the topping completely. But if the halves are small or if you use pieces, sprinkle them over the topping.

Bake for 35 to 40 minutes, reversing the position of the pan once during baking to insure even browning. If the cake puffs up during baking pierce it gently with a cake tester or a small, sharp knife to release the trapped air. Bake until the top is golden brown. Do not overbake; the bars should remain slightly soft in the center.

Cool the cake in the pan for 15 to 20 minutes. With a small, sharp knife cut around the sides of the cake to release. Then cover the cake pan with a cookie sheet and invert. If the cake does not fall out, bang the pan gently against the cookie sheet until it does. Cover the cake with a rack and invert to finish cooling right side up.

When the cake is completely cool transfer it to the freezer for about 20 minutes or to the refrigerator for about an hour until firm enough to cut.

If the cookies are cut with a plain, straight knife they will squash and look messy. Use a serrated bread knife and cut with a back-and-forth, sawing motion—they will cut perfectly. Cut into bars or squares.

These may be placed on a serving tray and covered with plastic wrap or they may be wrapped individually in clear cellophane or wax paper. Or they may be stored in a plastic freezer box.

Pecan Festival Bars

32 COOKIES

These are thin, crisp brown-sugar wafers topped with chopped pecans. This classic Southern recipe calls for long, slow baking.

½ pound (2 sticks) butter
1½ teaspoons vanilla extract
¼ teaspoon salt
1 cup strained light brown sugar, firmly packed
1 egg, separated
2 cups sifted all-purpose flour
6 ounces (generous 1⅔ cups) pecans, cut
    medium fine (see page 13)

Adjust rack one-third up from the bottom of the oven and preheat to 250 degrees. Butter a 10½-by-15½-by-1-inch jelly-roll pan.

In the large bowl of an electric mixer cream the butter. Add the vanilla, salt, and sugar and beat well. Beat in the egg yolk (reserve the white). On low speed gradually add the flour, scraping the bowl with a rubber spatula and beating only until the mixture is smooth and holds together.

Place spoonfuls of the dough all over the bottom of the buttered pan.

With the back of the spoon spread the dough as evenly as possible. This will make a very, very thin layer.

In a small bowl beat the egg white until it holds a soft shape, not stiff. Pour it over the layer of dough, and with a pastry brush, brush the white so that it covers the dough completely.

With your fingertips sprinkle the nuts evenly over the egg white. Cover with a large piece of wax paper. Press down gently with the palms of your hands to make a smooth, even layer of dough with the nuts pressed well into it. Remove the wax paper.

Bake for 1 hour and 50 minutes or until golden brown.

These cookies should be cut immediately, in the pan, while they are still hot; they will become crisp and brittle as they cool. Use a small, sharp knife and cut into even bars or squares. Transfer to racks to cool.

Pecan Chews

16 SQUARES OR
24 BARS

These are soft, tender, chewy squares from a recipe given to me by a Georgia pecan grower.

½ cup sifted all-purpose flour
¼ teaspoon double-acting baking powder
2 eggs
½ teaspoon vanilla extract
1 teaspoon instant coffee
1 cup dark brown sugar, firmly packed
6 ounces (generous 1⅔ cups) pecans, cut into
    medium-size pieces

Adjust a rack one-third up from the bottom of the oven and preheat to 350 degrees. Prepare a 9-inch-square cake pan as follows: Turn it upside down and place a 12-inch square of aluminum foil over the inverted pan. Turn down the sides and corners of the foil just to shape it. Remove the foil and turn the pan right side up. Place the foil in the pan. In order not to tear the foil place a folded towel or a pot holder in the pan and, pressing against the towel or pot holder, press the foil gently into place. Coat the foil with soft or melted butter, spreading it thin with a pastry brush or crumpled wax paper. Dust the foil lightly but thoroughly with flour and then invert the pan to shake out excess.

Sift together the flour and the baking powder and set aside. In the small bowl of an electric mixer beat the eggs lightly just to mix. Add the vanilla, instant coffee, and sugar and beat only to mix; do not overbeat. On low speed beat in the sifted dry ingredients only to mix. Mix in 1 generous cup (reserve remaining ⅔ cup) of the pecans.

Turn the dough into the prepared pan and spread it level. Sprinkle with the remaining ⅔ cup pecans.

Bake for 25 to 28 minutes—the cake will still be slightly soft inside. Remove from the oven and cool in the pan for about 20 minutes. Cover the pan with a cookie sheet and invert. Remove the pan and the aluminum foil. Cover with a rack or another cookie sheet and invert again, leaving the cake right side up to cool.

The cake will be very tender. Before cutting it into squares let it stand for several hours or chill it briefly in the freezer or refrigerator. Then gently transfer it to a cutting board. With a long, sharp knife, using the full length of the blade, cut the cake into squares or bars.

Aspen Oatmeal Bars

These are the height of ease and simplicity. Mixed in a saucepan, with no flour, they are chewy and crunchy with a butterscotch flavor, and very sweet.

24 SMALL BARS

¼ pound (1 stick) butter
1 cup light brown sugar, firmly packed
1 teaspoon double-acting baking powder
Scant ¼ teaspoon salt
2 cups old-fashioned or quick-cooking
    (not "instant") oatmeal

Adjust a rack to the center of the oven and preheat to 350 degrees. Butter an 8-inch-square cake pan.

Place the butter and sugar in a medium-size saucepan. Stir over moderate heat until melted.

Remove the pan from the heat. Through a fine strainer add the baking powder and stir until smooth. Stir in the salt and the oats. It will be a thick mixture.

Turn the dough into the buttered pan. Use your fingertips and the palm of your hand to press the dough into a smooth, compact layer.

Bake for 25 minutes. The cake will still be soft but it will harden as it cools. Do not bake any longer.

While the cake is still warm cut around the sides to release but then let the cake finish cooling in the pan.

With a small, sharp knife cut the cake into quarters. With a wide metal spatula transfer the quarters to a cutting board. Cut each quarter into 6 bars.

Texas Cowboy Bars

24 BARS

Rich, he-man oatmeal bars with a baked-in soft date filling.

FILLING

8 ounces (1 cup) pitted dates
1 cup water
1 cup granulated sugar
Finely grated rind of 1 large lemon

Cut the dates into medium-size pieces. Place the dates, water, and sugar in a heavy 2-quart saucepan over moderate heat and bring to a boil, stirring occasionally. Continue to boil, stirring occasionally, for 10 to 12 minutes until the mixture is thick. Watch it carefully toward the end: As it begins to thicken, it will bubble and splash; reduce the heat as necessary. Stir in the grated lemon rind and set aside to cool to lukewarm.

CRUST

1½ cups sifted all-purpose flour
½ teaspoon salt
1 cup dark brown sugar, firmly packed
1½ cups old-fashioned or quick-cooking
    (not "instant") oatmeal
2 ounces (generous ½ cup) walnuts or pecans,
    cut medium fine (see page 13)
½ pound (2 sticks) butter, melted

Adjust a rack one-third up from the bottom of the oven and preheat to 350 degrees. Prepare a 9-inch-square cake pan as follows: Turn the pan upside down and place a 12-inch square of aluminum foil over it. Turn down the sides and corners of the foil just to shape. Lift off the foil and turn the pan right side up. Place the foil in the pan. In order not to tear the foil place a folded towel or a pot holder in the pan and, pressing against the towel or pot holder, press the foil gently into place. Butter the foil; this is most easily done with melted butter and a pastry brush.

Place the flour, salt, and sugar in a mixing bowl and stir to mix. Mix in the oatmeal and nuts. Add the melted butter and stir well until completely mixed.

Remove 1 generous cup of the mixture and set it aside for the topping. Place the remaining crust mixture over the bottom of the prepared pan and press it firmly with your fingertips to make a smooth, even layer.

Cover the crust with the filling mixture and spread evenly. Sprinkle the reserved crust mixture evenly over the filling. Press gently with your fingertips to make a smooth, even layer.

Bake for 45 minutes.

Cool in the pan for 45 minutes. Cover with a rack or a cookie sheet and invert. Remove the pan and the aluminum foil. Cover with a rack and very gently invert again—handle with care.

Cool completely and then chill briefly in the freezer or refrigerator until the cake is firm enough to be cut.

Use a long, thin, sharp knife and cut the cake into squares or bars.

Honey Date-Nut Bars

32 BARS

These are soft and chewy like old-fashioned Date-Nut Bars but are made with honey instead of sugar.

1⅓ cups sifted all-purpose flour
1 teaspoon double-acting baking powder
Pinch of salt
3 eggs
1 cup honey
1 teaspoon vanilla extract
1 pound (2 cups) pitted dates, coarsely cut
8 ounces (2¼ cups) walnuts, cut or
 broken into medium-size pieces
Confectioners sugar (for sprinkling over the
 baked cookies)

Adjust a rack to the center of the oven and preheat to 350 degrees. Prepare a 15½-by-10½-by-1-inch jelly-roll pan as follows: Turn the pan upside down. Cut a piece of aluminum foil large enough to cover the pan and the sides. Place the foil over the inverted pan and fold down the sides and corners just to shape. Remove the foil. Wet the inside of the pan lightly— do not dry it (the wet pan will hold the foil in place). Place the foil in the pan. With a pot holder or a folded towel (so the foil doesn't tear) press the foil into place in the pan. Spread or brush the foil all over with very soft butter. Dust thoroughly with flour and then invert the pan to shake out excess flour. Set the prepared pan aside.

Sift together the flour, baking powder, and salt and set aside. In the large bowl of an electric mixer beat the eggs until they are slightly foamy. Beat in the honey and the vanilla. On low speed add the sifted dry ingredients, scraping the bowl with a rubber spatula and beating until thoroughly mixed. Add the dates and the nuts and stir or beat, preferably by hand, to mix well.

Turn the mixture into the prepared pan and spread it as evenly as possible. Bake for about 35 minutes, reversing the position of the pan once during baking, until the cake is golden brown. It is done when the top springs back firmly if it is lightly pressed with a fingertip.

Cool the cake for only a few minutes and then cover it with a large rack or a cookie sheet and invert. Remove the pan and the aluminum foil. Cover with a large rack and invert. Let the cake stand until it is completely cool.

Transfer the cake to a cutting board. With a long, thin, sharp knife, using the full length of the blade and pressing down firmly, cut the cake into bars.

Place the bars on a large piece of wax paper and cover them generously with confectioners sugar, pressing the sugar with your fingertips through a strainer held over the bars.

Aspen Date-Nut Fingers

48 SMALL FINGERS

These have whole-wheat flour, wheat germ, oatmeal, and honey. They may be made without a mixer.

3 eggs
¼ teaspoon salt
1 cup honey
1 cup <u>un</u>sifted all-purpose whole-wheat flour
    (stir lightly to aerate before measuring)
½ cup natural, untoasted wheat germ
    (available in health-food stores)
½ cup old-fashioned or quick-cooking
    (not "instant") oatmeal (see Note)
8 ounces (1 cup) pitted dates, coarsely cut
5 ounces (1¼ cups) pecans, cut into medium-
    size pieces
Confectioners sugar (for sprinkling over
    the tops)

Adjust two racks to divide the oven into thirds and preheat to 350 degrees. Butter two shallow 9-inch-square cake pans and dust them lightly but thoroughly with fine dry breadcrumbs.

This batter may be mixed with an electric mixer or a manual egg beater. In a large bowl beat the eggs with the salt only until the eggs are foamy. Beat in the honey. Add the flour, wheat germ, and oatmeal and beat or stir until smooth. Mix in the dates and nuts.

Divide the mixture between the two prepared pans. Spread to make smooth layers—they will be thin.

Bake for 25 to 30 minutes, reversing the pans top to bottom once during baking to insure even baking. The cakes are done when they are lightly colored and semifirm to the touch.

Cool the cakes in the pans for about 10 minutes. Cut around the sides if necessary to release them, then cover each pan with a rack or a cookie sheet and invert. Remove the pans. Cover each cake with a rack and invert again, leaving the cakes right side up. Let stand to cool slightly and then slide the cakes off onto a cutting board.

With a long, sharp knife cut each cake into three strips and then cut each strip into eight fingers.

Place the cookies on a large piece of wax paper. Cover the tops generously with confectioners sugar by pressing the sugar through a fine strainer held over the cookies.

Either wrap the cookies individually in clear cellophane or wax paper, or pack them in an airtight container.

NOTE: For these cookies I use El Molino Old-Fashioned Hull-less Rolled Oats that I buy in a health-food store, but you may use any quick-cooking kind.

Viennese Linzer Cookies

This is the classic Linzertorte, cut into small bars. It has a bottom crust, a raspberry-preserve filling, and a thin lattice topping of strips of the crust —all baked together. The filling keeps the cookies moist and juicy. These are made without a mixer.

24 BARS

1½ cups plus 2 tablespoons sifted
    all-purpose flour
½ teaspoon double-acting baking powder
1 teaspoon cinnamon
⅛ teaspoon powdered cloves
¼ teaspoon salt
¼ cup granulated sugar
½ cup dark brown sugar, firmly packed
¼ pound (1 stick) butter
2½ ounces (½ cup) blanched almonds
1 egg

Finely grated rind of 1 large lemon
¾ cup thick red or black raspberry preserves
1 egg yolk   ⎫ for glazing the tops
1 teaspoon water ⎭ of the cookies

Adjust an oven rack one-third up from the bottom and preheat to 375 degrees.

Sift together 1½ cups of the flour (reserve remaining 2 tablespoons), baking powder, cinnamon, cloves, salt, and granulated sugar into a large mixing bowl. Add the brown sugar and stir to mix well.

Slice the butter into ½-inch pieces; then, with a pastry blender, cut it into the dry ingredients until the mixture is fine and crumbly.

Grind the almonds to a fine powder in a nut grinder, a blender, or a food processor. Add the ground almonds to the dry ingredients and butter, and stir to mix well.

In a small bowl stir the egg lightly with a fork just to mix. Add the lemon rind to the egg and stir to mix. Then add the egg to the dough and, with a fork, stir well until the dry ingredients are evenly moistened. Remove and reserve ½ cup of the dough.

Place the remaining dough in an unbuttered 9-inch-square pan and set aside.

Replace the reserved ½ cup of dough in the mixing bowl. Add the reserved 2 tablespoons of flour. Stir together until the flour is all incorporated. With your hands form the dough into a flattened square and place it between two large pieces of wax paper. With a rolling pin, roll over the wax paper to roll the dough into a 9-inch square. (Keep the shape as square as you can, but if the sides are not exact don't worry—a few uneven strips will not really matter.) Slide a cookie sheet under the paper and transfer the dough to the freezer for a few minutes. When the dough is rolled out into a 9-inch square it will be very thin. You will have to be extremely careful handling it when cutting it into strips.

Meanwhile, flour your fingertips and press the dough that is in the pan to even it out on the bottom of the pan.

In a small bowl, stir the preserves slightly just to soften. Spread them evenly over the layer of dough in the pan, keeping the preserves ¼ to ⅓ inch away from the edges.

Now remove the chilled dough from the freezer. Remove and replace one piece of the wax paper just to loosen it. Turn the dough and both pieces of wax paper over. Then remove and do not replace the other piece of paper. With a long knife, cut the dough into ½-inch-wide strips; you will have 18 strips, each ½ inch wide and 9 inches long. Place half of the strips over the preserves, placing them ½ inch apart and parallel. Then place the remaining strips crosswise over the first ones, again placing them ½ inch apart, and forming a lattice top. (If the strips become too soft to handle while you are working with them, rechill as necessary.)

To make the glaze, stir the egg yolk and the water together lightly just to mix. With a soft brush, brush the glaze over the top of the lattice and the preserves.

Bake for 30 minutes or until the top is a rich golden brown.

Cool the cake completely in the pan. When completely cool, with a small, sharp knife cut around the cake to release it, then cut it into quarters, cut each quarter in half, and then cut each strip into thirds. With a metal spatula transfer the bars to a tray or serving plate.

Or cut the cake into quarters in the pan and, with a wide metal spatula, transfer the quarters to a cutting board. Then, with a long, heavy knife, cut into small bars.

If you wish, these may be wrapped individually in clear cellophane or wax paper. Or they may be stored in a covered box with plastic wrap or wax paper between the layers.

Polish Wedding Cakes

16 TWO-INCH SQUARES
OR 32 OR 48
SMALL BARS

These are called Mazurka in Polish. There are many versions, all rich and moist. This one has a crunchy crust and tart apricot filling.

APRICOT FILLING

4 ounces (about 24 halves) dried apricots
½ cup water
2 tablespoons sugar

Bring the apricots and the water to a boil, uncovered, in a small, heavy saucepan with a tight cover over high heat. Reduce the heat to low, cover the pan, and simmer until the apricots are very tender, about half an hour, depending on the apricots. The fruit should be very soft and the water should be partially but not completely absorbed.

Press the apricots with a potato masher or stir and mash vigorously with a fork. The mixture should be very thick. Add the sugar and stir until it dissolves. Cool to room temperature. (If you wish, this filling may be made ahead of time and refrigerated.)

POLISH PASTRY

This is not like American pastry. It will resemble a crumb mixture.

1¼ cups sifted all-purpose flour
¼ teaspoon salt
1 cup dark brown sugar, firmly packed
6 ounces (1½ sticks) cold butter, cut into
    ½-inch pieces
1¾ ounces (½ cup, firmly packed) shredded
    coconut
¾ cup old-fashioned or quick-cooking
    (not "instant") oatmeal
2 ounces (generous ½ cup) walnuts, cut
    medium fine (see page 13)

Adjust an oven rack one-third up from the bottom and preheat oven to 325 degrees.

Place the flour, salt, and sugar in a mixing bowl. With a pastry blender cut in the butter until the mixture resembles coarse meal. Stir in the coconut, oatmeal, and walnuts.

Place half (3 cups) of the mixture in an unbuttered 8-inch-square cake pan. Press it evenly with your fingertips. Cover with a piece of wax paper and with the palm of your hand press against the paper to make a smooth, compact layer. Remove the wax paper.

Spread the apricot filling smoothly over the pastry, staying ¼ to ½ inch away from the edges. Sprinkle the remaining pastry evenly over the filling and repeat the directions for covering with wax paper and pressing smooth. Remove the wax paper.

Bake for 60 to 70 minutes until the top is barely semifirm to the touch.

Cool in the pan for 15 minutes. Cut around the sides of the cake to release it. Cover with a rack or a cookie sheet. Invert, remove the pan, cover with a rack, and invert again so that the cake is right side up. Let cool completely and then refrigerate briefly—the cake cuts best if it is cold. Transfer it to a cutting board.

Use a long, thin, very sharp knife or a finely serrated one to cut the cake into squares or fingers.

OPTIONAL: These may be topped with confectioners sugar. Press it through a fine strainer held over the cookies to cover the tops generously.

Viennese Marzipan Bars

24 SMALL BARS

These fancy little cakes are really petits fours. They have a tender, buttery base, a thin layer of apricot preserves, a ground-almond filling, and a thin dark chocolate glaze.

CRUST

1 cup sifted all-purpose flour
½ teaspoon double-acting baking powder
2⅔ ounces (5⅓ tablespoons) butter
½ cup granulated sugar
1 egg yolk (reserve the white for the filling)
1 tablespoon milk

Adjust a rack one-third up from the bottom of the oven and preheat to 375 degrees. Butter the bottom and sides of an 8-inch-square cake pan.

Sift together the flour and baking powder and set aside. In the small bowl of an electric mixer cream the butter. Add the sugar and beat to mix well. Beat in the egg yolk and the milk. On low speed gradually add the sifted dry ingredients, scraping the bowl with a rubber spatula and beating only until the mixture holds together.

Place the dough in the prepared pan. Press it firmly with floured fingertips to make a smooth layer.

Bake for 12 to 15 minutes or until barely colored around the edges. The crust will sink slightly when it is removed from the oven.

Meanwhile prepare the following filling.

ALMOND FILLING

¼ cup apricot preserves
4 ounces (generous ¾ cup) blanched almonds
⅔ cup granulated sugar
¼ teaspoon salt
1 egg plus 1 egg white
½ teaspoon vanilla extract
Scant ¼ teaspoon almond extract
Few drops of green food coloring

In a small bowl stir the preserves just to soften and set aside.

Grind the almonds to a fine powder in a blender or nut grinder and place them in a bowl. Add the sugar and salt and stir with a rubber spatula to mix. Add the egg, egg white, vanilla and almond extracts, and 2 or 3 drops of food coloring. (Add another drop or two of food coloring if necessary to make a pale pea-green.) Stir to mix thoroughly.

Spread the preserves over the hot crust, leaving a ½-inch border—it will be a thin layer of preserves. Top with the almond filling and spread it to make an even layer.

Bake at 375 degrees for 25 minutes or until the top of the cake barely springs back when lightly pressed with a fingertip.

Cool completely and then prepare the following glaze.

CHOCOLATE GLAZE

½ cup confectioners sugar
½ ounce (½ square) unsweetened chocolate
1 tablespoon butter
½ teaspoon vanilla extract
1 tablespoon boiling water

Strain the sugar by pressing it with your fingertips through a strainer set over a bowl. Set aside.

Place the chocolate and the butter in the top of a small double boiler over hot water on moderate heat. Cover until it is melted and then stir smooth. Stir in the sugar, vanilla, and water and stir again until completely smooth.

Pour the glaze over the cooled cake and spread evenly. It will be a thin layer.

Let the cake stand in the pan for an hour or longer. Then, with a small, sharp knife, cut around the sides to release. Cut the cake into quarters. With a wide metal spatula transfer the quarters to a cutting board. If it is difficult to remove the first quarter, cut it into individual portions—bars or slices. Use a fork to ease out the first few portions, and then, with the wide metal spatula, transfer the remaining pieces to a cutting board and cut them into portions.

These little cakes are best after they stand for a few hours. Place them on a serving dish, cover with plastic wrap, and let stand at room temperature.

Icebox Cookies

NEW MEXICAN CHOCOLATE ICEBOX
   COOKIES

BLACK-AND-WHITE COCONUT SLICES

WIENERSTUBE COOKIES

MAXINES

COBBLESTONES

NEAPOLITANS

FRUITCAKE ICEBOX COOKIES

BUTTERSCOTCH THINS

PECAN BUTTERSCOTCH ICEBOX
   COOKIES

OATMEAL ICEBOX COOKIES

PEANUT-BUTTER PILLOWS

WHOLE-WHEAT PEANUT-BUTTER
   COOKIES

ICEBOX NUT COOKIES

SESAME FINGERS

CARAWAY CRISPS

ALMOND SPICEBOX COOKIES

ANISE ICEBOX COOKIES

CARDAMOM COOKIES FROM
   COPENHAGEN

PINWHEELS

Somehow the word "refrigerator" just doesn't sound right for icebox cookies. The dough is shaped, wrapped, and chilled until firm enough to be sliced. Most of these recipes may be prepared ahead of time and then sliced whenever you want to bake the cookies.

New Mexican Chocolate Icebox Cookies

66 COOKIES

These are not solid chocolate but filled with chopped chocolate chips

3½ cups sifted all-purpose flour
1 teaspoon baking soda
½ teaspoon salt
½ teaspoon nutmeg
6 ounces (1 cup) semisweet chocolate morsels
2⅔ ounces (5⅓ tablespoons) butter
⅓ cup vegetable shortening (such as Crisco)
2 cups dark brown sugar, firmly packed
1 tablespoon vanilla extract
1 egg
½ cup sour cream
3 ounces (generous ½ cup) pignoli (pine nuts) (see Note)

Prepare a 10-by-5-by-3-inch loaf pan as follows: Cut two long strips of wax paper or aluminum foil, one for the length and one for the width. The pieces should be long enough to fold over the top of the pan and cover the surface completely. Place them carefully in the pan. Set aside.

Sift together the flour, baking soda, salt, and nutmeg and set aside.

Grind the chocolate in a blender, or chop it fine with a long, heavy knife on a cutting board; it must be fine—any large chunks would make it difficult to slice the cookies. Set aside.

In the large bowl of an electric mixer cream together the butter and the shortening. Beat in the sugar and mix well, then beat in the vanilla and the egg and then the sour cream. On low speed add the sifted dry ingredients, scraping the bowl with a rubber spatula and beating only until thoroughly incorporated. Finally mix in the ground or chopped chocolate and the nuts.

Pack the dough firmly into the prepared pan. Fold the paper over the top and press down firmly to smooth the dough.

Freeze for 6 to 8 hours (or longer if you wish) until the dough is firm all the way through.

Adjust two racks to divide the oven into thirds and preheat to 400 degrees. Cut aluminum foil to fit cookie sheets.

Remove the block of dough from the pan. Remove the paper and place the dough on a cutting board. With a long, heavy knife, slice the block of dough in half the long way. Rewrap one piece and return it to the freezer.

With a sharp knife, cut the frozen dough into slices a generous ¼ inch thick. Place them about 1½ to 2 inches apart on the cut aluminum foil. (The reserved half of the dough may be sliced now or later, as you wish.)

Slide cookie sheets under the foil and bake the cookies about 10 minutes until they are semifirm to the touch. During baking, reverse the sheets top to bottom and front to back to insure even browning.

Slide the foil off the sheets, and with a wide metal spatula transfer the cookies to racks to cool.

NOTE: Other nuts may be substituted—walnuts, pecans, cashews, or hazelnuts—cut into medium-size pieces. Or you can leave out the nuts if you prefer.

Black-and-White Coconut Slices

56 COOKIES

Cream-cheese-coconut-nut centers wrapped on the outside edges with bittersweet-chocolate cookie dough.

FILLING

3½ ounces (1 cup, packed) shredded coconut
3 ounces cream cheese, preferably at room
    temperature
½ teaspoon vanilla extract
¼ teaspoon almond extract
⅓ cup granulated sugar
2 ounces (generous ½ cup) pecans, finely
    chopped (see page 13)

Place the shredded coconut on a large cutting board and chop it into shorter pieces, using a long, heavy knife, or chop for a few seconds in a food processor. Set aside.

In the small bowl of an electric mixer cream the cheese. Beat in the vanilla and almond extracts and the sugar. On low speed beat in the coconut and the nuts.

Tear off an 18-inch length of wax paper. Spoon the filling down the length of the paper to make a strip almost 14 inches long. Fold the long sides of the paper over the filling and, with your hands, form the filling into an even, compact roll or rectangle 14 inches long.

Wrap the filling in the paper, slide a cookie sheet under the roll, and transfer it to the freezer.

CHOCOLATE DOUGH

1½ cups sifted all-purpose flour
½ teaspoon baking soda
¼ teaspoon salt
2 ounces (2 squares) unsweetened chocolate
3 ounces (6 tablespoons) butter
1 teaspoon vanilla extract
1 cup confectioners sugar
1 egg

Sift together the flour, baking soda, and salt and set aside. Melt the chocolate in the top of a small double boiler over hot water on moderate heat. Set it aside to cool slightly. In the small bowl of an electric mixer cream the butter. Beat in the vanilla and sugar and mix well. Beat in the egg and then the chocolate. On low speed add the sifted dry ingredients, scraping the bowl with a rubber spatula and beating only until smooth.

Tear off a piece of wax paper about 12 inches long. Place the dough down the length of the paper, forming a strip about 8 inches long. Fold the long sides of the paper up around the dough and, with your hands, form the dough into a fat roll or a rectangle about 8 to 10 inches long. Refrigerate for about one-half hour or a little longer.

Tear off two 16-inch pieces of wax paper. Place the chocolate roll on one piece of the paper and cover it with the other piece. With a rolling pin, roll over the wax paper to form the chocolate dough into a 14-by-6-inch rectangle. If necessary, you may remove the top piece of paper, cut off some of the dough, and replace it where needed.

Unwrap the roll of filling and center it on the chocolate dough. Then wrap the chocolate dough firmly around the filling, overlapping the edges slightly and pressing firmly to make a smooth, compact roll.

Wrap the roll in the paper and freeze for a few hours or overnight; it must be firm in order to slice well.

Before baking adjust two racks to divide the oven into thirds and preheat to 375 degrees. Cut aluminum foil to fit cookie sheets.

Loosen the roll of frozen dough from the wax paper but do not remove it; just open the paper and leave the dough on it. With a sharp knife cut the roll into ¼-inch slices. If the dough starts to soften while you are slicing it, rechill the roll until it is firm. Or if the kitchen is warm cut the dough in half and work with only one-half at a time, keeping the other piece in the freezer. Place the slices 1½ to 2 inches apart on the cut aluminum foil.

Slide cookie sheets under the foil. Bake for 10 to 11 minutes, reversing the sheets top to bottom and front to back to insure even baking. When these are done the filling will feel barely semifirm to the touch; do not overbake or the chocolate will burn before you know it.

Slide the foil off the sheets and use a wide metal spatula to slip the cookies carefully off the foil and transfer them to racks to cool.

NOTE: These are not nearly as involved as they sound. Just follow the directions and you will find them really quite easy.

Wienerstube Cookies

48 COOKIES

These are Austrian. They are coal-black, chocolate, black-pepper cookies—buttery, crunchy, and spicy.

1½ cups sifted all-purpose flour
1½ teaspoons double-acting baking powder
¼ teaspoon salt
¾ teaspoon cinnamon
¼ teaspoon allspice

½ teaspoon finely ground black pepper
  (preferably freshly ground)
Pinch of cayenne pepper
¾ cup unsweetened cocoa
6 ounces (1½ sticks) butter
1½ teaspoons vanilla extract
1 cup granulated sugar
1 egg

Sift together the flour, baking powder, salt, cinnamon, allspice, black pepper, cayenne, and cocoa and set aside. In the large bowl of an electric mixer cream the butter. Add the vanilla and sugar and beat well. Beat in the egg to mix. On low speed gradually add the sifted dry ingredients, scraping the bowl with a rubber spatula and beating only until thoroughly mixed.

Tear off a strip of wax paper about 16 inches long. Place the dough by heaping tablespoonfuls down the length of the paper, forming a heavy strip about 10 inches long. Fold the long sides of the paper up around the dough. Pressing against the paper with your hands, shape the dough into an even oblong about 12 inches long, 2¾ inches wide, and 1 inch thick.

Wrap the dough in the paper. Slide a cookie sheet under the paper and transfer the dough to the freezer or refrigerator for several hours (or longer) until firm.

Adjust two racks to divide the oven into thirds and preheat to 375 degrees. Cut aluminum foil to fit cookie sheets.

Unwrap the firm dough. Place it on a cutting board and, with a sharp knife, cut the dough into ¼-inch slices. Place the slices 1 inch apart on the cut foil. Slide cookie sheets under the foil.

Bake for 10 to 12 minutes, reversing the sheets top to bottom and front to back to insure even baking. The cookies are done when the tops spring back if pressed with a fingertip. Do not overbake.

Slide the foil off the sheets and with a wide metal spatula transfer the cookies to racks to cool.

Maxines

Chewy, fudgy, chocolate-almond slices edged with a buttery brown-sugar layer.

24 COOKIES

CHOCOLATE MIXTURE

6 ounces (1 cup) semisweet chocolate morsels
1 tablespoon vegetable shortening
(such as Crisco)
⅓ cup sweetened condensed milk
½ teaspoon vanilla extract
¼ teaspoon almond extract
5 ounces (1 cup) blanched almonds, coarsely
cut (each almond should be cut into
3 or 4 pieces)

Place the chocolate and shortening in the top of a medium-size double boiler over hot water on medium heat, cover, and cook until partially melted. Uncover and stir until completely melted. Remove from heat. Stir in the condensed milk and the vanilla and almond extracts, then the almonds.

Tear off a piece of wax paper about 15 inches long. Place the dough by large spoonfuls the long way down the middle of the paper, forming a heavy strip about 10 inches long. Fold the sides of the paper up against the chocolate mixture. With your hands, press against the paper and shape the mixture into an even round or square roll 12 inches long and 1½ inches in diameter. Wrap in the paper. Slide a cookie sheet under the paper and transfer to the freezer or refrigerator until firm.

Meanwhile, prepare Brown-Sugar Dough.

BROWN-SUGAR DOUGH

1 cup sifted all-purpose flour
¼ teaspoon double-acting baking powder
¼ teaspoon salt
2 ounces (4 tablespoons) butter
½ teaspoon vanilla extract
½ cup light brown sugar, firmly packed
1 egg yolk

Sift together the flour, baking powder, and salt and set aside. In the small bowl of an electric mixer, cream the butter. Add the vanilla and sugar and beat well. Beat in the egg yolk, and then, gradually, on low speed, add the sifted dry ingredients. Beat only until thoroughly mixed. The mixture will be crumbly; remove it from the mixer and press it together with your hands until it forms a ball.

Place the ball of dough on a piece of wax paper a little more than 12 inches long. With your hands, shape it into a flattened oblong. Cover with another long piece of wax paper. Roll a rolling pin over the top piece of paper to form the dough into an oblong 12 inches long and 8 inches wide. While rolling, occasionally remove and then replace top wax paper; then invert and do the same with bottom wax paper, in order to keep both pieces of paper smooth and unwrinkled.

Remove the top piece of wax paper. Unwrap the chocolate roll and center it on the brown-sugar dough. Using the wax paper, lift one long side of the brown-sugar dough and press it firmly against the chocolate. Then lift the other side so that the sides of dough overlap slightly. (If the dough does not fit perfectly, the excess may be cut off and pressed into place where needed.)

Enclose the roll in the wax paper, then run your hands firmly over the roll to remove any air trapped between the dough and the chocolate mixture.

Rechill the roll only until it is firm enough to slice. (If the dough is frozen firm it will crack when sliced. If this happens, let it stand briefly at room temperature.)

Adjust two racks to divide the oven into thirds and preheat to 375 degrees.

Unwrap the roll of dough and place it on a cutting board. With a sharp knife, cut slices ½ inch thick—no thinner! Place the slices flat, 1 inch apart, on unbuttered cookie sheets. Bake about 12 minutes, until cookies are lightly colored. Reverse sheets top to bottom and front to back once during baking to insure even browning.

Let the cookies stand on sheets for a minute or so until firm enough to transfer, then with a wide metal spatula transfer cookies to racks to cool.

Cobble-
stones

These are thick, semisoft, and full of raisins and nuts. The name describes the shape, not the texture. The directions are for an unusual way of making icebox cookies.

3½ cups sifted all-purpose flour
1 teaspoon baking soda
½ teaspoon salt
1 teaspoon cinnamon
½ teaspoon nutmeg
¼ teaspoon powdered cloves
¼ teaspoon ginger
10 ounces (2 cups) raisins
Boiling water
5⅓ ounces (10⅔ tablespoons) butter
1 tablespoon instant coffee
1 tablespoon vanilla extract
1 cup light brown sugar, firmly packed
1 cup granulated sugar
1 egg
½ cup sour cream
7 ounces (2 cups) walnuts, cut or broken into
    medium-size pieces

Prepare a 10½-by-15½-by-1-inch jelly-roll pan as follows: Cut a piece of aluminum foil large enough to cover the bottom and sides of the pan. Invert the pan. Place the foil evenly on the pan and fold down the sides and corners to shape the foil. Now remove the foil and rinse the inside of the pan with water but do not dry it—the wet pan will hold the foil in place. Carefully place the foil in the pan and press it into place. Set aside.

Sift together the flour, baking soda, salt, cinnamon, nutmeg, cloves, and ginger and set aside.

In a bowl or a large measuring cup, pour the boiling water over the raisins to cover, and let them stand for about 10 minutes. Then pour into a strainer or a colander to drain. Spread the drained raisins on several thicknesses of paper towels and pat the top lightly with paper towels.

In the large bowl of an electric mixer cream the butter. Add the coffee, vanilla, and both sugars and beat to mix well. Beat in the egg. On low speed gradually add about one-third of the sifted dry ingredients, then the sour cream, and finally the remaining dry ingredients, scraping the bowl as necessary with a rubber spatula and beating only until smoothly incorporated. Remove from the mixer.

The dough will be stiff—use a heavy wooden spatula to stir in the raisins and nuts.

Place the dough by large spoonfuls into the lined pan. Cover with a large piece of wax paper. With your hands, press gently on the wax paper to spread the dough evenly. Now, with a small rolling pin or a straight-sided glass, roll over the wax paper to smooth the top of the dough. Do not remove the wax paper.

Chill the pan of dough in the freezer for several hours or more, or in the refrigerator overnight, until the dough is quite firm—the firmer the better.

Adjust two racks to divide the oven into thirds and preheat to 400 degrees. Cut aluminum foil to fit cookie sheets.

Lightly flour a section of a large cutting board, spreading the flour to cover a surface a little larger than the jelly-roll pan.

Slowly peel the wax paper off the dough. Invert the pan onto the floured surface. Remove the pan and peel off the foil. *Work quickly before the dough softens!!!* With a *long, heavy, sharp* knife, cutting down firmly with the full length of the blade, cut the dough into 48 bars, each measuring about 1¼ by 2½ inches (cut the cake into quarters, cut each piece across into thirds, and then cut each third into 4 bars). If the blade sticks, wipe it occasionally with a damp cloth.

Place the cookies 2 inches apart on the cut aluminum foil. Slide cookie sheets under the foil.

Bake for 12 to 13 minutes, reversing the sheets top to bottom and front to back once to insure even baking. The cookies are just done when the tops barely spring back if lightly pressed with a fingertip. Do not overbake or they will be hard and dry instead of semisoft.

Let the cookies stand on the sheets for a few seconds and then, with a wide metal spatula, transfer them to racks to cool.

Neapolitans

These Italian cookies present an interesting way of making icebox cookies. They are dramatic and unusual. You will make two entirely separate recipes for the dough—and it must chill overnight.

DARK DOUGH

3 cups sifted all-purpose flour
¼ teaspoon salt
1 teaspoon baking soda
½ teaspoon powdered cloves
½ teaspoon cinnamon
6 ounces (1 cup) semisweet chocolate morsels
½ pound (2 sticks) butter
2 teaspoons instant coffee
1½ cups dark brown sugar, firmly packed
2 eggs
5 ounces (1 cup) nuts, either whole pignoli
    (pine nuts) or green pistachios, or walnuts
    or pecans, cut into medium-size pieces

You will need an 11-by-5-by-3-inch loaf pan, or any other loaf pan with 8 to 9 cups' capacity (or use two smaller pans of equal capacity). To prepare the pan: Cut two strips of aluminum foil or two strips of wax paper (see Notes), one for the length and one for the width; they should be long enough so that they can be folded over the top of the pan when it is filled and should cover the whole surface. Place them in the pan and set aside.

Sift together the flour, salt, baking soda, cloves, and cinnamon and set aside. Grind the chocolate morsels in an electric blender (or they may be finely chopped, but they must be fine or it will be difficult to slice the cookies), and set aside. In the large bowl of an electric mixer cream the butter. Add the coffee and brown sugar and beat well. Add the eggs and beat to mix. Beat in the ground chocolate. On low speed gradually add the sifted dry ingredients, scraping the bowl with a rubber spatula and beating only until blended. Beat in the nuts.

Transfer the dough to another bowl, unless you have another large bowl for the electric mixer. Set the dough aside at room temperature and prepare the following light dough.

LIGHT DOUGH

2 cups sifted all-purpose flour
¼ teaspoon salt
¼ teaspoon baking soda
¼ pound (1 stick) butter
1 teaspoon vanilla extract
½ teaspoon almond extract
¾ cup granulated sugar
2 tablespoons water
1 egg
3½ ounces (¾ cup) currants, unchopped, or
    raisins, coarsely chopped
Finely grated rind of 1 large lemon
12 candied red cherries, cut into quarters
12 candied green cherries, cut into quarters

Sift together the flour, salt, and baking soda and set aside. In a clean large bowl of the electric mixer, with clean beaters, cream the butter. Add the vanilla and almond extracts, the sugar, and water and beat well. Add the egg and beat to mix. On low speed gradually add the sifted dry ingredients, scraping the bowl with a rubber spatula and beating only until blended. Mix in the currants, lemon rind, and both kinds of cherries.

To layer the doughs in the prepared pan: Use half (about 2¾ cups) of the dark dough and place it by spoonfuls over the bottom of the pan. Pack the dough firmly into the corners of the pan and spread it as level as possible. With another spoon, spread all of the light dough in a layer over the dark dough—again, as level as possible. Form an even top layer with the remaining dark dough. Cover the top with the foil or wax paper and, with your fingers, press down firmly to make a smooth, compact loaf.

Chill the dough overnight in its pan in the freezer or refrigerator.

To bake the cookies: Adjust two racks to divide the oven into thirds and preheat to 400 degrees. The cookies may be baked on unbuttered cookie sheets or on sheets lined with foil—either is O.K. Have the sheets ready.

To remove the dough from the pan: Use a small, narrow metal spatula or a table knife to release the dough from the corners of the pan. Fold back the foil or wax paper from the top of the loaf of dough, invert the pan onto a cutting board, and remove the pan and the foil or paper.

With a long, *heavy*, sharp knife cut the dough in half the long way.

Wrap one half and return it to the freezer or refrigerator while working with the other half.

With a very sharp knife cut the dough into slices about ¼ inch thick. Place the slices 1 to 1½ inches apart on the cookie sheets. (If you are using foil you can cut several pieces of foil to fit the cookie sheets, place the cookies on them, and then, later, slide the cookie sheets under the foil.)

The second half of the dough may be sliced and baked now or it may be frozen for future use.

Bake for about 10 minutes, reversing the cookie sheets top to bottom and front to back as necessary during baking to insure even browning. Bake until the light dough is lightly colored, but watch them carefully—the dark dough has a tendency to burn.

With a wide metal spatula transfer the cookies to racks to cool.

NOTES: When slicing the cookies, if the dough crumbles and is difficult to slice, it has not chilled enough. It should be wrapped and placed in the freezer for about an hour.

If you use wax paper instead of foil, each piece should be folded so that it is two or three thicknesses. Wax paper is weaker than foil and a single layer would tear.

Fruitcake Icebox Cookies

72 TO 80 COOKIES

2½ cups sifted all-purpose flour
¼ teaspoon cream of tartar
½ pound (2 sticks) butter
1 cup confectioners sugar
1 egg
½ pound (1 cup) candied pineapple, coarsely cut
½ pound (1 cup) candied cherries, left whole
6 ounces (generous 1⅔ cups) pecans, halves or large pieces

Sift together the flour and cream of tartar and set aside. In the large bowl of an electric mixer cream the butter. Add the sugar and beat to mix. Add the egg and beat well. On low speed gradually add the sifted dry ingredients, scraping the bowl with a rubber spatula and beating only until mixed. Remove from mixer.

With a heavy wooden spatula or with your bare hands mix in the fruit and nuts.

Tear off two 15-inch lengths of wax paper. Place one-half of the dough in a heavy strip about 9 inches long down the center of each piece of paper. Fold up the long sides of the paper and with your hands press against the paper to form the dough into rolls or oblongs 2 inches in diameter and 9 to 10 inches long. Squeeze and press firmly to smooth the sides. Wrap in the paper.

Slide a cookie sheet under the rolls and place them in the freezer for several hours or longer, until firm.

Adjust two racks to divide the oven into thirds and preheat to 375 degrees. Cut aluminum foil to fit cookie sheets.

The dough must be cold and very firm when you slice it. Unwrap one roll at a time, place it on a cutting board, and cut into ¼-inch slices. If the dough crumbles or is difficult to slice it needs more freezing.

Place the cookies ½ to 1 inch apart (these do not spread) on the cut foil. Slide a cookie sheet under the foil.

Bake 12 to 14 minutes, reversing sheets top to bottom and front to back during baking to insure even browning. The tops of the cookies will not color, but the cookies should be baked until the edges and the bottoms are golden brown. Check the color of the bottoms before removing them.

Slide the foil off the sheet and with a wide metal spatula transfer cookies to racks to cool.

NOTE: Green pistachio nuts are lovely in these cookies but they are hard to find. Shelled, unsalted green pistachios are generally available at specialty nut stores or wholesale nut dealers. You may add about 1 cup along with the pecans.

Butter-scotch Thins

96 COOKIES

1⅓ cups sifted all-purpose flour
¾ teaspoon baking soda
¼ pound (1 stick) butter, cut into
    4 or 5 pieces
6 ounces (1 cup) butterscotch morsels
⅔ cup light brown sugar, firmly packed
1 egg
¾ teaspoon vanilla extract
⅓ cup pecans, finely cut

Sift together the flour and baking soda and set aside. Place the butter and butterscotch morsels in the top of a small double boiler over hot water on moderate heat. Cover and cook for a few minutes until partially melted. Then uncover and stir (on the heat) until completely melted. The mixture will not be amalgamated; the butter will be a layer over the morsels. However, both must be completely melted.

Transfer the butterscotch mixture to the small bowl of an electric mixer and beat until smooth. Add the sugar, egg, and vanilla and beat again until very smooth. On low speed gradually add the sifted dry ingredients and then the nuts, scraping the bowl with a rubber spatula and beating only until well incorporated.

The dough will be soft. Place it, in the mixing bowl, in the refrigerator only until it is firm enough to shape. It will probably take less than half an hour; do not leave it much longer than that or it will become too stiff.

Tear off a piece of wax paper about 16 inches long. Spoon the dough lengthwise down the center of the paper in a heavy strip about 10 to 11 inches long. Fold the long sides of the paper up against the dough and, with your hands, press against the paper to shape the dough into a long roll or an oblong 12 inches long. Wrap the dough in the wax paper. Slide a cookie sheet under it and transfer to the freezer or refrigerator until very firm (or as much longer as you wish).

Adjust two racks to divide the oven into thirds and preheat to 375 degrees. Cut aluminum foil to fit cookie sheets.

Unwrap the dough and replace it on the wax paper. With a sharp knife cut the dough into very thin slices—⅛ inch, no more. (It is important that these be sliced thin, and as even as possible, or some will burn before the others have baked.) Place the cookies 1½ inches apart on the cut aluminum foil.

Slide cookie sheets under the foil and bake the cookies for about 6 to 8 minutes, until they are well browned. Reverse the sheets top to bottom and front to back to insure even browning. The cookies will rise as they bake and then flatten. The best way to time these is to leave them in the oven until all or almost all of the cookies have flattened. If they are under-baked they will be soft and chewy instead of crisp. But some people prefer them soft and chewy.

Slide the foil off the cookie sheets, let the cookies stand for about half a minute or a bit longer, and then, with a wide metal spatula, transfer them to racks to cool.

Pecan Butter-scotch Icebox Cookies

70 TO 80 COOKIES

An Early American recipe from Massachusetts. The recipe originated before baking powder was available; early recipes used baking soda plus cream of tartar. These are thin and crisp.

2 cups sifted all-purpose flour
½ teaspoon baking soda
½ teaspoon cream of tartar
¼ teaspoon salt
¼ pound (1 stick) butter
½ teaspoon vanilla extract
1 cup light brown sugar, firmly packed
1 egg
4 ounces (generous 1 cup) pecan halves or
    pieces

Sift together the flour, baking soda, cream of tartar, and salt and set aside. In the large bowl of an electric mixer, cream the butter. Add the vanilla and the sugar and beat well. Add the egg and beat until smooth. Gradu-ally, on low speed, add the sifted dry ingredients and beat until the mix-ture holds together. Mix in the nuts.

Turn the dough out onto a board, smooth work surface, or piece of wax paper. The dough will be firm enough to handle and not sticky. With your hands, shape it into a long rectangle.

Place it lengthwise on a piece of wax paper about 18 inches long. Fold the paper up on the sides and, with your hands, press and smooth over the paper to form a 12- to 14-inch roll about 2 inches in diameter.

Wrap the dough in the wax paper, slide a cookie sheet under it, and transfer to the freezer or refrigerator for several hours or overnight. The dough must be very firm, preferably frozen solid, in order to slice thin enough.

Adjust two racks to divide oven into thirds and preheat to 375 degrees. Cut aluminum foil to fit cookie sheets (see Note).

Unwrap the dough and place it on a cutting board. With a thin, sharp knife cut into very thin slices—⅛ to ¼ inch thick, or about 6 slices to an inch.

Place the slices 1 inch apart on the foil. Slide cookie sheets under the foil.

Bake for 8 to 10 minutes until cookies are golden brown all over, reversing the sheets top to bottom and front to back as necessary to insure even browning.

With a wide metal spatula, transfer to racks to cool.

NOTE: These may be baked without the foil on unbuttered cookie sheets. Without foil, the cookies will brown faster.

Oatmeal Icebox Cookies

80 COOKIES

These are thin, crisp, and crunchy.

1½ cups sifted all-purpose flour
½ teaspoon salt
1 teaspoon baking soda
1 teaspoon ginger
½ pound (2 sticks) butter
1 teaspoon vanilla extract
1 cup granulated sugar
1 cup dark brown sugar, firmly packed
2 eggs
3 cups old-fashioned or quick-cooking (not "instant") oatmeal
4 ounces (generous 1 cup) walnuts, cut medium fine (see page 13)

Sift together the flour, salt, baking soda, and ginger and set aside. In the large bowl of an electric mixer cream the butter. Add the vanilla and both sugars and beat well. Add the eggs one at a time and beat to incorporate after each addition. On low speed gradually add the sifted dry ingredients and then the oatmeal, scraping the bowl as necessary with a rubber spatula and beating only until thoroughly mixed. Stir in the nuts.

Spread out two pieces of wax paper, each about 13 to 15 inches long. Place spoonfuls of the dough lengthwise on each piece of paper to make strips about 9 to 10 inches long. Fold the long sides of the papers up against the dough and, pressing against the papers with your hands, shape the dough into oblongs about 10 inches long, 3 inches wide, and 1 to 1½ inches thick. Wrap the dough in the wax paper.

Slide a cookie sheet under the two oblongs of dough and place in the freezer for an hour or two, or in the refrigerator overnight, until the dough is firm enough to slice (or longer if you wish).

Adjust two racks to divide the oven into thirds and preheat to 350 degrees. Cut aluminum foil to fit cookie sheets.

Unwrap one piece of dough at a time. Place it on a cutting board. With a thin, sharp knife cut the dough into ¼-inch slices and place them on the cut foil 2 inches apart (these will spread). Slide cookie sheets under the foil.

Bake for 12 to 14 minutes, until the cookies are well browned. Reverse the sheets top to bottom and front to back as necessary to insure even browning.

Slide the foil off the cookie sheet and let stand for a few minutes until the foil can be easily peeled away from the backs of the cookies. Place the cookies on racks to finish cooling.

These must be stored airtight.

Peanut-Butter Pillows

16 TO 20 FILLED
COOKIES

Peanut butter is sandwiched between two peanut-butter icebox cookies and then the cookies are baked. They are crisp; the filling is soft.

1½ cups sifted all-purpose flour
½ teaspoon baking soda
¼ teaspoon salt
¼ pound (1 stick) butter
½ cup smooth (not chunky) peanut butter
½ cup granulated sugar
¼ cup light corn syrup
1 tablespoon milk
Additional peanut butter for filling (a scant
    ½ cup)

Sift together the flour, baking soda, and salt and set aside. In the small bowl of an electric mixer cream the butter. Add the peanut butter and sugar and beat until thoroughly mixed. Beat in the corn syrup and the milk. On low speed add the sifted dry ingredients, scraping the bowl as necessary with a rubber spatula and beating only until smooth.

Turn the dough out onto a large board or a smooth work surface. Knead it briefly and then, with your hands, form it into an even roll or oblong about 7 inches long and 2¼ to 2½ inches in diameter. Wrap the dough in wax paper. Slide a cookie sheet under the paper and transfer the dough to the refrigerator for several hours, or longer if you wish.

Adjust two racks to divide the oven into thirds and preheat to 350 degrees.

With a sharp knife cut half of the roll of dough into slices ⅛ to ¼ inch thick and, as you cut the slices, place them 2 inches apart on unbuttered cookie sheets.

Place 1 level measuring teaspoonful of the additional peanut butter in the center of each cookie. Then spread the peanut butter only slightly to flatten it, leaving a ½- to ¾-inch border.

Slice the remaining half of the roll of dough (same thickness) and, as you cut each slice, place it over one of the peanut-butter-topped cookies. Let the cookies stand for 2 or 3 minutes for the dough to soften slightly. Then seal the edges by pressing them lightly with the back of the tines of a fork, dipping the fork in flour as necessary to keep it from sticking. (Don't worry about slight cracks in the tops.)

Bake for 12 to 15 minutes, reversing the position of the cookie sheets top to bottom and front to back to insure even browning. (If you bake only one sheet at a time bake it high in the oven.) Bake until the cookies are lightly colored.

Let the cookies stand on the sheet for about a minute. Then, with a wide metal spatula, transfer them to racks to cool.

NOTE: This dough may be mixed without a mixer. Simply place the sifted dry ingredients and the sugar in a mixing bowl. With a pastry blender cut in the butter and the peanut butter until the mixture resembles coarse meal. Stir in the syrup and milk. Then, on a board or a smooth work surface, knead the dough briefly with the heel of your hand until it is smooth.

Whole-Wheat Peanut-Butter Cookies

48 COOKIES

These are extra crisp and crunchy, with a lovely sandy texture from the raw sugar.

1¼ cups <u>unsifted</u> whole-wheat pastry flour (available at health-food stores)
1 teaspoon baking soda
¼ teaspoon salt
¼ pound (1 stick) butter
½ cup smooth (not chunky) peanut butter
1 cup raw sugar
1 egg

Sift together the flour, baking soda, and salt and set aside. In the large bowl of an electric mixer cream the butter. Add the peanut butter and beat until smooth. Add the raw sugar and beat well, then add the egg and beat well again. On low speed gradually add the sifted dry ingredients, scraping the bowl with a rubber spatula and beating only until smooth.

Tear off a piece of wax paper about 16 inches long. Spoon the dough lengthwise down the center of the paper in a heavy strip about 10 to 11 inches long. Fold the long sides of the paper over the dough and, with your hands, shape the dough into a long, round or oblong roll, 12 inches long. Wrap the dough in the wax paper.

Slide a cookie sheet under the dough and transfer it to the freezer or refrigerator until firm (or as much longer as you wish).

Adjust two racks to divide the oven into thirds and preheat to 350 degrees.

Unwrap the dough and replace it on the wax paper. With a sharp knife cut the dough into slices ¼ inch thick and place them 1 to 1½ inches apart on unbuttered cookie sheets.

Bake for 15 minutes or a little longer, until the cookies are lightly colored and semifirm to the touch. Reverse the sheets top to bottom and front to back to insure even browning.

With a wide metal spatula transfer the cookies to racks to cool.

Icebox Nut Cookies

45 TO 50 COOKIES

This simple recipe is a popular teaparty specialty of a famous Washington hostess.

½ pound (2 sticks) butter
1 teaspoon mace or nutmeg
2 cups granulated sugar
2 eggs
3 cups sifted all-purpose flour
8 ounces (2¼ cups) walnut or pecan halves
   or large pieces
Finely grated rind of 1 large or 2 small lemons

In the large bowl of an electric mixer cream the butter. Add the mace or nutmeg and the sugar and beat well. Add the eggs one at a time and beat well after each addition. On low speed gradually add the flour, scraping the bowl with a rubber spatula and beating only until the mixture is smooth and holds together. Remove the bowl from the mixer and, with a heavy wooden spatula or with your bare hands, mix in the nuts and the lemon rind.

The cookies may now be shaped in one of two ways. Traditionally, the dough may be turned out onto a long piece of wax paper and, with floured hands, shaped into a long roll or oblong (or it may be divided in half and shaped into two rolls or oblongs). Wrap in the wax paper and place in the freezer or refrigerator.

Another way of shaping the dough is to line a 3- to 4-cup ice-cube tray (without dividers) with aluminum foil. Pack the dough into the lined tray. Cover with foil and press down firmly with the palm of your hand to smooth the top. Freeze or refrigerate until the dough is stiff—or longer if you want. Whichever way you shape the dough, it must be chilled until it is very firm—it may be sliced when it is frozen solid.

Adjust two racks to divide the oven into thirds and preheat to 350 degrees. Cut aluminum foil to fit cookie sheets (see Note).

Unwrap the dough and place it on a cutting board. With a thin, sharp knife cut the dough into ¼-inch slices. Place the slices ½ to 1 inch apart on the cut foil. Slide cookie sheets under the foil and bake for 18 to 20 minutes, until the cookies are lightly colored. Reverse the sheets top to bottom and front to back as necessary to insure even browning. Do not underbake; these should be very crisp when cool.

Slide the foil off the cookie sheets, and with a wide metal spatula transfer the cookies to racks to cool.

NOTE: These may also be baked on unlined and unbuttered cookie sheets if you prefer.

Sesame Fingers

48 COOKIES

There is an old saying in the South that sesame seeds, also known as benne seeds, bring good luck. These cookies from Charleston, South Carolina, are hard and dry and full of toasted sesame seeds. The dough should be chilled overnight in the freezer.

4 ounces (¾ cup) sesame seeds (see Note)
¼ pound (1 stick) butter
¾ teaspoon vanilla extract
¼ teaspoon salt
1 cup granulated sugar
1 egg
2 cups sifted all-purpose flour
¼ cup milk

Place the sesame seeds in a large, heavy frying pan over medium-low heat. Stir almost constantly and shake the pan frequently until the seeds are toasted to a golden-brown color. (Toasting brings out the sweet, nutty flavor of the seeds.) Be careful not to let them burn. Transfer the toasted seeds to a shallow plate and set aside to cool.

In the large bowl of an electric mixer cream the butter. Add the vanilla, salt, and sugar and beat to mix well. Add the egg and beat to mix. On low speed gradually add half of the flour, then all of the milk, and finally the remaining flour, scraping the bowl with a rubber spatula and beating only until smooth after each addition. Mix in the cooled toasted sesame seeds.

If the dough is too soft at this point to form it into a block for icebox cookies, chill it in the mixing bowl, stirring occasionally until it is slightly firm.

Then tear off a piece of wax paper about 18 inches long. Place the dough by large spoonfuls lengthwise down the center of the paper to form a heavy strip about 10 inches long. Fold up the two long sides of the paper. With your hands press against the paper to mold the dough into an oblong 12 inches long, ¾ inch wide, and 1 inch thick.

Slide a cookie sheet under the paper and transfer the dough to the freezer. Let stand overnight.

Adjust two racks to divide the oven into thirds and preheat to 375 degrees. Cut aluminum foil to fit cookie sheets.

Lightly flour a section of a cutting board a little larger than the oblong of dough. Unwrap the dough and place it on the floured board.

With a sharp, heavy knife, quickly cut the dough into ¼-inch slices, and place them 1 inch apart on the cut foil. Slide cookie sheets under the foil.

Bake for about 15 minutes, reversing the position of the sheets top to bottom and front to back as necessary to insure even browning. When done, the cookies will be slightly brown on the edges but still pale on the tops. (If you bake only one sheet at a time, use the higher rack.)

With a wide metal spatula transfer the cookies to racks to cool.

NOTE: Sesame seeds vary in color from so-called white (hulled) to gray-ish-tan (unhulled). I use the white.

Caraway Crisps

50 COOKIES

This is a classic Scottish recipe.

2⅔ cups sifted all-purpose flour
½ teaspoon baking soda
¼ teaspoon salt
Finely grated rind of 1 large lemon
2 tablespoons lemon juice
¼ pound (1 stick) butter
1 cup granulated sugar
1 egg
2 teaspoons caraway seeds

Sift together the flour, baking soda, and salt and set aside. Mix the lemon rind and juice and set aside. In the large bowl of an electric mixer cream the butter. Beat in the sugar and then the egg and the caraway seeds. On low speed gradually add the sifted dry ingredients, scraping the bowl with a rubber spatula and beating only until well mixed. Stir in the lemon rind and juice.

Place the dough on a large board or smooth work surface. Squeeze the dough between your hands and then knead it lightly just until the mixture holds together and is smooth. With your hands form the dough into a roll or an oblong 10 inches long and about 2 inches in diameter.

Wrap the dough in wax paper and slide a cookie sheet under it. Transfer to the freezer or refrigerator until it is firm enough to slice (or as much longer as you wish). This dough may be sliced when it is frozen solid.

Adjust two racks to divide the oven into thirds and preheat to 400 degrees.

With a sharp knife slice the cookies a scant ¼ inch thick and place them 1 inch apart on unbuttered cookie sheets.

Bake for 10 minutes, reversing the sheets top to bottom and front to back during baking to insure even browning. The cookies are done when they are lightly browned on the edges and barely sandy-colored in the centers.

With a wide metal spatula transfer cookies to racks to cool.

Almond Spicebox Cookies

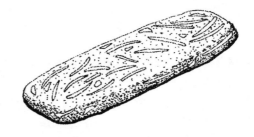

90 COOKIES

4 cups sifted all-purpose flour
3 teaspoons cinnamon
1 teaspoon ginger
½ teaspoon salt
1 teaspoon baking soda
½ pound (2 sticks) butter
2 teaspoons instant coffee
½ teaspoon almond extract
1 cup granulated sugar
1 cup dark brown sugar, firmly packed
3 extra-large or jumbo eggs
8 to 10 ounces (2½–3 cups) blanched and
    thinly sliced almonds

Sift together the flour, cinnamon, ginger, salt, and baking soda and set aside. In the large bowl of an electric mixer cream the butter. Add the coffee, almond extract, and both sugars and beat well. Add the eggs one at a time, beating until smooth after each addition. On low speed gradually add the sifted dry ingredients, scraping the bowl with a rubber spatula and beating only until the mixture is smooth. (When most of the dry ingredients have been added the mixture might start to crawl up on the beaters; if so, finish stirring it by hand with a wooden spatula; the dough will be stiff.) With a wooden spatula and/or your bare hands, mix in the almonds.

Spread out two pieces of wax paper, each about 16 inches long. Place large spoonfuls of the dough lengthwise on each piece of paper to form heavy strips about 10 to 11 inches long. Fold the long sides of the paper up against the dough and, pressing against the paper with your hands, shape each strip of dough into a smooth oblong 12 inches long, 3 inches wide, and about 1 inch thick. Wrap the dough in the wax paper.

Slide a cookie sheet under both packages of dough and transfer them to the freezer or refrigerator for several hours or overnight (or longer if you wish). This slices best when it is frozen solid.

Adjust two racks to divide the oven into thirds and preheat to 375 degrees.

Unwrap one roll of dough at a time. Place it on a cutting board. With a very sharp knife cut the dough into ¼-inch slices and place them 1 to 1½ inches apart on unbuttered cookie sheets.

Bake the cookies for about 12 minutes, reversing the position of the sheets top to bottom and front to back as necessary to insure even browning. The cookies are done when they are slightly colored and spring back if lightly pressed with a fingertip.

With a wide metal spatula transfer the cookies to racks to cool.

Anise Icebox Cookies

42 COOKIES

Anise is an herb. The seeds, which are used whole in this recipe, have a licorice flavor.

1¾ cups sifted all-purpose flour
¼ teaspoon salt
1½ teaspoons double-acting baking powder
¼ pound (1 stick) butter
½ teaspoon vanilla extract
1 cup granulated sugar
1 egg
1¾ teaspoons aniseed
Finely grated rind of 1 large lemon

Sift together the flour, salt, and baking powder and set aside. In the small bowl of an electric mixer cream the butter. Beat in the vanilla extract and the sugar. Add the egg and the aniseed and beat well. On low speed gradually add the sifted dry ingredients, scraping the bowl with a rubber spatula and beating only until thoroughly mixed.

Remove the bowl from the mixer and with a wooden spatula stir in the lemon rind.

Tear off a 15-inch piece of wax paper. Place the dough by large spoonfuls lengthwise down the middle of the paper, forming a heavy strip about 10 inches long.

Fold the paper up on the long sides. With your hands, press against the paper to shape the dough into an even oblong or roll about 11 inches long, 2½ inches wide, and 1 inch thick (or any other size you wish). Wrap the dough in the paper.

Slide a cookie sheet under the dough and transfer it to the freezer until it is firm (or as much longer as you wish—this dough may be sliced when frozen solid).

Adjust two racks to divide the oven into thirds and preheat to 400 degrees. Cut aluminum foil to fit cookie sheets.

Unwrap the frozen dough and place it on a cutting board. With a thin, sharp knife cut the dough into ¼-inch slices. Place the cookies on the foil 1 inch apart. Slide cookie sheets under the foil.

Bake for about 10 minutes, reversing the sheets top to bottom and front to back to insure even browning. These are done when they are golden brown. Do not underbake—these should be very crisp when cool.

Slide the foil off the cookie sheets and with a wide metal spatula transfer the cookies to racks to cool.

Cardamom Cookies from Copenhagen

40 COOKIES

This is a classic Danish butter cookie—plain, light, crisp, and dry, with a definite cardamom flavor.

2 cups sifted all-purpose flour
¼ teaspoon baking soda
1½ teaspoons ground cardamom
¼ pound (1 stick) butter
½ teaspoon vanilla extract
½ cup light brown sugar, firmly packed
⅓ cup light cream
2½ ounces (generous ½ cup) slivered almonds (julienne-shaped pieces)

Sift together the flour, baking soda, and cardamom and set aside. In the large bowl of an electric mixer cream the butter. Beat in the vanilla and then add the sugar and beat well. On low speed alternately add the sifted dry ingredients in three additions with the cream in two additions, scraping the bowl with a rubber spatula and beating only until thoroughly mixed. Remove from the mixer and, with a rubber or wooden spatula, stir in the almonds.

Turn the dough out onto a smooth work surface or a piece of wax paper. Knead it slightly and then, with your hands, form it into a smooth roll or oblong about 2 inches wide and 10 inches long.

Wrap the dough in plastic wrap or wax paper and place in the freezer for several hours or as much longer as you wish—this dough slices best when it is frozen solid.

Before baking, adjust two racks to divide the oven into thirds and preheat to 350 degrees.

Unwrap the dough and place it on a cutting board. With a long, heavy, sharp knife cut the dough into ¼-inch slices and place them 1 inch apart on unbuttered cookie sheets—these do not spread or change shape during baking.

Bake for about 15 minutes, until the cookies are only slightly sandy-colored on the edges—these barely color, if at all, on the tops. Reverse the position of the sheets top to bottom and front to back as necessary during baking to insure even browning.

With a metal spatula, transfer the cookies to racks to cool.

Pinwheels

56 COOKIES

This is an attractive crisp, black-and-white cookie (the two doughs are rolled together like a jelly roll). They are fancy cookies but not difficult to make.

> 1¾ cups sifted all-purpose flour
> ½ teaspoon double-acting baking powder
> ¼ teaspoon salt
> 1 ounce (1 square) unsweetened chocolate
> ¼ pound (1 stick) butter
> ½ teaspoon vanilla extract
> ¾ cup granulated sugar
> 1 egg
> 1 teaspoon powdered instant coffee (see Note)
> ¼ teaspoon almond extract
> ⅓ cup pecans, finely chopped

Sift together the flour, baking powder, and salt and set aside. Melt the chocolate in the top of a small double boiler over hot water on moderate heat. Set aside to cool.

In the large bowl of an electric mixer cream the butter. Add the vanilla and then the sugar and beat to mix well. Add the egg and beat well. On low speed gradually add the sifted dry ingredients, scraping the bowl with a rubber spatula and beating only until thoroughly mixed.

Place half (scant 1 cup) of the dough in another mixing bowl. To one-half of the dough add the melted chocolate and the coffee powder, mix thoroughly, and set aside.

To the other half of the dough add the almond extract and the pecans, mix thoroughly, and set aside.

Tear off four pieces of wax paper, each about 17 inches long. On one piece, place one of the doughs. Cover with another piece of paper. Flatten the dough well with your hands. With a rolling pin, roll over the paper to roll the dough into an oblong 14 by 9 inches. (During rolling, check both

152

pieces of wax paper—if the paper wrinkles, peel it off and then replace it to remove the wrinkles.) When the dough is almost the right size, remove the top piece of paper, cut away excess dough (from the sides), and place it where needed (in the corners). Be careful not to have the edges thinner than the center or there will be an air space in each end of the roll. Replace wax paper and roll the dough again to smooth it, check the size, then set it aside. Repeat with the remaining piece of dough.

Remove the top piece of wax paper from both of the rolled doughs. Place the white dough in front of you. Now, the chocolate dough must be inverted over the white dough, but you must be careful because you will not be able to move it if it is not placed correctly; the two doughs will stick together. So invert it cautiously over the white dough, lining up the edges as evenly as possible (see Notes). Then remove the piece of wax paper from the top of the chocolate dough. There will still be one piece of paper under the white dough; use that to help roll the doughs, jelly-roll fashion, starting with a long side.

Wrap the roll in the wax paper. Slide a cookie sheet under the roll in order to transfer it to the freezer or refrigerator to chill until firm. (This should be very firm, and may be sliced when frozen.)

Adjust two racks to divide the oven into thirds and preheat to 350 degrees.

Unwrap the dough and place it on a cutting board. Cut into ¼-inch slices. (If the dough softens while you are slicing it, rewrap and rechill it until firm.) Place the slices 1 inch apart on unbuttered cookie sheets.

Bake for about 12 minutes, until the cookies are slightly colored on the edges. Reverse the position of the sheets top to bottom and front to back as necessary to insure even browning. Do not overbake. (If you bake only one sheet at a time bake it on the higher rack.)

With a wide metal spatula transfer the cookies to racks to cool.

NOTES: Powdered coffee is better than granules for this recipe. If you do not have powdered coffee, any other instant type may be powdered in a blender. Or the coffee may be left out.

A wonderful trick that makes it easy to place one dough exactly over the other: slide a cookie sheet beneath each piece of waxed paper under the rolled-out dough. Transfer both doughs to the freezer and leave until they are firm. Then invert the chocolate dough over the white as directed. (Because the dough is firm, if you haven't placed the chocolated layer evenly it will be easy to correct.) Remove the top piece of waxed paper, then let the doughs stand at room temperature until they are completely thawed before rolling them up together.

Rolled Cookies

SWEDISH RYE WAFERS

WHOLE-WHEAT SQUARES

WHOLE-WHEAT HONEY WAFERS

WILD-HONEY AND GINGER COOKIES

HONEY GRAHAM CRACKERS

SWEDISH HONEY COOKIES

SWEDISH GINGER COOKIES

VIENNESE ALMOND WAFERS

ISCHLER COOKIES

VIENNESE CHOCOLATE COOKIES

TROPICAL SOUR-CREAM COOKIES

CARAWAY SOUR-CREAM COOKIES

RUM-RAISIN SHORTBREAD

HOT BUTTER WAFERS

CARAWAY HARDTACK

ARROWROOT WAFERS FROM
  BERMUDA

UPPAKRA COOKIES

GINGER SHORTBREAD COOKIES

DIONE LUCAS' SABLES

CORNELL SUGAR COOKIES

PLAIN OLD-FASHIONED SUGAR
  COOKIES

CHOCOLATE-CHIP PILLOWS

PRUNE PILLOWS

HAMANTASCHEN

RUGELACH

DANISH COFFEEHOUSE SLICES

BIG NEWTONS

*These are all rolled with a rolling pin and then cut into shapes with
cookie cutters, a knife, or a pastry wheel. Some, toward the end of this
section, are also filled, but they are just another variety of rolled cookie.*

*Cookie cutters come in a variety of shapes and sizes. In each recipe I
have specified the shape and size that I use—it is generally a plain round
shape. I like to see a neat row of plain round cookies, all exactly alike,
arranged overlapping each other on a long, narrow tray. Cookies, more
than cakes or puddings, express your own personality, your taste, and
your temperament. Me, I'm a Virgo—neat and orderly. But if variety or
even confusion suits you better, it's up to you. If you prefer to use different
sizes, different shapes, all alike or assorted designs, make them as you
wish. However, some cookie doughs do not lend themselves to fancy shapes
with intricate cutouts. They might not hold their forms when removed
from the cutter. Or some doughs will run slightly in baking; if they were cut
with a scalloped cutter they might lose their scalloped edge. Since
there is such a variety of cutters, I suggest that if a recipe calls for a plain
round cutter, and if you want to use a fancy one, please try a sample first to
see how it works.*

Swedish Rye Wafers

50 COOKIES

These are thin, crisp, buttery, and exotic, with caraway seeds. They may easily be made without a mixer; simply use a wooden spatula or your bare hands for creaming and mixing.

> ½ pound (2 sticks) butter
> ½ cup granulated sugar
> 1¼ cups strained rye flour (see Notes)
> 1¼ cups sifted all-purpose white flour
> Milk
> Caraway seeds

Adjust two racks to divide the oven into thirds and preheat to 350 degrees.

In the large bowl of an electric mixer cream the butter. Beat in the sugar and then on low speed gradually mix in both of the flours, scraping the bowl as necessary with a rubber spatula and beating only until thoroughly mixed.

Dust a pastry cloth and a rolling pin (if you have a stockinette cover for the pin, use it) with either white or rye flour or with untoasted wheat germ (see Notes). Do not use any more flour or wheat germ than is necessary to keep the dough from sticking.

Roll half of the dough at a time, rolling it to ⅛-inch thickness. If the dough is too sticky to roll, form it into a ball, flatten slightly, and let stand on the floured pastry cloth for 30 minutes to 1 hour before rolling out. Cut with a plain round 2½-inch cookie cutter. Then, with a very small round cutter, about ½ inch in diameter, cut a hole out of each cookie (see Notes). The hole should not be in the center of the cookie; it should be about ¾ inch from the edge. (In place of a very small round cookie cutter, use either the wide end of a pastry-bag decorating tube or a thimble.) Reserve the scraps and roll and cut them all at one time in order not to use any more flour than necessary.

With a metal spatula transfer the cookies to unbuttered cookie sheets, placing them about ½ inch apart.

Using a soft pastry brush, brush milk all over the top of each cookie and then sprinkle it with a moderate number of caraway seeds.

Bake 12 to 14 minutes, reversing the sheets top to bottom and front to back to insure even browning. Bake until cookies are lightly colored.

With a wide metal spatula transfer cookies to racks to cool.

NOTES: Since rye flour is too coarse to be sifted it must be strained to aerate it. With your fingertips press it through a large strainer set over a large bowl. The part that doesn't go through the strainer should be stirred into the strained part.

Rye flour and untoasted wheat germ are both available at health-food stores.

Traditionally the hole in these cookies is off center. You *could* cut them out with a doughnut cutter, and have the holes in the middle, but then the cookies would not have their classic and charming look.

Whole-Wheat Squares

36 TO 42 COOKIES

These are plain and not too sweet. The taste and texture will remind you of English wheatmeal biscuits. The recipe does not call for salt or flavoring, and does not require a mixer.

4 cups unsifted all-purpose whole-wheat flour
    (stir to aerate before measuring)
½ pound (2 sticks) butter
1 cup light brown sugar, firmly packed
1 teaspoon cream of tartar
1 teaspoon baking soda
1 egg
½ cup boiling water

Place the flour in a large mixing bowl. Slice the butter into ½- to 1-inch pieces, and with a pastry blender cut it into the flour until the particles are fine and the mixture resembles coarse meal. Stir in the sugar. Through a fine strainer add the cream of tartar and the baking soda. Beat the egg lightly just to mix and stir it in. Stir in the water.

Turn the mixture out onto a large board or smooth work surface and squeeze it between your hands until it holds together. Now "break" it by pushing off small pieces of the dough with the heel of your hand. Push against the work surface and smear it away from you. Re-form the dough and "break" it again.

The dough should be chilled before it is rolled. Form it into a flattened oblong with square corners, wrap in wax paper or plastic wrap, and refrigerate for one hour—no longer.

Adjust two racks to divide the oven into thirds and preheat to 350 degrees.

Cut the dough crossways into three equal pieces. Work with one piece at a time, letting the other pieces stand at room temperature. Place each piece on a floured pastry cloth. With a floured rolling pin roll out the dough. Roll it up around the rolling pin occasionally, reflouring the cloth if necessary, then unroll the dough other side down to keep both sides lightly floured. If the dough cracks while you are rolling it, use a bit from the edge to patch the crack—just put the patch in place and roll over it lightly with the rolling pin. Roll the dough into an even rectangle 9 by 12 inches and ¼ inch thick. (See Note.)

With a very long knife or a pastry wheel, trim the edges. (The scraps may be pressed together and rerolled.) Then cut the dough into 3-inch squares. Now score the cookies once lengthwise down the middle with the dull edge of a knife—the scoring should be deep enough to show but be careful that it does not cut through the cookie.

Use a wide metal spatula to transfer the cookies to unbuttered cookie sheets, placing them ½ to 1 inch apart.

Bake 20 to 30 minutes, until cookies are slightly colored. Reverse the sheets top to bottom and front to back as necessary during baking to insure even browning. Do not overbake. If the dough has been rolled unevenly the thinner cookies will be done first and should be removed as they are done. If you bake only one sheet at a time use the higher rack.

With a wide metal spatula transfer the cookies to racks to cool.

NOTE: These may be rolled a little thicker or a little thinner. I like them best a bit thick, or no less than ¼ inch. The baking time will depend on the thickness.

Whole-Wheat Honey Wafers

These are large, thin, crisp, and plain old-fashioned.

26 LARGE WAFERS

2 cups strained all-purpose whole-wheat flour (see Note)
½ teaspoon baking soda
½ teaspoon salt
1 teaspoon cinnamon
½ teaspoon ginger
¼ pound (1 stick) butter
2 teaspoons instant coffee
⅔ cup light brown sugar, firmly packed
⅓ cup honey
1 egg

Through a large strainer, set over a large bowl, strain together the flour, baking soda, salt, cinnamon, and ginger, pressing the ingredients through the strainer with your fingertips. Set aside.

In the large bowl of an electric mixer cream the butter. Beat in the instant coffee, brown sugar, honey, and egg. On lowest speed gradually add the strained dry ingredients, scraping the bowl as necessary with a rubber spatula and beating only until thoroughly mixed.

Divide the dough in half and wrap each half in a large piece of wax paper or aluminum foil. Refrigerate for a few hours (or longer if you wish) until the dough is firm enough to roll.

Adjust two racks to divide the oven into thirds and preheat to 375 degrees. Cut aluminum foil to fit cookie sheets.

Work with half of the dough at a time. Place the piece on a lightly floured pastry cloth and turn it over to flour the dough on all sides. With a lightly floured rolling pin, roll the dough until it is a scant ¼ inch thick. Cut cookies with a plain round 3-inch cookie cutter and place them 1 inch apart on the cut foil.

Reserve the scraps of dough and roll them all at once in order not to incorporate any more flour than necessary.

Slide cookie sheets under the foil and bake the cookies for 12 to 14 minutes, until the cookies are lightly colored. Reverse the sheets top to bottom and front to back as necessary to insure even browning. Do not underbake; these should be crisp.

Let the cookies stand on the foil for a few seconds until they can be transferred. With a wide metal spatula transfer the cookies to racks to cool.

These must be stored airtight.

NOTE: Since whole-wheat flour is generally too coarse to be sifted, it should be strained instead. Place a large strainer over a large bowl and, with your fingertips, work the flour through the strainer. Any particles too coarse to go through the strainer should be stirred into the strained flour.

Wild-Honey and Ginger Cookies

24 LARGE COOKIES

This is an old recipe that was originally made with wild honey, which has a very strong flavor. It may be made with any honey. The cookies are large, plain, and gingery. The dough has to be refrigerated 4 to 5 hours or longer.

2½ cups sifted all-purpose flour
1½ teaspoons baking soda
¼ teaspoon salt
1 tablespoon powdered ginger
½ pound (2 sticks) butter, cut into 1-inch pieces
12 ounces (1 cup) honey

Sift together the flour, baking soda, salt, and ginger into the large bowl of an electric mixer and set aside.

Place the butter and honey in a saucepan over moderate heat. Stir occasionally until the butter is melted and the mixture comes to a low boil.

Pour the hot honey and butter all at once over the sifted dry ingredients. On low speed mix until the dry ingredients are all absorbed and then on high speed for about a minute until the dough stiffens slightly.

Tear off a piece of aluminum foil large enough to wrap the dough. Pour a little vegetable oil onto the foil and, with your fingers, spread the oil thoroughly over the foil. The oil is necessary to keep this dough from sticking to the foil.

Place the dough on the foil, wrap, and refrigerate for 4 to 5 hours or overnight.

Adjust two racks to divide the oven into thirds and preheat to 350 degrees. Cut aluminum foil to fit cookie sheets.

Lightly flour a pastry cloth and rolling pin. Unwrap the dough, cut it in half, and work with one piece at a time. Place one piece on the pastry cloth and turn the dough to flour all sides. The dough will be quite stiff—pound it firmly with the rolling pin until it softens a bit. Roll out the dough, turning it over occasionally to keep both sides lightly floured. Roll it to ¼-inch thickness.

Cut the cookies with a plain round 3-inch cookie cutter. (Or, using a long, heavy knife or a pastry wheel, cut into large squares.) Reserve the scraps and roll them all together in order not to incorporate any more flour than necessary.

Place the cookies 2 inches apart on the cut foil. Slide cookie sheets under the foil.

Bake about 12 minutes, until the cookies are well colored. Reverse the cookie sheets top to bottom and front to back once during baking in order to insure even browning.

With a wide metal spatula transfer the cookies to racks to cool.

These must be stored airtight or they may become soft and limp. But they can be recrisped: Reheat them on foil-lined cookie sheets in a 325-degree oven for about 5 minutes. Let stand for a few seconds and then, with a wide metal spatula, transfer to racks to cool.

Honey Graham Crackers

24 TO 30 DOUBLE
CRACKERS

These are almost like the store-bought ones—plain, dry, crunchy squares.

1 cup sifted all-purpose bleached or unbleached white flour
1 teaspoon double-acting baking powder
½ teaspoon baking soda
¼ teaspoon salt
½ teaspoon cinnamon
¼ pound (1 stick) butter
1 teaspoon vanilla extract
½ cup dark brown sugar, firmly packed
¼ cup honey
2 cups <u>unsifted</u> all-purpose whole-wheat flour (stir lightly to aerate before measuring)
½ cup milk

Sift together the white flour, baking powder, baking soda, salt, and cinnamon and set aside. In the large bowl of an electric mixer cream the butter. Add the vanilla, brown sugar, and honey and beat well. On low speed, add the whole-wheat flour and the sifted ingredients in three additions, alternating with the milk in two additions. Scrape the bowl as necessary with a rubber spatula and beat only until smooth after each addition. If the mixture is not completely smooth, turn it out onto a large board or a smooth surface and knead it briefly with the heel of your hand.

Form the dough into an even, flattened oblong. Wrap it airtight and refrigerate for 2 to 3 hours or longer, overnight if you wish.

Adjust two racks to divide the oven into thirds and preheat to 350 degrees.

Cut the chilled dough into equal quarters and work with one piece at a time.

On a well-floured pastry cloth, with a floured rolling pin, roll the dough into an even 15-by-5-inch oblong. With a long, sharp knife trim the edges. (The trimmings should be reserved, pressed together, and re-rolled all at once in order not to incorporate any more flour than necessary.) Use a ruler as a guide and cut crosswise into six 5-by-2½-inch oblongs. With the back, or dull side, of a knife lightly score across the center of each cracker, dividing it into two halves, each 2½ inches square.

With a wide metal spatula transfer the crackers to unbuttered cookie sheets, placing them ½ to 1 inch apart. With a fork, prick the crackers evenly in parallel rows at ½-inch intervals.

Bake for 12 to 14 minutes, reversing the sheets top to bottom and front to back to insure even browning. If you bake only one sheet at a time bake it high in the oven. Bake until the crackers are lightly colored.

Swedish Honey Cookies

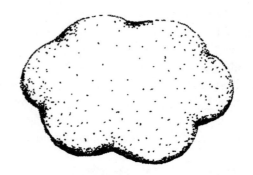

32 TO 42 COOKIES

These are a Swedish classic; they have a mild and interesting flavor. The dough must be well chilled before rolling.

2 cups sifted all-purpose flour
½ teaspoon baking soda
½ teaspoon salt
½ teaspoon cinnamon
¼ pound (1 stick) butter
1 teaspoon ground coriander seeds (see Note)
⅔ cup light brown sugar, firmly packed
⅓ cup honey
1 egg

Sift together the flour, baking soda, salt, and cinnamon. In the large bowl of an electric mixer, cream the butter. Add the coriander seeds and beat well. Gradually beat in the sugar and honey and then the egg. On low speed gradually add the sifted dry ingredients, scraping the bowl with a rubber spatula and beating only until mixed.

Turn the dough out onto a large piece of wax paper or aluminum foil, wrap, and chill for at least several hours (or longer) in the freezer or refrigerator.

Adjust two racks to divide the oven into thirds and preheat to 375 degrees. Cut aluminum foil to fit cookie sheets.

Flour a pastry cloth and a rolling pin. Cut the dough in half and work with one piece at a time, keeping the other piece chilled. Turn the dough over several times on the pastry cloth to flour both sides. If the dough is very firm pound it well with the rolling pin to soften it slightly. Roll out the dough, turning it over occasionally to keep both sides floured. Work quickly before the dough softens, and roll it to ⅛-inch thickness.

Quickly cut the dough with a plain or scalloped round 2½- or 3-inch cookie cutter. These cookies are traditionally scalloped but the scallops must be wide and deep or the design will run together.

With a wide metal spatula place the cookies 1 inch apart on the cut aluminum foil. Reserve the scraps, press them together, wrap and rechill before rolling them.

Slide cookie sheets under the foil. Bake for 10 to 12 minutes, reversing the sheets top to bottom and front to back as necessary to insure even browning. The cookies are done when they are medium brown and semi-firm to the touch.

Slide the foil off the cookie sheets. Let stand for a minute or so and then, with a wide metal spatula, transfer the cookies to racks to finish cooling.

These must be stored airtight in order for them to remain crisp.

NOTE: Whole coriander seeds may be ground in a blender or well crushed with a mortar and pestle—they do not have to be powdered or strained.

Swedish Ginger Cookies

Although these do not have to be hung on a Christmas tree, this is a good recipe for making cookies to hang. I am including directions for hanging, but the cookies may be cut with a plain or fancy cookie cutter, and not hung. I have also used this recipe for Christmas-card cookies; using a long knife, cut the dough into oblongs, bake, and then write the greeting on the baked cookies with the following Royal Icing. Once I tripled the recipe and made one huge cookie, as large as my oven would hold. It was made of many different layers that were pasted together with melted chocolate. Although it could have been eaten, it was strictly for show—it won first prize in a professional baking olympics. The design was a large flower. I pasted petals on top of petals and decorated the whole thing with thin, wiggly lines of Royal Icing. If you're artistic and creative and want to design things, use this recipe. Or if you simply want to make plain round or square ginger cookies that are wonderfully good, use this recipe.

⅔ cup dark or light molasses
⅔ cup granulated sugar
1 tablespoon ginger
1 tablespoon cinnamon
5⅓ ounces (10⅔ tablespoons) butter, at
    room temperature
¾ tablespoon baking soda (see Note)
1 egg
5 cups sifted all-purpose flour

If you are making small cookies, adjust two racks to divide the oven into thirds and preheat to 325 degrees. If you are making something very large and thick on one cookie sheet, adjust a rack to the center of the oven and preheat to 300 degrees. Cut aluminum foil to fit cookie sheets.

In a heavy 2-quart saucepan over moderate heat, bring the molasses, sugar, ginger, and cinnamon just to a low boil, stirring occasionally.

Meanwhile, cut the butter into 1-inch pieces and place them in a large mixing bowl.

When the molasses mixture comes to a boil, add the baking soda and stir until the mixture foams up to the top of the saucepan. Then pour it over the butter and stir to melt the butter.

With a fork, stir the egg lightly just to mix and then stir it into the molasses mixture. Gradually stir in the flour with a rubber or wooden spatula.

Turn the dough out onto a large board or smooth work surface and knead lightly until it is mixed thoroughly.

If you are making thin cookies, work with half of the dough at a time, but for thick cookies work with it all.

Place the dough on a lightly floured pastry cloth, turn it to flour all sides, and form it into a ball. With a lightly floured rolling pin, roll the dough to the desired thickness. If the dough is rolled thick, and if the cookies are not baked until thoroughly dry, they will be similar to gingerbread. But if they are rolled thin and baked dry, they will be like crisp gingersnaps. (I have used this recipe for cookies ranging from a scant ⅛-inch to a generous ½-inch thickness.) Cut the shapes as you wish—with cookie cutters (which should be floured as necessary if the dough sticks to them); with a long knife, cutting squares or oblongs; or with a small knife, either cutting freehand or tracing around your own pattern. Place the cookies on the cut aluminum foil. Slide a cookie sheet under the foil. Reserve all scraps. Try not to incorporate any more flour (from the cloth) than necessary. Press scraps together, knead well until smooth, and then reroll them.

If you bake two sheets at a time, reverse them once top to bottom and front to back to insure even browning. Bake until cookies feel firm to the touch. A rough guide is if the cookies are rolled ⅛ inch thick and baked 13 to 15 minutes they will be very crisp. If the cookies are ¼ inch thick and baked 15 minutes they will be slightly soft. If they are ⅜ inch thick and baked 15 minutes the cookies will be semisoft like gingerbread. This timing will vary depending on the diameter of the cookies—small shapes will take a bit less time, large shapes a bit more. If you make something extremely large and thick the baking time should be longer. It might take 45 minutes or more at 300 degrees. You will be able to judge by the feel of the cookie.

With a wide metal spatula transfer the cookies to racks to cool. If you are making a very large shape, as large as the cookie sheet, let it cool briefly on the foil and then use a cookie sheet as a spatula to transfer the cookie to the rack to cool.

NOTE: To measure ¾ tablespoon, first measure 1 level tablespoon and then, with a table knife or small metal spatula, mark it into quarters and return one quarter to the box.

HOW TO PREPARE COOKIES TO BE USED AS CHRISTMAS-TREE ORNAMENTS

Before baking, sew a length of heavy cotton or linen thread through each cookie, sewing from the front of the cookie to the back, about ¼ to ½ inch in from the edge, depending on the size of the cookie. Place the cookies on the foil, carefully arranging the threads so that they do not touch other cookies. After baking and cooling the cookies, tie the threads for hanging.

Another way is to use a small pastry tube (the kind that fits into a decorating bag) to cut a small hole near the edge of the cookie. But, if you do, bake one sample first to make sure that the hole is not so small that it closes during baking. After baking and cooling the cookies, thread string or ribbon through the holes.

A third method is to place a small piece of spaghetti upright, inserting it from the front to the back near the edge of the cookie (do this after the cookies are placed on the foil). After baking, while the cookies are still warm, push the spaghetti out through the back of the cookie and thread a thin string through the hole.

ROYAL ICING FOR DECORATING

(*This makes a generous amount.*)

1 pound (3½ cups, packed) confectioners
    sugar
⅓ cup egg whites (2–3 eggs), at room
    temperature
¼ teaspoon cream of tartar

Strain the sugar by pressing it with your fingertips through a large strainer set over a large bowl. In the small bowl of an electric mixer beat the egg whites with about half of the sugar at high speed for 5 minutes. Beat in the cream of tartar. Continue to beat while gradually adding more of the sugar, about ½ cup at a time, beating thoroughly after each addition, until the icing reaches the desired consistency. The icing should be thick enough to hold its shape without running or flattening when it is pressed through a pastry bag, but not so thick that it is difficult to press it through the bag. Also, if it is too stiff it will not stick to the cookies. It will probably not be necessary to add all of the sugar. If the icing is too stiff, add a bit more egg white or a few drops of water, very little at a time. If it is too soft, add a little more sugar. Keep the icing covered with a damp cloth to prevent a crust from forming.

For fine line decorating or lettering: Use a pastry bag fitted with a tube that has a small round opening. Or use a cone made of a triangle of parchment paper (or baking-pan liner paper). Traditionally the triangle is made by cutting a 15-inch square in half diagonally, but it may be a little smaller than that if you wish. Cut a very small opening in the tip of the cone. First cut off just a tiny bit and try it with some icing. You can always cut away more if necessary.

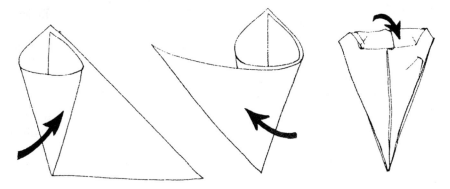

Practice first on a piece of paper to be sure that the icing is the correct consistency.

(If you wish, the icing may be colored with food coloring—you may divide the icing and make several different colors—but the cookies will be dark and I prefer white icing.)

Just a suggestion: It is fun to use silver dragées. I spread them out on a piece of wax paper, and to place them where I want them on the icing before it dries, I transfer the dragées with tweezers.

Viennese Almond Wafers

These are rich and buttery, simple but elegant. The recipe makes a small amount; if you double it, roll only half at a time.

9 LARGE SQUARES OR
24 SMALL OBLONGS

3¾ ounces (¾ cup) sliced blanched almonds (see Note), frozen
¼ pound (1 stick) butter
Scant ⅛ teaspoon salt
¼ teaspoon almond extract
⅓ cup granulated sugar
¾ cup plus 1 tablespoon sifted all-purpose flour
1 egg white

Adjust two racks to divide the oven into thirds and preheat to 350 degrees.

The almonds should be coarsely crushed; this is most easily done if they are frozen. Place them in a plastic bag and press them with your fingers to break them into coarse pieces. Set aside.

In the small bowl of an electric mixer cream the butter with the salt and almond extract. Beat in the sugar and then the flour, beating only until mixed.

If the dough is too soft to be rolled, chill it briefly. It may be chilled in the mixing bowl and should be stirred occasionally.

Transfer the dough to a well-floured pastry cloth, turn it over to flour all sides, and form it into a square or an oblong. With a well-floured rolling pin (continue to flour the pin as necessary to keep it from sticking) roll the dough into an even square with straight edges; the square will be about 9 to 10 inches across and the dough will be a scant ⅛ inch thick.

Trim the edges of the dough with a pastry wheel, or use a long, thin, sharp knife and wipe the blade after each cut to keep the dough from sticking. Cut the dough into even squares or oblongs.

Beat the egg white until foamy, but not at all stiff. With a pastry brush, brush some of the white generously over each cookie. Sprinkle the almonds evenly over the egg white. Press down gently with the palms of both hands to press the nuts slightly into the dough. Carefully brush the remaining egg white over the almonds—it will help to keep them from falling off after the cookies have been baked.

With a wide metal spatula transfer the cookies to unbuttered cookie sheets, placing them ½ to 1 inch apart.

Bake about 20 minutes, reversing the position of the cookie sheets top to bottom and front to back to insure even browning. If you bake only one sheet at a time use the higher rack. Bake until the cookies are lightly browned; do not underbake.

With a wide metal spatula transfer the cookies to racks to cool.

NOTE: "Sliced" almonds are those that have been cut into very thin slices—they are the ones to use for this recipe. The fatter, oblong, julienne-shaped pieces are called "slivered" and are too thick for these cookies.

Ischler Cookies

24 SANDWICHED
COOKIES

This is a classic and elegant Viennese cookie made of two rich and fragile almond cookies sandwiched together with preserves and partially covered with chocolate glaze. These are made without a mixer. They should be stored in the refrigerator and served cold.

8 ounces (1⅔ cups) blanched almonds
2¼ cups sifted all-purpose flour
⅔ cup granulated sugar
10 ounces (2½ sticks) cold butter, cut into
    ½-inch slices
½ to ¾ cup smooth, thick apricot preserves

In a nut grinder, a blender, or a food processor, grind the almonds to a fine powder and place them in a large mixing bowl. Add the flour and sugar and stir to mix. With a pastry blender cut the butter into the dry ingredients until the mixture resembles a coarse meal.

Turn the dough out onto a large board or smooth work surface, then squeeze it between your hands until it holds together. Form the dough into a ball, flatten slightly, and then "break" it as follows. Using the heel of your hand start at the farther end of the dough and push off small pieces (about 2 tablespoons), smearing it against the work surface and away from you. Continue until all the dough has been pushed off. Re-form the dough and then push it off or "break" it again.

Work with half of the dough at a time. Form it into a ball and place it on a large piece of wax paper. Cover with another large piece of wax paper. With your hand flatten the dough slightly, and then, with a rolling pin, roll over the paper to roll the dough until it is ¼ inch thick. If the wax paper wrinkles, peel it off and then replace it in order to remove the wrinkles. (During rolling check both pieces of wax paper for wrinkles.)

Slide a cookie sheet under the dough (still between the two pieces of wax paper) and transfer to the freezer or refrigerator until the dough is firm and the paper may be pulled off easily.

Repeat with the second half of the dough.

While the dough is chilling, adjust two racks to divide the oven into thirds and preheat to 350 degrees.

When the dough is firm, peel off one piece of the wax paper just to release it, then replace it. Turn the dough in both pieces of paper over. Then peel off but do not replace the second piece of paper.

With a plain round cookie cutter measuring 2¼ to 2½ inches in diameter, cut out cookies and place them (with the help of a metal spatula if necessary) 1 inch apart on unbuttered cookie sheets. The dough must be firm enough for the rounds to hold their shape when they are transferred. Reserve scraps and roll, chill, and cut them. You should have about 48 cookies. (See Notes.)

Bake for 15 to 18 minutes, reversing the sheets top to bottom and front to back as necessary to insure even baking. When done the cookies should be sandy-colored or lightly golden but not brown.

Let stand for a few seconds and then, with a wide metal spatula, transfer the cookies to racks to cool.

If the cookies are different sizes (because the dough was not all rolled to the same thickness), match them up into pairs of equal size. Place one cookie from each pair upside down.

Then, holding the cookie in your hand (carefully because these are fragile), spread the under side with a thin layer of the apricot preserves, keeping it a bit away from the edges. Cover this with another cookie and press them together very gently.

Prepare the following glaze.

CHOCOLATE GLAZE

> 12 ounces (2 cups) semisweet chocolate
>   morsels
> 2 tablespoons vegetable shortening (such as
>   Crisco)

Place the chocolate and shortening in the top of a small double boiler over warm water on low heat. Cover until partially melted. Then uncover and stir until completely melted and smooth. Transfer the glaze to a small narrow bowl for ease in handling. A soup cup is good.

Line cookie sheets with wax paper. Hold a cookie sandwich between your fingers so that you are touching the two cookies, not the open ends. Dip it, edge down, into the glaze. Dip it deeply enough so that the glaze covers about half of the sandwich, both top and bottom. Gently wipe the edge of the sandwich against the top of the bowl to remove excess glaze. Place the cookie on the wax-paper-lined cookie sheet, laying it on either of the glazed sides.

Glaze the remaining cookies.

When the cookie sheet is covered with glazed cookies transfer it to the freezer or refrigerator to chill until the glaze is set and the cookies may be lifted from the paper easily and don't stick.

Then place the cookies on a tray or in a freezer box with plastic wrap over each layer to make them airtight. Refrigerate until serving time and serve cold.

NOTES: These directions make rather large cookies, which is traditional for this recipe. However, they may be rolled thinner and/or cut smaller if you wish.

If there is any glaze left over it may be saved for some other time, some other cookies. Line a small bowl with aluminum foil, pour in the glaze, and let stand (or chill) until the glaze is firm. Then remove it—with the foil—from the bowl. Place it in a freezer bag or wrap it in enough foil to protect it. It may stand at room temperature for a few days, or for longer storage it may be refrigerated or frozen. When ready to use, remove it from the foil, chop it coarsely, and melt slowly over hot water.

Viennese Chocolate Cookies

24 LARGE COOKIES

These are crisp-crunchy, bittersweet, and mildly spiced. Made without a mixer, but you will need a blender or food processor.

12 blanched almonds (for topping the cookies)
1¼ cups sifted all-purpose flour
Pinch of salt
½ teaspoon cinnamon
Scant ¼ teaspoon powdered cloves
½ cup plus 2 tablespoons granulated sugar
2 ounces (2 squares) unsweetened chocolate
2 ounces (2 squares) semisweet chocolate
5 ounces (1 cup) blanched almonds
5 ounces (1¼ sticks) cold butter, cut into
    ½-inch slices
Finely grated rind of 1 lemon
2 egg yolks
1 egg white (for the topping)

To prepare the almonds for topping the cookies, they must be split into halves and lightly toasted. First, in order to soften them for splitting, place them in a small pan, cover with boiling water, and boil over high heat for 2 to 3 minutes. Drain the nuts and then, quickly, while they are still warm, insert the tip of a small, sharp knife into the natural cracks to split them in half the long way. Now, to dry them, place them in a small, shallow pan in a 350-degree oven. Bake for about 7 minutes, stirring the nuts or shaking the pan occasionally, until they are barely colored. Set the nuts aside to cool.

Adjust two racks to divide the oven into thirds and preheat to 350 degrees.

Sift together into a large bowl the flour, salt, cinnamon, cloves, and sugar and set aside.

On a cutting board, with a long, heavy knife, chop both chocolates coarsely and then place them in a blender (or a food processor) and grind them to a powder. Set the chocolates aside.

Without washing the blender (or processor), grind the 5 ounces of blanched almonds to a powder and set aside.

With a pastry blender cut the butter into the sifted dry ingredients until the particles are fine and the mixture resembles a coarse meal. Stir in the lemon rind, ground chocolates, and ground almonds. Beat in the egg yolks.

The mixture will be uneven. Turn it out onto a large board or a smooth work surface and squeeze it between your hands until it holds together. Now, "break" the dough as follows: Form it into a ball. Using the heel of your hand, start at the farther end of the dough and push off small pieces (about 2 tablespoons), smearing it against the work surface and away from you. Continue until all the dough has been pushed off. Re-form the dough and push it off or break it again. All the ingredients should be completely mixed by now, but if not, break the dough again.

Work with half of the dough at a time. Form it into a ball. Place it on a long piece of wax paper, flatten the dough slightly, and then cover it with another long piece of wax paper. With a rolling pin, roll over the top piece of wax paper until the dough is ⅜ inch thick.

Remove the top piece of wax paper just to loosen it and then replace it. Turn the dough over (still between the two pieces of paper). Now remove and do not replace the second piece of paper.

Cut the cookies with a plain round cookie cutter 2¼ to 2½ inches in diameter. With a small metal spatula transfer the cookies to unbuttered cookie sheets, placing them 1 inch apart. Reroll the scraps and cut again.

Beat the egg white only until it is slightly foamy, and, with a soft brush, brush it over the cookies. Place a prepared almond half on each cookie, flat side down. And then brush some more egg white over the almonds.

Bake the cookies for 15 minutes, reversing the sheets top to bottom and front to back once or twice to insure even baking. Do not overbake—these burn easily.

With a wide metal spatula transfer the cookies to racks to cool.

Tropical Sour-Cream Cookies

St. Augustine, Florida, is the oldest city in the United States. This recipe is adapted from one of the first cookbooks published in St. Augustine. The cookies are large, plain, and semisoft, with a tropical orange and lemon flavor. Plan to chill the dough overnight before baking.

20 LARGE COOKIES

2 cups sifted all-purpose flour
½ teaspoon baking soda
⅛ teaspoon salt
Finely grated rind of 1 large, deep-colored orange
Finely grated rind of 1 large lemon
1 tablespoon lemon juice
¼ pound (1 stick) butter
1 cup light brown sugar, firmly packed (see Note)
1 egg
½ cup sour cream
Granulated sugar

Sift together the flour, baking soda, and salt and set aside. In a small cup mix the orange rind, lemon rind, and lemon juice and set aside. In the large bowl of an electric mixer cream the butter. Add the sugar and beat well. Add the egg and beat to mix well. On low speed gradually beat in half of the sifted dry ingredients, then all of the sour cream, and finally the remaining dry ingredients, scraping the bowl with a rubber spatula and beating only until blended. Remove the bowl from the mixer and stir in the rinds and juice.

The dough will be soft. Turn it out onto a large piece of aluminum foil, wrap it in the foil, and place it in the freezer or refrigerator overnight.

Adjust two racks to divide the oven into thirds and preheat to 375 degrees. Cut aluminum foil to fit cookie sheets.

The dough will soften quickly and become sticky at room temperature, so work quickly. Work with half of the dough at a time, keeping the remainder chilled.

Generously flour a pastry cloth and a rolling pin. Turn the dough over on the floured cloth to flour all sides and then form it into a ball and flatten it slightly. With the rolling pin, roll the dough to a generous ¼-inch thickness, turning the dough over occasionally while rolling, and adding additional flour to the cloth or pin if necessary to keep the dough from sticking.

Quickly cut the cookies with a plain round 3- to 3½-inch cookie cutter. And then, quickly, transfer the cookies with a wide metal spatula to the cut aluminum foil, placing them about 1 inch apart—these spread only slightly in baking.

Reserve the scraps of dough, press them together, rechill, and roll them all out together in order not to incorporate any more flour than necessary.

Sprinkle the tops of the cookies with granulated sugar. Slide cookie sheets under the foil.

Bake for about 15 minutes, until the cookies are lightly colored. Reverse the cookie sheets top to bottom and front to back as necessary to insure even browning.

With a wide metal spatula transfer the cookies to racks to cool.

NOTE: If the brown sugar has any hard lumps it must be strained; place it in a large strainer set over a large bowl and, with your fingertips, press the sugar through the strainer.

Caraway Sour-Cream Cookies

Many old English cookie recipes call for caraway seeds. This recipe comes from New Hampshire and has been handed down through several generations. These are large, thin, and crisp with a mild caraway flavor. It is best to mix the dough a day before baking.

38 COOKIES

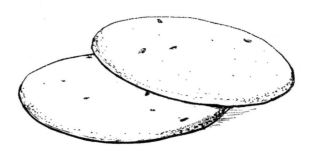

2 cups sifted all-purpose flour
¼ teaspoon salt
½ teaspoon nutmeg
¼ pound (1 stick) butter
1 cup granulated sugar
1 egg
½ cup sour cream
½ teaspoon baking soda
½ teaspoon caraway seeds

Sift together the flour, salt, and nutmeg and set aside. In the large bowl of an electric mixer cream the butter. Add the sugar and beat well. Add the egg and beat to mix well. On low speed add half of the sifted dry ingredients, scraping the bowl with a rubber spatula and beating only until they are incorporated. Place the sour cream in a small bowl. Add the baking soda and stir together with a rubber spatula. Then add the sour cream to the dough, beating only until smooth. Add the remaining dry ingredients and the caraway seeds and beat only until smooth.

Transfer the dough to a large piece of wax paper or aluminum foil, wrap well, and place the dough in the freezer for several hours or preferably overnight.

When ready to bake the cookies, adjust two racks to divide the oven into thirds and preheat to 375 degrees.

Work with half of the dough at a time, keeping the remainder in the freezer. Work quickly as the dough will become soft and sticky at room temperature.

Place the dough on a well-floured pastry cloth. Turn it over to flour all sides. Form it into a ball and flatten slightly. With a well-floured rolling pin, roll the dough to ⅛-inch thickness. While rolling the dough, in order to keep it from sticking, roll it up around the rolling pin occasionally, re-flour the pastry cloth, and then unroll the dough bottom side up.

With a floured plain round 3-inch cookie cutter, cut rounds very close to each other and quickly transfer the rounds with a wide metal spatula to unbuttered cookie sheets, placing them ½ to 1 inch apart.

Press the scraps together, wrap, and refreeze them before rolling.

Bake for 12 to 15 minutes, reversing the sheets top to bottom and front to back as necessary to insure even browning. Bake until the cookies are lightly colored—they will be slightly darker around the edges. If they have been rolled thicker than ⅛ inch they will take a little longer to bake. (If you bake only one sheet at a time use the higher rack.)

With a wide metal spatula transfer the cookies to racks to cool.

Rum-Raisin Shortbread

These are large and thick, with rum-soaked raisins all through them. The dough is very short; the cookies are rather delicate and quite unusual. The raisins must be prepared several hours ahead of time or the day before.

15 LARGE COOKIES

RAISINS

5 ounces (1 cup) raisins
½ cup dark rum

Bring the raisins and the rum to a boil in a small saucepan over moderate heat. Remove from the heat, cover, and let stand for several hours or overnight. When ready to bake the cookies drain the raisins in a strainer set over a small bowl; use any leftover rum for something else.

COOKIE DOUGH

2 cups sifted all-purpose flour
¼ teaspoon double-acting baking powder
¼ teaspoon salt
½ pound (2 sticks) butter
½ cup confectioners sugar

Sift together the flour, baking powder, and salt and set aside. In the large bowl of an electric mixer cream the butter until it is very soft. Add the sugar and beat well until completely smooth. On low speed gradually add the sifted dry ingredients, scraping the bowl with a rubber spatula and beating until smooth. Stir in the prepared raisins.

Transfer the dough to a large piece of wax paper or aluminum foil, wrap, flatten slightly, and refrigerate for about 1½ to 2 hours. Do not freeze the dough or it will become too firm to roll.

When ready to bake the cookies adjust two racks to divide the oven into thirds and preheat to 375 degrees.

Place the dough on a lightly floured pastry cloth and turn it over to flour all sides lightly. With a floured rolling pin roll the dough gently only until it is ½ inch thick, no thinner! Use a plain round cookie cutter about 2½ inches in diameter. Dip the cutter in flour before cutting each cookie and cut them as close to each other as possible. When cutting a cookie press the cutter very firmly into the dough and rotate it slightly in order to cut through the raisins. Press the scraps together, chill them, and reroll.

Place the cookies 1 to 2 inches apart on unbuttered cookie sheets.

Bake the cookies for 20 minutes, or until cookies are golden brown. Reverse the sheets top to bottom and front to back to insure even browning.

With a wide metal spatula transfer the cookies to racks to cool.

Since these are fragile I like to wrap them individually in clear cellophane. However you store them—handle with care.

Hot Butter Wafers

60 WAFERS

An early Colonial recipe reportedly used by Dolley Madison and served at the White House. These are very plain, thin, crisp, and buttery. They may be served as a plain cookie, or as a cracker with soup or salad. The absence of salt, flavoring, and leavening is typical of Early American cookies.

4 cups sifted all-purpose flour
½ pound (2 sticks) butter
½ cup granulated sugar
3 eggs

Place the flour in the large bowl of an electric mixer. Cut the butter into 1-inch pieces and melt it in a small, heavy saucepan over moderate heat. Pour the hot butter all at once into the flour. Beat at low speed to mix—the mixture will be crumbly. Beat in the sugar and then the eggs, one at a time. Beat only until the last egg is incorporated.

Turn the dough out onto a large floured board or a smooth work surface and knead briefly only until completely smooth.

Wrap the dough in wax paper or aluminum foil and chill it in the freezer for 15 minutes—no longer!

Adjust two racks to divide the oven into thirds and preheat to 350 degrees.

Cut the dough into quarters. Work with one piece at a time, keeping the remainder covered at room temperature.

Turn the dough over several times on a floured pastry cloth to flour all sides lightly. Roll the dough with a floured rolling pin, turning it over frequently to keep both sides floured. Reflour the cloth and pin as necessary but don't use any more flour than you really need. Roll the dough until it is paper thin. (Each quarter of the dough should be rolled until it is 15 inches or more in diameter.)

Cut the cookies with a plain round 4-inch cookie cutter. Or use a long knife or a pastry wheel, and trim the edges of the dough, then cut it into 4-inch squares. Prick the cookies all over with a fork at ½-inch intervals.

With a wide metal spatula transfer the cookies to unbuttered cookie sheets. These may be placed on the sheets actually touching each other since, instead of spreading, they shrink slightly when baked.

Reserve scraps of dough, knead them together briefly, and roll them all together in order not to incorporate any more flour than necessary (see Note).

Bake the cookies for 13 to 18 minutes, reversing the cookie sheets top to bottom and front to back as necessary to insure even browning. Bake until the cookies are golden brown all over with no white spots remaining.

With a wide metal spatula remove the cookies individually as they are done and place them on racks to cool.

NOTE: After the dough has been rolled twice it becomes rubbery and difficult to roll thin enough. So try to end up with as few scraps as possible. (The first time the dough is rolled you might cut it into rounds and then, the second time, cut into squares, thereby eliminating scraps.) In any event, roll it thin, thin, thin.

Caraway Hardtack

55 COOKIES

These are similar to the previous Hot Butter Wafers but they are not so plain—these are sweeter and have the additional flavoring of caraway seeds.

4 cups sifted all-purpose flour
½ pound (2 sticks) butter
2 cups granulated sugar
3 eggs
Milk (for brushing over the cookies)
Caraway seeds (for sprinkling on top)

Place the flour in the large bowl of an electric mixer. Cut the butter into 1-inch pieces and melt it in a small, heavy saucepan over moderate heat. Pour the hot butter all at once into the flour. Mix at low speed, scraping the bowl with a rubber spatula until the flour is all moistened—the mixture will be crumbly. Beat in the sugar and then the eggs, one at a time, continuing to scrape the bowl with the spatula and beating until the mixture is smooth.

Place the dough, still in the mixing bowl, in the freezer for 10 minutes (no longer) or in the refrigerator for 15 to 20 minutes.

Adjust two racks to divide the oven into thirds and preheat to 350 degrees. Cut aluminum foil to fit cookie sheets.

Generously flour a pastry cloth and a rolling pin. Work with one-third of the dough at a time, letting the rest stand at room temperature. (If the dough is too sticky to roll, let it stand at room temperature for 15 to 20 minutes, or longer if necessary.)

Place the dough on the floured cloth and turn it to flour all sides. With the floured rolling pin (reflour it frequently) roll the dough until it is ⅛ inch thick. Cut out cookies with a plain round 3½-inch cookie cutter.

With a wide metal spatula transfer the cookies to the cut aluminum foil, placing them ½ inch apart (these do not spread).

Reserve the scraps, press them together, and reroll them.

With a pastry brush, brush the tops of the cookies generously with milk and then, before the milk dries, sprinkle a generous pinch of caraway seeds over the top of each cookie. Slide cookie sheets under the foil.

Bake the cookies for 15 to 20 minutes, until the cookies are lightly browned. Reverse the sheets top to bottom and front to back as necessary to insure even browning.

Remove the cookies individually as they are ready, leaving the lighter ones until done. With a wide metal spatula transfer them to racks to cool.

Arrowroot Wafers from Bermuda

46 COOKIES

Arrowroot is the root of a tropical plant that has been dried and then ground to a powder similar to flour. Since it is a highly nutritive and easily digested form of starch, it is often thought of as food for young children and invalids. But everyone likes these cookies, which are thin, plain, dry, and extremely light. Arrowroot is available in small (3⅛-ounce) jars in the spice section of food stores. One of these jars holds half a cup.

½ cup <u>unsifted</u> arrowroot
1 cup sifted all-purpose flour
¼ teaspoon double-acting baking powder
¼ teaspoon salt
2 tablespoons butter, at room temperature
½ teaspoon vanilla extract
⅓ cup granulated sugar
2 eggs

Sift together the arrowroot, flour, baking powder, and salt and set aside. In the small bowl of an electric mixer, cream the butter with the vanilla and sugar until smooth. Add the eggs one at a time, beating until thoroughly mixed. On low speed, gradually add the sifted dry ingredients, scraping the bowl with a rubber spatula and beating until smooth.

The dough will be soft and sticky. Transfer it to a small bowl (or leave it in the mixer bowl if you prefer), cover airtight, and place in the freezer for a few hours. (See Note.)

Adjust two racks to divide the oven into thirds and preheat to 350 degrees. Cut aluminum foil to fit cookie sheets.

Generously flour a pastry cloth and rolling pin. Work with half of the dough at a time, keeping the remainder in the freezer. With a heavy spoon, transfer half of the dough to the floured cloth. Turn it over to flour both sides. *Work very quickly as the dough will soften and become sticky at room temperature!!!* With the floured rolling pin, roll the dough to a scant ⅛-inch thickness (that's thin), turning it over once or twice to keep both sides floured. Cut quickly with a 2½-inch round cookie cutter and, with a wide metal spatula, immediately transfer cookies to the foil, placing them about ½ inch apart. These may be close to each other, as they do not spread; actually they shrink a little. Replace scraps in the bowl and freeze again until firm enough to reroll.

Slide cookie sheets under the foil and bake 10 to 15 minutes, reversing sheets top to bottom and front to back to help them brown evenly. Bake only until lightly colored, very pale—a few spots may remain white. Some cookies will color sooner than others and should be removed individually when done. With a wide metal spatula (or with your fingers if you don't mind the heat) transfer cookies to racks to cool.

NOTE: If the dough has been frozen too long it will be too hard to roll. Place it on a floured pastry cloth and pound it heavily with a floured rolling pin, turning it over a few times, until soft enough to roll. Do not just let it stand at room temperature or it will become sticky.

Uppåkra Cookies

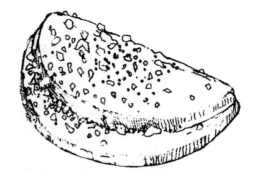

50 COOKIES

These traditional Swedish cookies are thin and delicate and dainty enough for a teaparty. The batter calls for potato flour, which adds to their light, flaky quality.

½ pound (2 sticks) butter
½ teaspoon almond extract
⅓ cup granulated sugar
¾ cup sifted potato flour (see Notes)
1¾ cup sifted all-purpose flour

In the large bowl of an electric mixer, cream the butter. Add the almond extract and sugar and beat well. On low speed, gradually add the potato flour and then the all-purpose flour, scraping the bowl with a rubber spatula and beating only until the flours are thoroughly incorporated and smooth.

Transfer the dough to a large piece of wax paper or aluminum foil, wrap and refrigerate for only about 30 minutes. (If the dough is chilled longer, it will become too hard to roll. If this happens, let it stand at room temperature until it softens enough to roll.)

While the dough is chilling, adjust two racks to divide oven into thirds and preheat to 350 degrees. Cut aluminum foil to fit cookie sheets.

Work with half of the dough at a time. Unless the kitchen is very warm, the other half may wait, wrapped, at room temperature.

The dough is fragile and must be handled with care. On a lightly floured pastry cloth, with a floured rolling pin, roll the dough to ⅛-inch thickness—that's thin; measure it. While rolling the dough, flour the pin as frequently as necessary to keep it from sticking. With a plain round cookie cutter about 2½ inches in diameter, cut the cookies, and then, with a small metal spatula, transfer them to a cutting board.

With a sharp knife, cut each cookie into two unequal pieces, one one-third of the cookie, one two-thirds. After all are cut, flip the smaller pieces over on top of the larger pieces, lining up the straight edges together.

Repeat with the remaining half of the dough. Reserve all scraps and roll them all at once in order not to incorporate any more flour than necessary.

With a metal spatula, transfer the cookies to the foil, placing them about ½ inch apart—these don't spread.

TOPPING

1 egg
⅓ cup blanched almonds, finely chopped
3 tablespoons pearl sugar (see Notes)

In a small bowl, beat the egg lightly just to mix and set aside. Stir the almonds and the sugar together.

With a soft pastry brush, brush the egg over the tops of the cookies and then sprinkle with the almond-sugar mixture.

Slide cookie sheets under the foil and bake about 20 minutes, reversing the sheets top to bottom and front to back as necessary to insure even browning. Bake only until cookies are lightly browned.

With a wide metal spatula, transfer cookies to racks to cool.

Handle with care—these are fragile.

NOTES: Potato flour, also called potato starch, is generally available in Jewish or Scandinavian grocery stores.

Pearl sugar is commonly used to sprinkle over European cookies and pastries before baking. It is also called "crystal sugar" and in German it is Hagelzucker. It is coarser than granulated sugar and, although it is available in some specialty food stores, it is hard to find. You may substitute crushed lump sugar or granulated sugar. It is available under the name "crystal sugar" at Paprikas Weiss, 1546 Second Avenue, New York, N.Y. 10028.

Ginger Shortbread Cookies

This is an unusual brown-sugar spice cookie from Scotland.

26 COOKIES

26 whole blanched almonds
1½ cups sifted all-purpose flour
⅛ teaspoon salt
1 teaspoon ginger
1 teaspoon cinnamon
¼ teaspoon powdered cloves
¼ teaspoon mustard powder
6 ounces (1½ sticks) butter
¾ teaspoon instant coffee
½ cup dark brown sugar, firmly packed
1 egg yolk ⎱ for glazing the tops of the
1 teaspoon water ⎰ cookies

Adjust a rack one-third down from the top of the oven and preheat to 350 degrees.

Place the almonds in a small, shallow pan and bake them, shaking the pan occasionally, for about 10 minutes until they are thoroughly dried and only slightly colored. Set aside to cool completely.

Sift together the flour, salt, ginger, cinnamon, cloves, and mustard and set aside. In the large bowl of an electric mixer cream the butter together with the instant coffee. Add the brown sugar and beat to mix well. On low speed gradually add the sifted dry ingredients, scraping the bowl with a rubber spatula and beating only until the ingredients are thoroughly mixed and the dough holds together.

Turn the dough out onto a large piece of wax paper and cover it with another large piece of wax paper. Flatten the dough slightly with your hand. Then, with a rolling pin, roll over the top piece of paper until the dough is ⅜ inch thick (no thinner). Slide a cookie sheet under the bottom paper and transfer the dough to the freezer or refrigerator for 5 to 10 minutes until the dough is firm enough to be cut with a cookie cutter and the wax paper can be peeled away cleanly, leaving a smooth surface on the dough.

Remove and then replace the top piece of wax paper just to loosen it. Invert the dough still between both papers. Then remove and do not replace the second piece of paper.

Cut cookies with a plain round cookie cutter about 1¾ inches in diameter. Place the cookies 1 inch apart on an unbuttered cookie sheet.

If the dough is very firm let the cookies stand at room temperature for 2 or 3 minutes to soften slightly.

(Meanwhile, you can press together the scraps of dough, reroll, and chill them.)

Place a baked, blanched almond on each cookie and press it very gently into the dough. (If, when you press on the almond, the dough is still so cold and firm that it cracks, let it stand a few moments longer. But don't let the unbaked cookies stand any longer than necessary in a warm kitchen or the edges will run unevenly during baking.)

Stir the egg yolk and water together just to mix. With a soft brush, brush lightly over the tops of the cookies and the almonds to give a shiny finish.

Bake for about 15 minutes, until the cookies darken slightly and are barely semifirm to the touch. Reverse the cookie sheet front to back once to insure even baking. Do not overbake or the cookies will become too hard.

With a wide metal spatula transfer the cookies to a rack to cool.

NOTE: The chances are that you will bake these cookies only one sheet at a time. (Almost all of them will fit on one sheet, and the remainder that you reroll from the scraps of dough will probably have to chill while you are baking the first sheet.) However, if you do bake two sheets together, adjust two racks to divide the oven into thirds. Then, during baking, reverse the sheets top to bottom once or twice (as well as front to back) to insure even baking. Baking two sheets together generally takes a bit more baking time.

Dione Lucas' Sablés

These French almond cookies are similar to shortbread. Sablé is French for "sandy," which describes the texture of these cookies. Dione Lucas, one of the greatest cooks of our time, served these for dessert along with a cold soufflé at a memorable formal dinner party.

36 COOKIES

2½ ounces (½ cup) blanched almonds
6 ounces (1½ sticks) butter
Pinch of salt
½ cup confectioners sugar
2 tablespoons rum (I use Myer's dark rum)
2 cups sifted all-purpose flour
1 egg yolk
1 teaspoon water
38 whole blanched almonds

Adjust a rack to the top position in the oven and preheat to 350 degrees.

Grind the ½ cup blanched almonds either in a nut grinder or in a blender—they must be ground to a powder. Set aside.

In the large bowl of an electric mixer cream the butter well. Add the salt and the sugar and beat until smooth. Beat in the rum and then the ground almonds. On lowest speed gradually add the flour, scraping the bowl with a rubber spatula and beating only until smooth.

Turn the dough out onto a large board or a smooth work surface. Work the dough with your hands, first squeezing it between your fingers, and then pushing it away from you, a bit at a time, with the heel of your hand, until very smooth.

Form the dough into a ball and flatten it slightly. Place it on a large piece of wax paper and cover with another large piece of wax paper. With a rolling pin, roll over the top of the paper until the dough is a scant ⅜ inch thick (don't make these too thin) and perfectly level. If the wax paper wrinkles during the rolling, remove and then replace the paper to remove the wrinkles.

Slide a cookie sheet under the bottom wax paper and transfer the dough to the freezer for about 10 minutes, or a little longer in the refrigerator, until the dough is almost firm.

Remove the top piece of wax paper just to release it, then replace it. Turn the dough over, still between the two pieces of paper. Remove the second piece of wax paper and do not replace it.

Cut the cookies with a round 1¾-inch cookie cutter. Place them ½ inch apart on an unbuttered cookie sheet; these barely spread at all in baking and may be placed quite close to each other. Press the scraps together. Reroll and chill before cutting.

In a small cup mix the egg yolk with the water. With a soft brush, brush the egg wash over the tops of the cookies. Place a whole blanched almond on top of each cookie and press gently until the almond is slightly imbedded—if the cookies are too firm, let them stand for a few minutes to soften slightly.

Now brush the egg wash over each cookie again, generously covering the top of the cookie and the almond.

Bake for 15 to 17 minutes, reversing the position of the cookie sheet front to back to insure even browning. Bake only until the cookies are slightly colored; do not overbake.

With a wide metal spatula transfer the cookies to racks to cool.

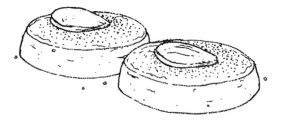

Cornell Sugar Cookies

16 TO 18 VERY LARGE
COOKIES

I created these cookies but they were inspired by a health-food formula devised by Dr. Clive M. McCay at Cornell University. The formula was originally planned for a nutritious high-protein bread. The special features that make it "Cornell" are the additions of soy flour, nonfat dry powdered milk, and wheat germ. People do not have to be health-food devotees to like these. They are large and plain old-fashioned.

2¼ cups sifted all-purpose unbleached white flour
¼ cup <u>unsifted</u> soy flour (see Note)
1 teaspoon double-acting baking powder
½ teaspoon baking soda
½ teaspoon salt (you may substitute sea salt if you wish; see Note)
½ teaspoon nutmeg
¼ teaspoon allspice
¼ pound (1 stick) butter
1½ teaspoons vanilla extract
1 cup raw sugar (see Note)
2 eggs
2 tablespoons natural untoasted wheat germ (see Note)
2 tablespoons nonfat dry powdered milk
1 tablespoon milk

Sift together the white flour, soy flour, baking powder, baking soda, salt, nutmeg, and allspice and set aside. In the large bowl of an electric mixer cream the butter. Add the vanilla and sugar and beat well. Add the eggs one at a time. Beat in the wheat germ, powdered milk, and then the milk. Beat until smooth. On low speed gradually add the sifted dry ingredients, scraping the bowl with a rubber spatula and beating only until smooth.

Transfer the dough to wax paper or foil, wrap, and refrigerate overnight.

Adjust two racks to divide the oven into thirds and preheat to 425 degrees.

Place the dough on a well-floured pastry cloth. If the dough is very hard pound it briefly with a floured rolling pin to soften slightly. Turn the dough over and over and press down on it gently to flour both sides. Work quickly before the dough softens and becomes sticky. Roll it with a floured rolling pin, turning it over once or twice as you roll to keep it from sticking. Roll the dough to a scant ¼-inch thickness. Cut with a plain round 3½-inch cookie cutter. Or use a long, heavy knife and cut into large squares. Press scraps together and reroll.

Place the cookies 2 inches apart on unbuttered cookie sheets.

Bake about 8 to 10 minutes, until cookies are golden-colored. Reverse the sheets top to bottom and front to back to insure even browning. If you bake only one sheet at a time bake it high in the oven.

With a wide metal spatula transfer cookies to racks to cool.

NOTE: Soy flour, raw sugar, natural untoasted wheat germ, and sea salt are all available in health-food stores.

Plain Old-Fashioned Sugar Cookies

20 EXTRA-LARGE COOKIES

These cookies are traditionally made very large, almost saucer size, but you can make any size or shape you want.

3¼ cups sifted all-purpose flour
2½ teaspoons double-acting baking powder
Scant ½ teaspoon salt
6 ounces (1½ sticks) butter
1½ teaspoons vanilla extract
1½ cups granulated sugar
2 eggs
1 tablespoon milk
Additional granulated sugar (for topping)

Sift together the flour, baking powder, and salt and set aside. In the large bowl of an electric mixer cream the butter. Add the vanilla and sugar and beat well. Beat in the eggs one at a time and then add the milk. On low speed gradually add the sifted dry ingredients, scraping the bowl as necessary with a rubber spatula and beating only until thoroughly mixed.

Divide the dough in two and wrap each half separately in wax paper or aluminum foil. Chill the dough in the refrigerator for 3 hours or longer if you wish. (Chilling the dough in the freezer makes it too hard to roll.)

Adjust two racks to divide the oven into thirds and preheat to 400 degrees.

Place one piece of the dough on a lightly floured pastry cloth. Turn it over to flour all sides and form it into a ball. With a floured rolling pin, roll the dough to the desired thickness: For very large cookies roll to a generous ¼ inch. Cut the cookies as you wish. If you want very large cookies, cut with a plain round 4-inch cookie cutter.

With a wide metal spatula transfer the cookies to unbuttered cookie sheets. If the cookies are large and thick, place them 1½ to 2 inches apart. They may be closer if they are small and thin.

Sprinkle the tops of the cookies generously with granulated sugar.

Bake until the cookies are lightly browned, reversing the position of the sheets top to bottom and front to back as necessary during baking to insure even browning. Large, thick cookies will need to bake for 10 to 12 minutes.

With a wide metal spatula transfer the cookies to racks to cool.

Chocolate-Chip Pillows

18 COOKIES

Chocolate chips are sandwiched between two thin, buttery, brown-sugar cookies and baked together.

1⅓ cups sifted all-purpose flour
½ teaspoon salt
¼ teaspoon baking soda
¼ pound (1 stick) butter
½ teaspoon vanilla extract
2 tablespoons granulated sugar
¼ cup dark brown sugar, firmly packed
1 egg yolk
2 ounces (⅓ cup) semisweet chocolate morsels (see Note)

Adjust two racks to divide the oven into thirds and preheat to 425 degrees.

Sift together the flour, salt, and baking soda and set aside. In the small bowl of an electric mixer cream the butter. Add the vanilla and both sugars and beat well. Beat in the egg yolk and then, on low speed, gradually add the sifted dry ingredients, scraping the bowl with a rubber spatula and beating until the dough holds together.

Tear off two pieces of wax paper, each about 16 to 18 inches long. Place the dough on one piece of the paper and flatten it slightly. Cover with the other piece of paper and, with a rolling pin, roll over the wax paper until the dough is ⅛ inch thick—it will be about 14 inches long and almost as wide as the paper.

Slide a cookie sheet under the dough and papers and transfer to the freezer or refrigerator very briefly, only until the dough is firm enough to cut and handle. (It will take only a few minutes in the freezer.)

Pull off the top piece of wax paper just to loosen it and then replace it. Turn the dough, still between both papers, over. Pull off the second piece of paper and do not replace it.

Now work quickly before the dough softens. Cut about half of the rolled dough with a plain round 2-inch cookie cutter. Place the cookies 1½ to 2 inches apart on unbuttered cookie sheets, using a small metal spatula if necessary to transfer the cookies.

Replace the remaining rolled dough in the freezer or refrigerator to keep it firm until you are ready to use it.

Place 6 chocolate morsels in the center of each round of dough on the cookie sheets.

Then remove the reserved chilled dough and, following the above directions, cut it into rounds. Place a round of the dough over each cookie.

Reroll and form the scraps of dough the same way, chilling the dough as necessary.

Seal the edges of the sandwiched cookies by pressing them with the back of the tines of a fork.

Bake for about 10 minutes, reversing the sheets top to bottom and front to back once to insure even browning. Bake until the cookies are lightly browned.

With a wide metal spatula transfer the cookies to a rack to cool.

NOTE: You may use the midget-size morsels if you wish. Just use as many as you can easily sandwich between the two cookies.

Prune
Pillows

*These are large, old-fashioned, homey cookies
with a tender crust and a thick, baked-in prune-
nut filling. It is best to make both the crust
and the filling the day before. If not, plan on at
least several hours for the crust to chill. You will
need two large, plain round cookie cutters, one
½ inch smaller than the other. Mine measure
3¼ inches and 2¾ inches, but you may make
these either a little larger or a little smaller.*

CRUST

2½ cups sifted all-purpose flour
¼ teaspoon baking soda
Scant ½ teaspoon salt
¼ pound (1 stick) butter
1 teaspoon vanilla extract
1 cup granulated sugar
2 eggs

Sift together the flour, baking soda, and salt and set aside. In the large bowl
of an electric mixer cream the butter. Add the vanilla and sugar and beat
to mix well. Beat in the eggs to mix well. On low speed gradually add the
sifted dry ingredients, scraping the bowl with a rubber spatula and beating
until thoroughly incorporated.

Transfer the dough to a large piece of wax paper or aluminum foil,
wrap well, flatten slightly, and refrigerate overnight or for at least several
hours. (The dough may be placed in the freezer until it is very cold and

partially firm, but if it is left in the freezer too long it will become too solid to roll out.)

FILLING

1 one-pound-nine-ounce jar or can of stewed prunes (about 28 medium-size prunes— you may use dried prunes and stew them yourself)
½ cup granulated sugar
3 tablespoons lemon juice
3 ounces (scant 1 cup) walnuts, cut or broken into medium-size pieces

Confectioners sugar for topping

Pit the prunes and place them in a strainer set over a bowl to drain. Then place them on a cutting board and with a long, heavy knife chop them rather fine to make 1¼ cups of pulp.

Bring the prune pulp with the sugar and lemon juice to a boil in a medium-size heavy saucepan over moderate heat, stirring almost constantly. Let the mixture boil very slowly for about 8 minutes until it is slightly thickened. Set aside to cool and then stir in the nuts. If you have made the filling a day or more ahead, cover and refrigerate it. If it is to be used within a few hours it may wait at room temperature but it must not be warm when used.

When you are ready to bake the cookies, adjust two racks to divide the oven into thirds and preheat to 400 degrees. Line two 15½-by-12-inch cookie sheets with aluminum foil.

Work with half the dough at a time, keeping the remainder refrigerated. Work quickly before the dough softens. Place the dough on a well-floured pastry cloth and turn it over several times to flour all sides. If the dough is too firm to roll, pound it with a rolling pin to soften it slightly. With a floured rolling pin, roll the dough until it is a scant ⅛ inch thick (make it thin enough), reflouring the cloth and pin as necessary to keep the dough from sticking.

With a plain round 3¼-inch cookie cutter, cut the first half of the dough into rounds. With a small metal spatula transfer the rounds to a foil-lined cookie sheet—they may be placed less than 1 inch apart in order to fit 12 rounds on each sheet. Reserve the scraps, rechill, and reroll them.

Place a rounded teaspoonful of the filling in the center of each cookie, mounding the filling high in the center and keeping it well away from the edges.

Roll out the other half of the dough, which you had left in the refrigerator, cut it the same way as the first half, and use these rounds for tops. Cover each cookie with a top, and then with floured fingertips press down gently around the edges.

Now, to seal and trim the edges, the cookies should be cut again, with the smaller cutter. Since the dough will have softened and become sticky by now, the smaller cutter must be dipped into flour frequently. Recut the cookies with the 2¾-inch cutter. (Don't worry about any small spots where the rounds of dough are not sealed to each other—or any small cracks in the top rounds of dough.) Remove the excess dough, and if it does not have any of the filling mixed in with it, it may be reused.

Bake for about 15 minutes until the cookies are delicately browned. Reverse the cookie sheets top to bottom and front to back as necessary to insure even browning.

With a wide metal spatula transfer the cookies to racks to cool.

Place the racks of cooled cookies over wax paper. Cover the tops generously with confectioners sugar, pressing it with your fingertips through a fine strainer held over the cookies.

Haman-taschen

27 HAMANTASCHEN

The name Hamantaschen is derived from Haman's hat. Haman was a wicked man who wanted to destroy the Jewish people, but Queen Esther did him in first. Haman wore a hat shaped like Napoleon's—triangular— and these cookies are made to resemble that shape. These are traditionally served during Purim, the feast of Esther, which is the most joyous day of the Hebrew year, and traditionally they are filled with prune jam, called lekvar, or with a poppy seed and honey mixture. This version is slightly different. (The pastry must be refrigerated overnight.)

PASTRY

2 cups sifted all-purpose flour
2 teaspoons double-acting baking powder
¼ teaspoon salt
¾ cup granulated sugar
¼ pound (1 stick) butter, cold and firm
1 egg
Finely grated rind of 1 bright-colored orange
1½ tablespoons orange juice

Sift together, into a large mixing bowl, the flour, baking powder, salt, and sugar. Cut the butter into ½-inch slices, and with a pastry blender cut it into the dry ingredients until the particles are fine and the mixture resembles coarse meal. Beat the egg lightly just to mix. Stir the egg, orange rind, and juice into the dough. Mix thoroughly and then stir well until the dough is completely moistened and smooth. Wrap in wax paper or plastic wrap, flatten the dough slightly, and refrigerate overnight.

The filling may be made the next day or it may be made ahead of time and kept at room temperature for a day or two or refrigerated for a longer time.

FILLING

*12 ounces unsweetened dried pitted prunes
(about 2 cups, lightly packed)*
*6 ounces unsweetened dried apricots (about
1 cup, lightly packed)*
1 cup water
1 tablespoon lemon juice
½ cup honey (see Notes)
*2½ ounces (¾ cup) walnuts, cut into
medium-size pieces*

Cut the prunes and apricots into small pieces. Place them in a saucepan with the water. Bring to a boil, cover, and lower the heat so that they just simmer for 10 to 15 minutes until very soft. (Some fruits are drier than others—if the water evaporates before the fruit is soft add another spoon or two of water and cook a bit longer.) Add the lemon juice and honey. Cook, stirring almost constantly, for about 5 minutes (it should not get too thick; it will thicken more while cooling). Stir in the nuts and set aside to cool.

When you are ready to bake, adjust two racks to divide the oven into thirds and preheat to 400 degrees. Cut aluminum foil to fit cookie sheets.

Work with half of the pastry at a time; refrigerate the other half. Work quickly or the dough will become sticky. On a floured pastry cloth with a floured rolling pin roll out the dough, turning it over occasionally to keep both sides floured. Roll it to an even ⅛-inch thickness (that is thin but be careful—if you roll the dough too thin it will be hard to handle). With a plain round 3-inch cookie cutter, cut the dough into rounds. (Reserve the scraps of dough, press them together, and rechill until firm enough to roll.)

Hold one round in your hand. Place a rounded teaspoonful of the filling in the center, mounding it rather high—it will not run out in baking. Fold up two sides of the dough—each side should be a third of the circle— and pinch them together where they meet. Now fold up the third side and pinch together at both sides, forming a triangle and leaving a generous opening at the top. The filling should extend above the top of the pastry. (If the rounds of pastry become soft or sticky before you shape them, transfer them with a wide metal spatula to a tray or cookie sheet and chill briefly in the freezer or refrigerator only until they are firm enough to handle.)

Place the Hamantaschen 1½ to 2 inches apart on the cut foil. Slide cookie sheets under the pieces of foil. Bake 12 to 15 minutes until the cookies are barely colored on the sides, slightly darker on the edges. Reverse the sheets top to bottom and front to back to insure even browning. If you bake only one sheet at a time bake it high in the oven.

With a wide metal spatula transfer the Hamantaschen to racks to cool, or serve them warm. If anyone is in the kitchen with me when I bake these, very few if any actually have a chance to cool.

NOTES: These are better with a mild clover honey than with a strongly flavored one.

There might be a little filling left over. If so, it makes a wonderful conserve. Serve with crackers, toast, or biscuits, and, if you wish, butter or cottage cheese. You might like it so much that you decide to make it especially for that purpose. If you do, don't cook it until it gets as dry as for the Hamantaschen. If it becomes too dry from standing, stir in a bit of orange juice, prune juice, or apricot nectar.

Rugelach

(Walnut Horns)

36 COOKIES

This is a traditional Jewish recipe that my grandmother used to make. Like all pastry— best when very fresh. They freeze perfectly. The dough must be refrigerated overnight.

CREAM-CHEESE PASTRY

½ pound (2 sticks) butter
½ pound cream cheese
½ teaspoon salt
2 cups sifted all-purpose flour

In the large bowl of an electric mixer cream the butter and cream cheese together until completely blended and smooth. Beat in the salt and on low speed gradually add the flour. While beating in the flour, toward the end, the dough might start to run up on the beaters. If so, the last of it may be stirred in by hand. When the dough is smooth, flour your hands lightly and, with your hands, form it into a short, fat roll. Cut the roll into three equal pieces. Form each piece into a round ball, flatten slightly, and wrap each individually in plastic wrap or wax paper. Refrigerate the balls of dough overnight.

When you are ready to bake, prepare the following filling and then adjust two racks to divide the oven into thirds. Preheat the oven to 350 degrees. Cut aluminum foil to fit cookie sheets.

FILLING

½ cup plus 2 tablespoons granulated sugar
3 teaspoons cinnamon
3 tablespoons butter, melted
¾ cup currants
5 ounces (1¼ cups) walnuts, finely chopped
    (see page 13)

Stir the sugar and cinnamon together and set aside. (Do not mix the remaining ingredients.)

Place one ball of dough on a floured pastry cloth. With a floured rolling pin pound the dough firmly to soften it slightly. On the floured cloth, with the floured rolling pin, roll out the dough (turning it over occasionally) into a 12-inch circle—don't worry about slightly uneven edge.

With a pastry brush, brush the dough with 1 tablespoon of the melted butter and, quickly, before the cold dough hardens the butter, sprinkle with one-third of the sugar-cinnamon mixture. Then sprinkle with one-third of the currants and the nuts. With the rolling pin, roll over the filling to press the topping slightly into the dough.

With a long, sharp knife, cut into 12 pie-shaped wedges. Roll each wedge jelly-roll fashion, rolling from the outside toward the point. Then place each little roll, with the point down, 1 inch apart on the cut aluminum foil.

Repeat with remaining dough and filling. Since some of the filling will fall out while you are rolling up the horns, after preparing each third of the dough it will be necessary to clean the pastry cloth; either shake it out or scrape it with a dough scraper or a wide metal spatula and then re-flour it.

GLAZE

1 egg yolk
1 teaspoon water

In a small cup, with a fork, stir the yolk and water just to mix. With a pastry brush, brush the glaze over the tops of the horns. Slide a cookie sheet under each piece of foil.

Bake two sheets at a time for about 30 minutes, until the horns are golden brown. Reverse the sheets top to bottom and front to back once to insure even browning. If you bake one sheet at a time use the higher rack.

With a wide metal spatula immediately transfer the horns to racks to cool.

Danish Coffeehouse Slices

Delicate orange pastry is wrapped jelly-roll fashion around a raisin-nut filling; the rolls are baked and then sliced. These are more like pastry or coffee cake than typical cookies but they may be served with, or in place of, cookies.

30 SLICES

ORANGE PASTRY

2 cups <u>unsifted</u> all-purpose flour
½ teaspoon baking soda
Pinch of salt
½ cup granulated sugar
Finely grated rind of 1 large, deep-colored orange
¼ cup orange juice
¼ pound (1 stick) butter, cold and firm
1 egg

Cut a piece of aluminum foil to cover the length of a 14-by-17-inch cookie sheet and place it on the sheet. Or line two smaller sheets with foil. For one large sheet adjust an oven rack one-third down from the top. For two sheets adjust two racks to divide the oven into thirds. Preheat the oven to 350 degrees.

Sift together into a large mixing bowl the flour, baking soda, salt, and sugar. In a small cup mix the orange rind and juice and set aside. Cut the butter into ½-inch slices, then with a pastry blender cut the butter into the dry ingredients until the particles are fine and the mixture resembles coarse meal. In a small bowl, with a fork, stir the egg lightly just to mix. Mix the egg with the orange mixture and stir into the dough until the dry ingredients are completely absorbed.

Turn the dough out onto a floured pastry cloth. Knead the dough lightly until it is smooth, and then with your hands form it into a flattened oblong about 5 by 6 inches. Let the dough stand at room temperature while you prepare the filling.

FILLING

¾ cup apricot preserves, or any other thick jam, jelly, preserves, or marmalade
3 tablespoons granulated sugar
3 teaspoons cinnamon
3½ ounces (¾ cup) currants or raisins

2½ ounces (¾ cup) walnuts, cut or broken
into medium-size pieces

Confectioners sugar for topping

Stir the preserves to soften them and set aside. Stir together the sugar and cinnamon and set aside. Do not mix the remaining ingredients together.

The dough is delicate—handle it lightly and work quickly. Cut the dough into equal thirds and set aside two pieces; work with one piece at a time. On the floured pastry cloth, turn the piece of dough over and over to flour all sides. With a floured rolling pin roll the dough, turning it over occasionally. Roll it into a 6-by-10-inch oblong. Keep the shape as even as possible but don't worry about trimming the edges.

Use a spoon to spread ¼ cup of the preserves over the dough, leaving a 1-inch border all around. Then sprinkle the preserves with ¼ cup of the currants or raisins and ¼ cup of the walnuts, and then with 4 teaspoons of the sugar-cinnamon mixture.

Fold over 1 inch of each short side of the dough and press down on the corners to seal. Then roll the dough jelly-roll fashion, starting at a long side. Now with both hands, quickly and carefully transfer the roll, seam side down, to the foil-covered sheet. If you are using one large cookie sheet place the rolls across the short way, three on the sheet, leaving 3 inches between the rolls. If you are using two smaller sheets place two rolls lengthwise on one sheet and one on the other. If the rolls are thicker on the ends use your hands to flatten them slightly.

Bake for 30 minutes, reversing the one large sheet front to back, or the two smaller sheets top to bottom and front to back, to insure even browning. Bake until the rolls are golden brown.

Slide the foil off the sheet and, immediately, using a small cookie sheet as a spatula, carefully transfer the rolls to a large cutting board.

Let the rolls stand for about 5 minutes and then while they are still warm cut them into diagonal slices ¾ to 1 inch thick. With a wide metal spatula transfer the slices to racks to cool.

Place the slices on the rack over a large piece of wax paper. Sprinkle confectioners sugar through a fine strainer to coat the tops of the slices lightly.

These are best while very fresh. They may be frozen.

NOTE: This is a very fragile pastry and must be handled gently, quickly, and as little as possible. The finished product is worth the extra care it takes. The tops of the rolls might crack and open slightly during baking but don't worry—if the dough has not been rolled thinner than the directions specify, the cracks will be minor and O.K.

Big Newtons

30 LARGE
BIG NEWTONS

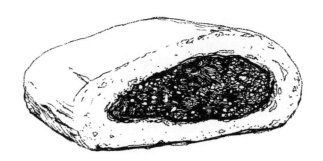

A thick, juicy version of the Fig Newtons you buy at the store.

PASTRY

1 cup sifted all-purpose white flour
1 teaspoon double-acting baking powder
½ teaspoon baking soda
½ teaspoon salt
2 cups <u>unsifted</u> all-purpose whole-wheat flour
¼ pound (1 stick) butter
½ cup light brown sugar, firmly packed
½ cup honey
1 egg

Sift together into a bowl the white flour, baking powder, baking soda, and salt. Add the whole-wheat flour and stir to mix well. Set aside.

In the large bowl of an electric mixer cream the butter. Add the sugar and beat well. Beat in the honey and then the egg. On low speed gradually add the dry ingredients, scraping the bowl with a rubber spatula and beating until completely mixed.

Turn out onto a large piece of wax paper, flatten slightly, and wrap airtight. Refrigerate for several hours or overnight, or freeze for an hour or two, until the dough is firm enough to be rolled.

Meanwhile, prepare the filling. Or the filling may be made days ahead and refrigerated.

FILLING

1½ pounds of dried brown figs (although technically they are "dried," they should be soft and moist; do not use them if they are dry and hard)
¾ cup honey
3 tablespoons water
2 tablespoons lemon juice
2 tablespoons orange juice

Remove the tough stems from the figs. On a large board with a long, heavy chef's knife, chop the figs very fine to make 3 cups of finely chopped figs. Or if you have some way of grinding them—in a food processor or a meat grinder—do.

In a large, heavy saucepan mix the figs with the honey, water, lemon juice, and orange juice. Place over moderate heat and cook, stirring almost constantly, for about 10 minutes, until very hot but not boiling. Transfer to a dinner plate or a shallow tray to cool. When cool, refrigerate. The filling must be cold when it is used.

Adjust a rack to the highest position in the oven and preheat to 400 degrees. Cut two pieces of aluminum foil the size of your largest cookie sheet.

Work with half of the dough at a time; reserve the other half in the refrigerator. Work on a floured pastry cloth with a floured rolling pin. If the dough is too hard to roll, place it on the cloth and pound it with the rolling pin until it softens slightly. Roll the dough into an even oblong 15 inches long, 6 inches wide, and ¼ inch thick. Use a ruler as a guide and trim the edges evenly. If necessary, excess cut-off dough may be used to fill in where needed. Work quickly before the dough becomes sticky.

With two teaspoons, one for picking up and one for pushing off, spoon half of the filling evenly down the middle of the dough, lengthwise, forming a band of filling 1 inch deep and 2 inches wide. Stop it ½ inch away from the narrow ends. Smooth it with the back of a spoon but do not flatten it.

Use the pastry cloth to help fold the two long sides of the pastry over the filling. They should overlap each other by ¼ to ½ inch. Press lightly to seal. Use the pastry cloth again to help turn the roll over so that it is now seam side down. Do not worry about any shallow surface cracks.

With both hands, one on each long side of the roll, quickly and carefully transfer the roll to a piece of the cut foil, placing the roll either lengthwise down the middle, or on an angle from one corner to the opposite corner. With your hands, perfect the shape of the roll so that it is smooth and even. Press down gently on the two narrow open ends to seal the dough.

If your cookie sheet is big enough (14 by 17 inches) to fit both rolls, by all means bake them together. Otherwise, prepare the second roll while the first is baking.

Slide a cookie sheet under the foil and bake for 15 minutes, reversing the position of the sheet during baking to insure even browning. When the roll is golden brown all over slide the aluminum foil off the cookie sheet and let the roll stand for about 10 minutes, until it is firm enough to be removed from the foil. Transfer the roll to a rack to finish cooling.

When cool, refrigerate the rolls briefly—the strips are easier to cut when cold.

Use a very sharp knife or a finely serrated one to cut the roll crossways into 1-inch slices. If necessary, wipe the blade occasionally with a damp cloth.

Hand-Formed Cookies

FUDGE MALLOWS

CHOCOLATE AGGIES

CHOCOLATE OATMEAL CRISPIES

CHOCOLATE AND PEANUT-BUTTER
  CRESCENTS

SENORITAS

FRENCH FILBERT MACAROONS

DANISH BUTTER SANDWICHES

COCONUT WASHBOARDS

COCONUT PENNIES

CRACKER-BARREL RAISIN COOKIES

AUSTRIAN WALNUT CRESCENTS

SOUR CREAM AND PECAN DREAMS

CHARLIE BROWN'S PEANUT COOKIES

ENGLISH GINGERSNAPS #1

ENGLISH GINGERSNAPS #2

ITALIAN SESAME STICKS

Rolling the dough between your hands to shape these cookies might take a little time, but it is creative, expressive, and gratifying.

Fudge Mallows

Semisoft chocolate cookies with a pecan hidden underneath, a marshmallow on top, and then a thick chocolate icing.

28 COOKIES

1¾ cups sifted all-purpose flour
1 teaspoon baking soda
¼ teaspoon salt
½ cup unsweetened cocoa, strained
    or sifted
¼ pound (1 stick) butter
1 teaspoon vanilla extract
1 cup granulated sugar
2 eggs
28 large pecan halves (see Notes)
14 large marshmallows (see Notes)

Adjust two racks to divide the oven into thirds and preheat to 350 degrees. Cut aluminum foil to fit cookie sheets.

Sift together the flour, baking soda, salt, and cocoa and set aside. In the large bowl of an electric mixer, cream the butter. Add the vanilla and the sugar and beat to mix well. Add the eggs one at a time and beat until smooth. On low speed, gradually add the sifted dry ingredients, scraping the bowl with a rubber spatula and beating only until thoroughly mixed.

Place a large piece of wax paper on the work surface. Use a heaping teaspoonful of dough for each cookie—place them on the wax paper, making about 28 mounds.

Wet your hands under cold running water, shake off excess water—your hands should be damp but not too wet. Pick up a mound of dough and roll it between your hands into a round ball. Press a pecan half into the ball of dough, placing the curved side (top) of the nut into the dough. Do not enclose it completely.

Place the cookie on the foil so that the flat side of the pecan is on the foil, on the bottom of the cookie. Continue to wet your hands as necessary while you shape the remaining cookies, placing them 2 inches apart on the foil. Slide cookie sheets under the foil.

Bake 16 to 18 minutes, reversing sheets top to bottom and front to back once to insure even baking. Bake until cookies are barely done—not quite firm to the touch. Do not overbake.

While cookies are baking, cut the marshmallows in half crosswise. (Easily done with scissors.)

Remove the cookie sheets from the oven. Quickly place a marshmallow half, cut side down, on each cookie. Return to the oven for 1 to 1½ minutes. Watch the clock! If the marshmallows bake any longer they will melt and run off the sides of the cookies—they should not melt and they should stay on top. These should not actually melt at all—only soften very slightly—and not get soft enough to change shape.

Let cookies stand for a few seconds until they are firm enough to be moved and then, with a wide metal spatula, transfer to racks to cool.

Prepare the following icing.

CHOCOLATE ICING

½ cup unsweetened cocoa
Pinch of salt
1½ cups confectioners sugar
2⅔ ounces (5⅓ tablespoons) butter
About 3 tablespoons boiling water

Place the cocoa, salt, and sugar in the small bowl of an electric mixer. Melt the butter and pour the hot butter and 3 tablespoons of boiling water into the bowl. Beat until completely smooth. The icing should be a thick, semi-fluid mixture. It should not be so thin that it will run off the cookies. It might be necessary to add a little more hot water, but add it very gradually—only a few drops at a time. (If the sugar has not been strained or sifted before measuring, you might need as much as 2 or 3 additional teaspoons of water.) If you add too much water and the icing becomes too thin, thicken it with additional sugar. If the icing thickens too much while you are icing the cookies, thin it carefully with a few drops of water. Transfer the icing to a small bowl for ease in handling.

Lift a cookie and hold it while you partially frost it with a generous teaspoonful of the icing. Allow some of the marshmallow to show through —preferably one side of the marshmallow—the contrast of black and white is what you want. Also, don't try to cover the entire top of the cookie itself or you will not have enough for all the cookies. Replace cookie on rack. Ice all the cookies and then let them stand for a few hours to set.

NOTES: If you do not have large pecan halves you may use several small pieces—just put them on the bottom of the cookies any which way.

If you use your own homemade marshmallows (page 267) they will be smaller than the regular-size commercial ones. Don't cut them in half, use them whole.

Chocolate Aggies

These are dense, chocolaty, rather thick, and semisoft. They are mixed in a saucepan, and are rolled in confectioners sugar before baking.

40 TO 45 COOKIES

2 cups sifted all-purpose flour
2 teaspoons double-acting baking powder
¼ teaspoon salt
2 ounces (4 tablespoons) butter
4 ounces (4 squares) unsweetened chocolate
2 cups granulated sugar
4 extra-large or jumbo eggs
2 ounces (generous ½ cup) walnuts, cut medium fine (see page 13)
About 1 cup confectioners sugar; you might need a bit more (to be used when cookies are shaped)

Sift together the flour, baking powder, and salt and set aside. In a heavy 3-quart saucepan over low heat melt the butter and the chocolate. Stir occasionally until smooth and then remove from the heat. With a heavy wooden spatula stir the granulated sugar into the warm chocolate mixture. Then stir in the eggs one at a time. Add the sifted dry ingredients and stir until smooth. Stir in the nuts.

It will be a soft dough and it must be refrigerated. It may be left in the saucepan or transferred to a bowl. Either way, cover and refrigerate, preferably for 1½ hours (but the dough may be refrigerated longer or overnight if you wish).

Adjust two racks to divide the oven into thirds and preheat to 300 degrees. Cut aluminum foil to fit cookie sheets.

Press the confectioners sugar through a strainer and spread it out on a large piece of wax paper. Sugar the palms of your hands with some of the confectioners sugar. Roll the dough into 1- to 1¼-inch balls, using a heaping teaspoonful of dough for each cookie. Roll the balls around in the confectioners sugar and place them 2 inches apart on the aluminum foil. (If the dough was refrigerated overnight and if the cookies are not baked immediately after being shaped, the confectioners sugar will become wet. If this happens, the cookies should be rolled around in the sugar again and then rolled between your hands again—the cookies will be more attractive if the confectioners sugar coats them heavily.)

Slide cookie sheets under the foil and bake the cookies for 20 to 22 minutes, until the tops of the cookies are barely semifirm to the touch. Reverse the position of the sheets top to bottom and front to back once during baking to insure even baking. Do not overbake—these should be slightly soft in the centers. (If you bake only one sheet at a time bake it high in the oven.)

Slide the foil off the cookie sheets and with a wide metal spatula transfer the cookies to racks to cool.

VARIATION: The above recipe may be made with vegetable oil (not olive oil) in place of butter. Melt the chocolate in the top of a small double boiler over hot water on moderate heat. Transfer the melted chocolate to a large mixing bowl. Add ½ cup vegetable oil (yes, ½ cup vegetable oil in place of ¼ cup butter) and the sugar and stir to mix. Then follow the above directions to stir in the eggs, dry ingredients, and nuts. Continue with directions above.

Chocolate Oatmeal Crispies

These are large, flat cookies that are crisp-crunchy and have a dry, meringue-like texture.

28 TO 30 COOKIES

6 ounces (1 cup) semisweet chocolate morsels
1 cup sifted all-purpose flour
½ teaspoon baking soda
¼ teaspoon salt
¼ pound (1 stick) butter
1 teaspoon vanilla extract
½ teaspoon almond extract
1 cup granulated sugar
1 egg
1 cup old-fashioned or quick-cooking
  (not "instant") oatmeal
3½ ounces (1 cup, firmly packed) shredded
  coconut

Adjust two racks to divide the oven into thirds and preheat to 350 degrees. Cut aluminum foil to fit cookie sheets.

Partially melt the chocolate morsels in the top of a small double boiler over hot water on moderate heat. Remove from the heat and stir until completely melted. Set aside to cool for a few minutes.

Meanwhile, sift together the flour, baking soda, and salt and set aside. In the small bowl of an electric mixer cream the butter. Add the vanilla and almond extracts and the sugar, and beat until blended. Beat in the egg and the melted chocolate. On low speed gradually add the sifted dry ingredients, scraping the bowl with a rubber spatula and beating only until incorporated. Mix in the oatmeal and the coconut.

To divide the dough evenly: On a long piece of wax paper or aluminum foil place the dough by rounded tablespoonfuls in 28 to 30 equal mounds. Roll each mound between your hands to form a ball and place the balls on the cut aluminum foil at least 2 to 2½ inches apart, no closer.

Press the tops of the cookies with the back of the tines of a fork to flatten them to ½-inch thickness. First press all in one direction and then in the opposite direction. Slide cookie sheets under the foil.

Bake for about 15 minutes, reversing the sheets top to bottom and front to back once to insure even baking. When done, the cookies will feel crusty on the tops but semisoft in the centers—they will harden as they cool.

With a wide metal spatula transfer the cookies to racks to cool.

Chocolate and Peanut-Butter Crescents

66 COOKIES

These are small, candylike cookies that take time and patience. They have a crisp chocolate dough wrapped around a peanut-butter filling and are formed into crescent shapes.

COOKIE DOUGH

2 cups sifted all-purpose flour
⅓ cup unsweetened cocoa
¼ teaspoon salt
¼ pound (1 stick) butter
1 teaspoon vanilla extract
¾ cup granulated sugar
1 egg

Sift together the flour, cocoa, and salt and set aside. In the large bowl of an electric mixer cream the butter. Beat in the vanilla and sugar. Add the egg and beat until thoroughly mixed. On low speed gradually add the sifted dry ingredients, scraping the bowl with a rubber spatula and beating until the mixture holds together. Transfer the dough to a small bowl for ease in handling and set aside at room temperature.

Prepare the following filling.

FILLING

¾ cup smooth (not chunky) peanut butter
½ cup strained or sifted confectioners sugar

In a small bowl thoroughly mix the peanut butter and the sugar.

Adjust a rack to the center of the oven and preheat to 325 degrees.

To shape the cookies: On a large piece of wax paper or aluminum foil place the cookie dough in mounds, using a slightly rounded teaspoonful (no more) of the dough for each mound—in order not to make them too large it is best to measure with a measuring spoon. Instead of doing all at once you may prefer to measure only a fourth or a half of the dough at one time.

Then do the same with the filling, using a level ½ measuring teaspoon for each mound. Place these mounds on other pieces of wax paper or foil.

Pick up one mound of the dough, roll it between your hands into a ball, and flatten it between your palms until it is very thin. Then, with a small metal spatula or a table knife, lift up and place one mound of the filling in the center of the flattened dough. With your fingers bring the dough around the filling and pinch the edges to seal. Roll the filled dough between your hands into a cylindrical shape about 2 inches long with very slightly tapered ends. Place the cookie on an unbuttered cookie sheet and as you do, turn the ends down slightly to form a short, fat crescent.

Continue shaping the cookies and placing them ½ to 1 inch apart—these do not spread.

Bake for 13 to 15 minutes, or until the cookies are firm to the touch. Reverse the cookie sheet front to back once to insure even baking.

OPTIONAL TOPPING: *Confectioners sugar or vanilla sugar (see Note).* While the cookies are baking spread out a large piece of wax paper or aluminum foil and sift or strain 1 to 2 cups of the sugar onto the paper or foil, forming a mound of sugar.

As soon as the cookies are done immediately transfer them with a wide metal spatula to the mound of sugar and roll the cookies around to coat them thoroughly with the sugar.

Then place the cookies on another piece of paper or foil to cool. When the cookies are cool, roll them again in the sugar.

NOTE: *How to make vanilla sugar:* This must be prepared ahead but can be kept for a long time (and can be used for topping all kinds of cakes and cookies). You will need a whole vanilla bean (available in specialty food stores). Place the bean on a board and with a sharp knife split it the long way. Fill a 1-quart jar that has a tight cover with confectioners sugar and bury the bean in the sugar. Cover tightly and let stand for at least several days or a week before using—the sugar will have absorbed the flavor of the bean. Sift or strain the sugar immediately before using, as it will absorb some moisture from the bean and become lumpy—it will have to be strained again even if it was done beforehand. As the sugar is used it may be replaced. If you replace the sugar often, the bean itself should be replaced after a month or two.

Señoritas

These are crisp, crunchy, and chewy with toasted chopped almonds and a butterscotch flavor.

5 ounces (1 cup) blanched almonds, coarsely
    chopped or diced (they must not be fine)
3 cups sifted all-purpose flour
1 teaspoon baking soda
½ teaspoon cream of tartar
½ teaspoon salt
6 ounces (1½ sticks) butter
½ teaspoon vanilla extract
Scant ½ teaspoon almond extract
1 cup granulated sugar
1 cup dark brown sugar, firmly packed
2 eggs

Adjust two racks to divide the oven into thirds and preheat to 400 degrees. Cut aluminum foil to fit cookie sheets.

Place the almonds in a small, shallow pan and toast them in the preheated oven, shaking the pan frequently, for about 8 minutes until they are golden brown. Set aside to cool.

Sift together the flour, baking soda, cream of tartar, and salt and set aside. In the large bowl of an electric mixer cream the butter. Add the vanilla and almond extracts and then, gradually, both sugars and beat well. Add the eggs and beat well. On low speed gradually add the sifted dry ingredients, scraping the bowl with a rubber spatula and beating only until thoroughly mixed. With a wooden spatula stir in the cooled toasted almonds.

Place a large piece of wax paper in front of you. Use a heaping teaspoonful of the dough for each cookie, placing the mounds on the wax paper and forming 48 mounds.

Roll the mounds of dough between your hands, forming them into balls and placing them at least 2 inches apart (no closer) on the cut aluminum foil.

Slide cookie sheets under the foil. It is very important to time the baking of these cookies exactly. Bake for 10 minutes (no longer), reversing the position of the sheets top to bottom and front to back once to insure even baking. When the 10 minutes are up the cookies will still feel soft, but they harden as they cool and if they are baked any longer they will become too hard—they should remain slightly soft and chewy in the centers.

Slide the foil off the cookie sheets and with a wide metal spatula transfer the cookies to racks to cool.

French Filbert Macaroons

24 MACAROONS

These are traditional Christmas holiday cookies in France. They are made extra soft and chewy with chopped cherries and a bit of jam. You will not need an electric mixer.

8 ounces (1⅔ cups) unblanched filberts (hazelnuts) (see Notes)
1 cup granulated sugar
Pinch of salt
1 tablespoon smooth jam or preserves (see Notes)
About ¼ cup egg whites (1½–2 eggs, depending on size)
12 glacéed cherries, finely chopped
Confectioners sugar (for powdering your hands and sprinkling over the baked cookies)

Adjust a rack to the center of the oven and preheat to 325 degrees. Line a cookie sheet with aluminum foil.

Grind the nuts to a fine powder in a nut grinder, a blender, or a food processor. Place them in a bowl with the sugar and salt and stir to mix thoroughly. Add the jam or preserves and the egg whites. Stir, then, in order to mix the dough thoroughly, squeeze it between your hands until it is smooth. The mixture should be slightly moist but not wet—if it is crumbly and too dry to hold together easily, add a few drops of additional egg white as necessary. Then add the cherries and work the dough again with your hands until they are evenly distributed.

Spread out a large piece of wax paper. Use a slightly rounded measuring tablespoonful of dough for each cookie, making 24 mounds of dough, and placing them on the wax paper.

If necessary, powder your hands lightly with confectioners sugar and roll each mound of dough into a smooth, round ball. Place them 1 inch apart on the foil-lined cookie sheet.

Bake for 20 minutes, reversing the cookie sheet front to back once to insure even baking. Do not overbake—these should remain chewy-soft in the centers.

Slide the foil off the cookie sheet and let the macaroons stand on the foil for about 10 minutes. Then, with a wide metal spatula, carefully remove them from the foil (these have a tendency to stick to the foil) and transfer them to a rack to finish cooling.

When cool, place the rack over wax paper. Sprinkle the tops generously with confectioners sugar, pressing the sugar with your fingers through a strainer held over the macaroons.

NOTES: Using unblanched nuts (nuts from which the skins have not been removed) will only affect the color, not the taste.

Any jam or preserves may be used (I like black raspberry) but it must be smooth. If it is chunky, strain it.

If the macaroons have baked too long and are hard or dry instead of moist and chewy, place them (before sugaring the tops) in an airtight container with a slice of bread, or a lemon, or an orange, or half an apple (placed cut side up on top of the macaroons). Let stand for a day or two until they soften and then remove the bread or fruit.

Danish Butter Sandwiches

These are crisp brown-sugar butter cookies sandwiched together with a browned-butter filling.

½ pound (2 sticks) butter
¾ cup light brown sugar, firmly packed
1 egg yolk
2¼ cups sifted all-purpose flour

Adjust two racks to divide the oven into thirds and preheat to 325 degrees.

In the large bowl of an electric mixer cream the butter. Add the sugar and beat to mix. Add the egg yolk and beat to mix. On low speed gradually add the flour, scraping the bowl with a rubber spatula and beating until the mixture holds together.

Place a long piece of wax paper in front of you. Use a slightly rounded teaspoonful of the dough for each cookie, and place the mounds of dough on the wax paper, making 48 mounds.

Roll the mounds between your hands into round balls, and place them 1½ to 2 inches apart on unbuttered cookie sheets.

With the heel of your hand, or with your fingertips, flatten each mound into a round cookie about ¼ inch thick.

Have a little extra flour in a cup or on a piece of wax paper. Dip a fork into the flour and then press the back of the tines firmly onto the top of a cookie, forming deep indentations, in one direction only. Reflour the fork each time you use it, and make the indentations on all of the cookies.

Bake for 15 to 20 minutes (depending on the thickness of the cookies), reversing the cookie sheets top to bottom and front to back as necessary to insure even baking. Do not allow the cookies to brown—when done they should be a pale golden color.

With a wide metal spatula transfer the cookies to racks to cool.

Since these cookies are shaped by hand, they will not all be exactly the same size. They should be matched into even pairs before they are filled.

After matching them, place each pair, open, flat side up, on a long piece of wax paper.

Prepare the following filling.

BROWNED-BUTTER FILLING

2 tablespoons butter
1¼ cups strained or sifted confectioners sugar
½ teaspoon vanilla extract
About 5 to 6 teaspoons heavy cream

Melt the butter in a small saucepan over moderate heat. Bring it to a boil and let boil until it browns slightly, shaking the pan gently during the last part of heating to prevent the sediment from burning. Remove from the heat when the butter has a rich golden color, and immediately add the sugar, vanilla, and 5 teaspoons of the cream. Stir until completely smooth. If necessary, add another teaspoon or so of the cream to make a thick filling.

Transfer the filling to a small custard cup or bowl for ease in handling.

Place a scant teaspoonful of the filling in the center of a cookie. Repeat with 4 or 5 cookies. Cover each cookie with its matching cookie and, as you do so, press the cookies gently together to spread the filling just to the edges of the sandwich. It is best to hold the cookies in your hands while you do this, and turn the cookies around so that you can see just where the filling is going.

Repeat, filling the remaining cookies, doing about 4 or 5 at a time. While working with the filling you will find it will thicken and will need to have a few drops of additional cream stirred in. Add only a few drops at a time in order not to make the filling too thin.

Let the sandwiches stand for a few hours for the filling to set.

NOTE: Without the filling these are delicious plain butter cookies.

Coconut Wash- boards

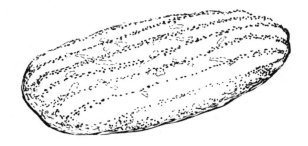

24 EXTRA-LARGE
COOKIES

Years ago when we lived on a farm in Connecticut the local general store sold these by the pound from a large wooden barrel. They are extra-large, plain, semisoft, and nostalgic. The dough must be well chilled before the cookies are shaped.

> 2 cups sifted all-purpose flour
> ¾ teaspoon double-acting baking powder
> ¼ teaspoon baking soda
> ⅛ teaspoon salt
> ¼ pound (1 stick) butter
> ½ teaspoon vanilla extract
> 1 cup light brown sugar, firmly packed
> 1 egg
> 2 tablespoons water
> 3½ ounces (1 cup, firmly packed) shredded coconut

Sift together the flour, baking powder, baking soda, and salt and set aside. In the large bowl of an electric mixer cream the butter. Beat in the vanilla. Add the brown sugar and beat to mix. Add the egg and the water and beat to mix well (the mixture will appear curdled—it's O.K.). On low speed gradually add the sifted dry ingredients, scraping the bowl with a rubber spatula and beating only until incorporated. Stir in the coconut.

Cut a piece of wax paper to fit a cookie sheet. Use a heaping teaspoon-ful of the dough for each cookie (remember these are large). Place them close to each other on the wax paper, forming 24 mounds.

Slide a cookie sheet under the wax paper and transfer the mounds of dough to the freezer or refrigerator to chill until they are firm enough to be handled. (If they are in the freezer, watch them carefully—they should not be frozen solid.)

In the meantime, adjust two racks to divide the oven into thirds and preheat to 375 degrees. Cut aluminum foil to fit cookie sheets. Have some flour handy for flouring your hands, and a fork.

Flour your hands. Pick up a mound of the dough and roll it between your palms into a sausage shape about 3 inches long. Place it on a piece of the foil. Continue shaping the remaining mounds and placing them 3 inches apart (no closer).

Flour the fingertips of one hand and, with your fingertips, flatten each sausage-shaped roll of dough until it is only ¼ inch thick, 3½ inches long, and 2 inches wide.

Now, to form the traditional ridges that give these cookies their name, dip a fork into the flour and press the back of the tines onto the cookies, forming deep indentations. Since the cookies are so large it will be necessary to press the fork onto each cookie four times, once for each quarter of the cookie surface. The ridges should be parallel and should go lengthwise with the shape of the cookie.

Slide cookie sheets under the foil. Bake the cookies for about 12 minutes, reversing the sheets top to bottom and front to back once to insure even browning. Bake until the cookies are golden brown all over—do not underbake. If you bake only one sheet at a time, use the higher rack.

Let the cookies stand for a few seconds and then, with a wide metal spatula, transfer them to racks to cool.

Coconut Pennies

These are smaller, richer, crisper, and fancier than the previous Coconut Washboards. This dough too must be well chilled before shaping.

60 COOKIES

2 cups sifted all-purpose flour
¾ teaspoon double-acting baking powder
⅛ teaspoon salt
¼ teaspoon cinnamon
¼ teaspoon nutmeg
½ pound (2 sticks) butter
1 teaspoon vanilla extract
½ teaspoon almond extract

1 cup dark brown sugar, firmly packed
1 egg
7 ounces (2 cups, packed) shredded coconut

Sift together the flour, baking powder, salt, cinnamon, and nutmeg and set aside. In the large bowl of an electric mixer, cream the butter. Add the vanilla and almond extracts and the sugar and beat to mix well. Beat in the egg. On low speed, gradually add the sifted dry ingredients, scraping the bowl with a rubber spatula and beating only until incorporated. Mix in the coconut.

Place the dough on a large piece of wax paper or aluminum foil, wrap, flatten slightly, and refrigerate for about 1½ to 2 hours. Do not use the freezer—the dough would become too firm to handle.

Adjust two racks to divide the oven into thirds and preheat to 375 degrees. Cut aluminum foil to fit cookie sheets (see Note).

Cut the dough into quarters. Work with one piece at a time. On a floured board, with floured hands, form the dough into a roll 15 inches long. Cut the roll into 1-inch pieces. (Or use a slightly rounded tablespoonful of the dough for each cookie.) Keeping your hands lightly floured, roll each piece into a ball.

Place the balls 2 inches apart on the cut foil. With the back of the tines of a floured fork, press each cookie in one direction only to form indentations and flatten the cookie to ⅓-inch thickness.

Slide cookie sheets under the foil. Bake about 10 minutes, until cookies are lightly colored. Reverse sheets top to bottom and front to back as necessary to insure even browning. The cookies will be slightly darker at the edges. Slide the foil off the cookie sheets.

With a wide metal spatula, transfer cookies to racks to cool.

NOTE: These may be baked on unbuttered cookie sheets without the foil, but since you probably won't have enough cookie sheets, the foil is recommended so you can shape them all at once.

Cracker-Barrel Raisin Cookies

72 COOKIES

These semisoft and chewy old-fashioned cookies are especially good for the cookie jar, for the lunch box, or for mailing.

4 cups sifted all-purpose flour
1 teaspoon baking soda
1 teaspoon salt
½ teaspoon nutmeg
15 ounces (3 cups) raisins
Boiling water
½ pound (2 sticks) butter
1½ teaspoons vanilla extract
¾ cup granulated sugar
¾ cup light brown sugar, firmly packed
1 egg
⅔ cup sour cream
Finely grated rind of 1 large or 2 small lemons

Sift together the flour, baking soda, salt, and nutmeg and set aside.

Pour boiling water over the raisins to cover and let stand for about 10 minutes. Drain the raisins in a strainer or a colander and then spread them out on several thicknesses of paper towels and lightly pat the tops with more paper towels. (The raisins do not have to be absolutely dry; they add moisture to the cookies.)

In the large bowl of an electric mixer cream the butter. Beat in the vanilla and both sugars. Add the egg and beat well. On low speed mix in half of the sifted dry ingredients, then all of the sour cream, and finally the remaining dry ingredients, scraping the bowl with a rubber spatula and beating only until thoroughly mixed. Remove the bowl from the mixer.

With a heavy wooden spatula stir in the lemon rind and then the raisins.

Now the dough has to be chilled before you roll it into balls (see Note). Spread out three or four large pieces of wax paper, divide the dough —an equal part on each piece of the paper—wrap, and chill in the freezer or the refrigerator until firm enough to handle.

Adjust two racks to divide the oven into thirds and preheat to 375 degrees. Cut aluminum foil to fit cookie sheets.

Work with one portion of the dough at a time, keeping the remainder chilled. Use a well-rounded teaspoonful of dough for each cookie. Flour your hands as necessary to keep the dough from sticking. Roll the dough between your hands into balls and place them 2 to 2½ inches apart on the cut aluminum foil.

With the back of the tines of a floured fork (reflour the fork as necessary) press the cookies first in one direction and then in the opposite direction to flatten them to ¼- to ½-inch thickness.

Slide cookie sheets under the foil and bake the cookies for about 15 minutes, until the cookies are golden brown all over. Reverse the sheets top to bottom and front to back as necessary to insure even browning.

Slide the foil off the sheets and, with a wide metal spatula, transfer the cookies to racks to cool.

NOTE: An easier, time-saving way of shaping these cookies without having to chill the dough is to treat them as drop cookies. The shapes will not be quite as even but since these are very homey, old-fashioned cookies, you might prefer this method.

Adjust the racks, preheat the oven, and cut the aluminum foil before mixing the dough. After stirring the raisins into the dough, transfer it to a small bowl for ease in handling. Place the dough by well-rounded teaspoonfuls 2 to 2½ inches apart on the cut foil. Flatten the cookies as above with a floured fork. Bake, etc., as above.

Austrian Walnut Crescents

56 COOKIES

These classic Viennese cookies are delicate, fragile, and elegant.

5¼ ounces (1½ cups) walnuts
½ pound (2 sticks) butter
2 teaspoons vanilla extract
⅔ cup granulated sugar
2½ cups sifted all-purpose flour
Confectioners sugar or vanilla sugar (see pages 14 and 217) for sprinkling over the baked cookies

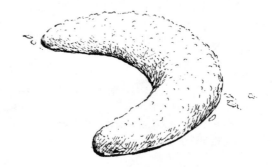

Adjust two racks to divide the oven into thirds and preheat to 325 degrees.

The walnuts must be ground very fine—this may be done in a nut grinder, a blender, or a food processor. (In a blender or food processor, grind half of the nuts at a time. Ground in a blender or processor the nuts may become oily and pasty—that doesn't matter for this recipe.) Set the ground nuts aside.

In the large bowl of an electric mixer cream the butter. Beat in the vanilla and then the ground nuts and mix well. Add the granulated sugar and beat well. On low speed gradually add the flour, scraping the bowl with a rubber spatula and beating until thoroughly mixed.

Place a large piece of wax paper in front of you. Use a rounded teaspoonful of the dough for each cookie, placing the mounds on the wax paper and forming 56 mounds.

Pick up one mound of dough at a time, rolling it between your hands into a small cigar shape about 4 inches long, with tapered ends and thicker in the middle. Place it on an unbuttered cookie sheet, curving the ends to form the cookie into a crescent shape. Continue shaping the cookies and placing them about 1 inch apart.

Bake the cookies for 18 to 20 minutes, reversing the position of the sheets top to bottom and front to back as necessary to insure even baking.

Bake only until the cookies are golden-colored on the tips and the bottoms —the center parts of the cookies should remain light. If you bake only one sheet at a time, use the higher rack.

Remove the cookie sheets from the oven but let the cookies stand for a minute or two until they are firm enough to be moved. These are very fragile—handle with care. With a wide metal spatula, gently transfer the cookies to racks set over wax paper.

Immediately, while the cookies are still warm, cover them generously with confectioners or vanilla sugar by pushing the sugar through a strainer held over the cookies.

When the cookies are cool, gently and carefully transfer them to a tray or serving dish. Or, if the cookies are to be stored in a box, package them with plastic wrap between the layers.

If necessary, sugar the tops of the cookies again before serving.

NOTE: From Nancy Nicholas, my editor: "I made these Walnut Crescents, my favorite kind of cookie, with black (as opposed to brown?) walnuts just to see and they came out very well. It is a stronger taste, but I thought delicious."

Sour Cream and Pecan Dreams

48 COOKIES

These are rather fancy. They are semisoft brown-sugar cookies with a baked-on sour cream and pecan topping.

2 cups sifted all-purpose flour
½ teaspoon baking soda
¼ teaspoon salt
¼ pound (1 stick) butter
1 teaspoon vanilla extract
1 cup dark brown sugar, firmly packed
1 egg

Adjust two racks to divide the oven into thirds and preheat to 350 degrees.

Sift together the flour, baking soda, and salt and set aside. In the large bowl of an electric mixer, cream the butter. Add the vanilla and sugar and beat well. Add the egg and continue to beat for a few minutes, scraping the bowl as necessary with a rubber spatula and beating until the mixture lightens in color. On low speed gradually add the sifted dry ingredients, scraping the bowl with the spatula and beating only until the mixture is smooth.

Use a slightly rounded teaspoonful of dough for each cookie—make these a little smaller than average. (To be sure that you are not making the cookies too large, before rolling any of the dough into balls you may divide the dough into 48 equal mounds on wax paper.) Roll the dough between your hands into round balls and place them 2 inches apart—no closer—on unbuttered cookie sheets.

With your fingertip or with the handle end of a large wooden spoon make a wide, round depression in the center of each cookie—reaching almost to the edges and leaving a rim.

Prepare the following topping.

SOUR CREAM AND PECAN TOPPING

½ cup dark brown sugar, firmly packed
½ teaspoon cinnamon
¼ cup sour cream
4 ounces (generous 1 cup) pecans, finely
    chopped (these should not be ground or
    chopped so fine that they are powdery)

Place the sugar, cinnamon, and sour cream in a small mixing bowl. With a rubber spatula stir until smooth. Stir in the nuts.

With a demitasse spoon or a small measuring spoon, place some of the topping in each cookie. The topping should be mounded fairly high above the rims of the cookies.

Bake for 13 to 15 minutes, reversing the cookie sheets top to bottom and front to back once to insure even baking. If you bake only one sheet at a time use the higher rack.

With a wide metal spatula transfer the cookies to racks to cool.

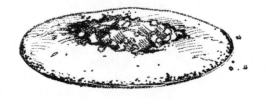

Charlie Brown's Peanut Cookies

36 COOKIES

These are coated with chopped peanuts and have a baked-on topping of peanut butter and chocolate morsels. They are fancy and take a little longer to make than many other cookies, but they are worth the time, and are fun to make.

2 cups sifted all-purpose flour
1 teaspoon double-acting baking powder
½ teaspoon cinnamon
½ pound (2 sticks) butter
1 cup dark brown sugar, firmly packed
2 eggs (leave 1 egg whole and separate the other)
1 teaspoon water
10 ounces (2¼ cups) salted peanuts (preferably dry roasted), chopped medium fine (see page 13)
Scant ¾ cup smooth (not chunky) peanut butter (it is not necessary to measure this; you may use it right from the jar)
4 ounces (⅔ cup) semisweet chocolate morsels (see Notes)

Sift together the flour, baking powder, and cinnamon and set aside. In the large bowl of an electric mixer cream the butter. Add the sugar and beat to mix. Beat in 1 whole egg and 1 egg yolk (reserve the second white). On low speed gradually add the sifted dry ingredients, scraping the bowl with a rubber spatula and beating only until thoroughly mixed.

Place a long piece of wax paper on the work surface. Divide the dough into 36 equal mounds on the wax paper. Use a heaping teaspoonful for each mound. Flour your hands and roll each mound into a round ball, continuing to flour your hands before rolling each ball. As you roll the balls, replace them on the wax paper.

Adjust two racks to divide the oven into thirds and preheat to 375 degrees. Cut aluminum foil to fit cookie sheets.

In a small, shallow bowl beat the reserved egg white with the water, beating only until mixed and barely foamy.

Place the chopped peanuts on a long piece of aluminum foil or wax paper.

Pick up a cookie and use your fingers to roll it around in the egg white and then place it on the chopped nuts. Next, roll it around in the nuts to coat the cookie thoroughly. Coat 4 or 5 cookies at a time. Place the nut-covered cookies 2 inches apart on the cut aluminum foil. Continue to prepare all of the cookies the same way.

Now, form a depression in the top of each cookie. Either do it with the handle end of a large wooden spoon or, if your fingernails are not too long, do it with your thumb. Either way it will probably be necessary to flour the end of the wooden spoon or your thumb to keep the dough from sticking. Make the depression rather deep and wide but not so deep that you make the bottom of the cookie too thin.

With a small, demitasse spoon or a ½ teaspoon-size measuring spoon, place a generous ½ teaspoonful of the peanut butter into each indentation.

Place about 5 or 6 chocolate morsels on the top of each cookie, pressing them slightly into the peanut butter.

Slide cookie sheets under the foil and bake the cookies for 12 to 13 minutes, reversing the sheets top to bottom and front to back once to insure even browning.

Let the cookies cool for a minute or two before removing them with a wide metal spatula to racks to cool.

When the cookies have reached room temperature place them in the refrigerator very briefly—only long enough to set the chocolate morsels.

NOTES: In place of the semisweet chocolate morsels you may, if you wish, use butterscotch morsels. Or use chocolate on half of the cookies and butterscotch on the others. Or you may use the midget-size morsels, in which case use as many as it takes to cover the peanut butter.

Don't worry about placing the morsels exactly in position because as the cookies spread in baking, the morsels will slide out over the tops and won't stay where you put them anyhow.

English Ginger-snaps #1

This is a classic recipe for large, dark, semisoft gingersnaps.

22 LARGE COOKIES

2¼ cups sifted all-purpose flour
2 teaspoons baking soda
½ teaspoon salt
1 teaspoon cinnamon
1 teaspoon ginger
½ teaspoon powdered cloves
¼ teaspoon allspice
¼ teaspoon finely ground black pepper
6 ounces (1½ sticks) butter
1 cup dark brown sugar, firmly packed
1 egg
¼ cup molasses
Granulated sugar (to roll the cookies in)
Optional: blanched almonds, halved, sliced, or coarsely chopped

Sift together the flour, baking soda, salt, cinnamon, ginger, cloves, allspice, and black pepper and set aside. In the large bowl of an electric mixer cream the butter. Add the brown sugar and beat well. Add the egg and the molasses and beat for a few minutes until the mixture is light in color. On low speed gradually add the sifted dry ingredients, scraping the bowl with a rubber spatula and beating only until incorporated.

Refrigerate the dough briefly (in the mixing bowl if you wish) until it can be handled; 10 to 15 minutes might be enough.

Adjust two racks to divide the oven into thirds and preheat to 375 degrees. Cut aluminum foil to fit cookie sheets.

Spread some granulated sugar on a large piece of wax paper. Use a rounded tablespoonful of dough for each cookie. Roll it into a ball between your hands, then roll it around in the granulated sugar, and place the balls 2½ to 3 inches apart on the cut aluminum foil.

Slide cookie sheets under the foil.

Bake the cookies for about 13 minutes, reversing the cookie sheets top to bottom and front to back once during baking to insure even browning. The cookies are done when they feel semifirm to the touch.

With a wide metal spatula transfer the cookies to racks to cool.

NOTE: If you wish, these cookies may be baked on unbuttered cookie sheets without the aluminum foil.

English Ginger- snaps #2

This is a variation of the previous recipe. These are made smaller, and are more crisp and gingery.

70 TO 80 COOKIES

Follow the recipe for English Gingersnaps #1 with the following changes: Use only 2 cups plus 2 tablespoons flour, increase the ginger to 2 teaspoons, use light brown sugar instead of dark brown, and stir in the finely grated rind of 1 small lemon and 1 orange.

Because of the slightly smaller amount of flour in this recipe the dough will need a bit more chilling time, and then it is best to work with one-fourth of the dough at a time and keep the remainder refrigerated.

Use one very slightly rounded teaspoonful of dough for each cookie, roll into balls, roll in sugar as above, and place the cookies about 1½ inches apart.

Bake for 10 to 12 minutes.

Italian Sesame Sticks

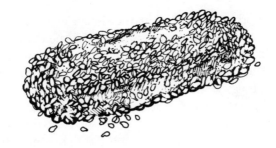

66 COOKIES

These are dry, light, crisp-crunchy, and plain. The recipe comes from a trattoria on Mulberry Street in New York's Little Italy. I had them with espresso as I watched the regulars dunk one after another in red wine.

4 cups sifted all-purpose flour
1 tablespoon plus 1 teaspoon double-acting
  baking powder
½ teaspoon salt
½ pound (2 sticks) butter
1 teaspoon vanilla extract
1 cup granulated sugar
3 eggs
Milk
About 10 ounces (2 cups) sesame seeds (use
  the seeds that are labeled "hulled" and are
  white in color)

Adjust two racks to divide the oven into thirds and preheat to 350 degrees. Cut several pieces of aluminum foil to fit cookie sheets and set aside.

Sift together the flour, baking powder, and salt and set aside. In the large bowl of an electric mixer cream the butter. Add the vanilla and sugar and beat very well. Add the eggs one at a time, scraping the bowl with a rubber spatula and beating until thoroughly incorporated after each addition. The mixture will look curdled at this point—it's O.K. On low speed gradually add the sifted dry ingredients, continuing to scrape the bowl and beating only until smooth.

Remove from the mixer and place the bowl of dough in the refrigerator, stirring occasionally for about 15 minutes only until the dough can be handled.

Meanwhile, pour some milk to a depth of approximately 1 inch in a small bowl. Also, spread the sesame seeds on a large piece of wax paper near you. And lightly flour a large cutting board.

Work with ½ cup of the dough at a time. Place it on the floured board. With lightly floured hands, roll the dough into a long, thin roll—it should be rolled until it is 20 inches long and about ¾ inch in diameter.

The dough is delicate; handle it gently. Cut the roll into pieces 2½ inches long. With one hand, transfer several of the pieces at a time to the milk. Then, with the other hand (see Notes), lift them out and place them on the seeds, rolling them to coat thoroughly. Finally place the cookies at least 1 inch apart on the cut aluminum foil. Repeat with remaining dough.

Slide cookie sheets under the foil. Bake for 20 minutes or until the sticks are golden brown—do not overbake. Reverse the sheets top to bottom and front to back once to insure even browning. If you bake one sheet at a time, use the upper rack.

With a wide metal spatula transfer the cookies to racks to cool.

NOTES: The directions for using one hand for dipping the cookies in milk and the other for rolling them in the seeds are a trick I learned from a restaurant chef. For any breading procedure, if you use one hand for wet and the other for dry, you will find it much more efficient than using both hands for both steps. It takes a bit of practice to get used to it, but then you will not have to stop and wash your hands every few minutes. And, in this case, if you don't do it this way, you will waste a lot of the seeds in the milk.

Any seeds that are left over on the wax paper, even if they are wet from the milk, should not be thrown away. Place them in a small shallow pan in a moderate oven, shake them occasionally, and bake until they are dry and golden brown. Reserve them to use for other cookies that call for toasted sesame seeds (or sprinkle them on salads or vegetables).

Et Cetera

CRAIG CLAIBORNE'S CHOCOLATE
    MACAROONS
ALMOND MACAROONS
FUDGE DELICES
CHOCOLATE MERINGUE LADYFINGERS
CHOCOLATE TARTLETS
ALMOND TARTLETS
CONNECTICUT DATE SLICES
CONNECTICUT STRIPPERS
FRENCH SUGAR FANS
SWEDISH FRIED TWISTS
BASLER BRUNSLI
HAZELNUT RUSKS
BLACK-AND-WHITE RUSKS
PALM ISLAND BRANDY SNAPS
MARSHMALLOWS
CHEESE PENNIES

A variety of recipes that do not fit into any of the previous categories and might call for some special equipment.

Craig Claiborne's Chocolate Macaroons

24 MACAROONS   *Hip hip hooray and three cheers for Craig for creating these sensational macaroons—they are moist, soft, dark, bittersweet, and very elegant. You will need a pastry bag fitted with a large star-shaped tube.*

> 5 ounces (1 cup) almonds, blanched or
>   unblanched
> 2 ounces (2 squares) unsweetened chocolate
> ¾ cup granulated sugar
> 5 liquid ounces egg whites (3–5 eggs,
>   depending on size)
> ½ teaspoon almond extract
> 12 glacéed cherries, cut into halves

Adjust a rack to the center of the oven and preheat to 400 degrees. Line a 12-by-15½-inch cookie sheet with aluminum foil.

Grind the almonds to a powder (they must be fine) in a nut grinder, a blender, or a food processor. Place the ground almonds in a large, heavy frying pan. Now grind the chocolate; the whole squares may be ground in a nut grinder, or the chocolate may be chopped coarsely and then ground in a blender or food processor. Add the ground chocolate to the almonds. Add the sugar and egg whites. Stir to mix—it will be a thick mixture.

Place the frying pan over medium heat and, with a wooden or rubber spatula, stir constantly, scraping the bottom and sides. The heat will melt the chocolate and sugar, which will cause the mixture to become a little thinner. Then, as the egg whites start to cook, the mixture will begin to thicken. Do not let the mixture boil, and be careful that it does not burn. The mixture should cook, stirred constantly, until it starts to thicken to the consistency of soft mashed potatoes—it should take about 5 minutes altogether.

Remove from the heat and transfer to a bowl in order to stop the cooking. Add the almond extract, and stir occasionally for about 10 minutes until the mixture is tepid.

It is best to use a pastry bag about 12 inches long (although you may use a larger one). And it is best to use a #8 star tube (although you may use one slightly smaller if necessary). Insert the tube in the bag. Fold down a deep cuff on the outside of the bag. Place the bag in a tall, narrow glass or jar in order to hold it upright. Transfer the dough to the bag. Unfold the cuff and twist the top of the bag closed.

Hold the bag over the foil-lined cookie sheet. Press from the top of the bag to press out rosettes of the dough about 1 inch in diameter, shaping them moderately high and placing them ½ to 1 inch apart. (If the mixture was cooked long enough in the frying pan, these will not spread in baking. If it was cooked too long, the dough will be stiff and difficult to press through the pastry bag.)

Place half of a glacéed cherry, cut side down, on each macaroon.

Bake for 12 to 13 minutes, reversing the cookie sheet front to back once to insure even baking. The macaroons will feel dry to the touch but they will be soft and flexible. Do not overbake—these must remain soft and moist inside.

Slide the foil off the cookie sheet and let stand for 5 to 10 minutes. Then, with a wide metal spatula, remove the macaroons and transfer them to racks to finish cooling.

Almond Macaroons

These are classic French macaroons—soft and chewy. They are formed with a pastry bag and a large star-shaped tube. They may be made without an electric mixer.

28 MACAROONS

8 ounces (1⅔ cups) blanched almonds
⅔ cup granulated sugar
½ cup egg whites (3–4 eggs, depending on size)
½ teaspoon almond extract
14 glacéed cherries, cut into halves, or about 3 tablespoons slivered (julienne-shaped) blanched almonds

Adjust two racks to divide the oven into thirds and preheat to 350 degrees. Line two cookie sheets with aluminum foil and set aside.

The almonds must be ground to a very fine powder. They may be ground in a nut grinder, a blender, or a food processor. If they are ground in a blender they will probably become oily and lumpy—if so they must be strained to aerate them; place a large strainer over a large bowl and, with your fingertips, force the nuts through the strainer.

Place the ground nuts and the sugar in a medium-size mixing bowl and stir them together until they are thoroughly mixed.

Beat the egg whites until they hold a firm shape and are stiff but not dry, adding the almond extract toward the end of the beating. Fold the whites into the ground almond and sugar mixture.

Fit a 12-inch pastry bag with a #8 star-shaped tube. Fold down a deep cuff on the outside of the bag. Support the bag by placing it in a tall, narrow glass or jar. Place the macaroon mixture in the bag and, quickly, before the mixture runs out through the tube, unfold the cuff, twist the top of the bag closed, and turn the bag tube end up.

Hold the bag at a right angle to a foil-lined sheet. Press from the top of the bag to press out rosettes of the dough 1½ to 1¾ inches in diameter, placing them 1 inch apart.

Top each macaroon with a glacéed cherry half or a few pieces of slivered almonds.

Bake for about 20 minutes, until the macaroons are lightly colored. Reverse the sheets top to bottom and front to back as necessary to insure even browning. These are more attractive if they are not too pale, but do not overbake. They should be a golden color on the ridges and the edges, but they may still be pale between the ridges.

Slide the foil off the cookie sheets and let stand for about 5 minutes. Then peel the foil away from the backs of the macaroons and transfer them to racks to finish cooling.

Fudge Délices

23 COOKIES

A fancy French recipe, buttery shells filled with dark baked-in fudge. It is necessary to have small French tartlet pans for these. The recipe is written for 23 (see Note) plain round pans measuring 2¼ inches across the top and ⅜ inch in depth. These are generally available at specialty kitchen-equipment stores. You will also need a plain round 2¾-inch cookie cutter.

PASTRY

1 cup sifted all-purpose flour
¼ teaspoon double-acting baking powder
¼ teaspoon salt
2⅔ ounces (5⅓ tablespoons) cold butter, cut into ½- to 1-inch slices
1 extra-large or jumbo egg

Into a mixing bowl sift together the flour, baking powder, and salt. Then, with a pastry blender, cut the butter into the dry ingredients until the particles are fine and the mixture resembles coarse meal.

In a small bowl beat the egg lightly just to mix, and stir it into the flour mixture. Turn the dough out onto a large board or smooth work surface. Flour your hands. Form the dough into a ball. (The dough will be sticky—use a dough scraper or a wide metal spatula when necessary to remove it from the work surface.) With the heel of your hand, break off small amounts of the dough (about 2 tablespoons at a time), pushing it away from you against the work surface. Re-form the dough into a ball and, if it is not completely smooth and well blended, push it off again. Re-form the dough and flatten it slightly.

Place the dough on a floured pastry cloth and turn it over to flour both sides. With a floured rolling pin, roll the dough until it is 1/16 inch thick —that's *very* thin. While rolling, occasionally roll the dough up on the pin and then unroll it with the other side down in order to keep both sides floured. (Reflour the cloth as necessary, but lightly.)

With a plain round 2¾-inch cookie cutter, cut 23 rounds (see Note).

Put the pastry rounds into the tartlet pans and press them gently into place. Arrange the lined pans on a jelly-roll pan or a large cookie sheet.

Adjust a rack one-third up from the bottom of the oven and preheat to 350 degrees.

Prepare the following filling.

FILLING

6 ounces (1 cup) semisweet chocolate morsels
⅓ cup granulated sugar
1 tablespoon butter
1 tablespoon milk
1 teaspoon vanilla extract
1 extra-large or jumbo egg
23 pecan halves

Partially melt the chocolate in the top of a small double boiler, covered, over hot water on moderate heat. Uncover and stir until the chocolate is completely melted and smooth. Add the sugar, butter, milk, and vanilla. Stir until the butter is melted and then remove the top of the double boiler from the heat.

In a small bowl beat the egg just to mix and, *very gradually*, stir it into the chocolate mixture.

Place a slightly rounded teaspoonful of the filling in each pastry shell. They will be only about ⅓ to ½ full, but the filling will rise during baking.

Place a pecan half on the top of each tartlet.

Bake for 22 to 25 minutes, reversing the jelly-roll pan or cookie sheet once to insure even browning. Bake until the pastry is barely colored. Do not overbake—the filling should remain slightly chewy.

Cool the tartlets in the pans for about 10 minutes, and then, with your fingers, remove them from the pans and place them on racks to finish cooling.

NOTE: Twenty-three is a strange number of cookies to make but I like the filling to be generous. If you make 24, the filling is a little too shallow—and if you make 22, it's a little too deep. But 23 is just right.

Chocolate Meringue Lady-fingers

36 COOKIES

Dry, crisp meringue in the shape of ladyfingers. This is a classic French recipe. You will need a candy thermometer, a 15-inch pastry bag fitted with a plain round ½-inch tube, and an electric mixer with both a large and a small bowl.

1¼ cups sifted or strained confectioners sugar
⅓ cup unsweetened cocoa
⅓ cup water
1 cup granulated sugar
½ cup egg whites (3–4 eggs, depending on size)
Pinch of salt
1 teaspoon vanilla extract

Adjust two racks to divide the oven into thirds and preheat to 275 degrees. Line two 12-by-15½-inch cookie sheets with aluminum foil, placing the foil shiny side up.

Sift together the confectioners sugar and cocoa and set aside.

Place the water and the granulated sugar in a 3-cup saucepan (that's a very small one and it should preferably be narrow and deep instead of shallow and wide, or the thermometer will not register accurately because it might not be deep enough in the syrup). With a small wooden spatula stir over high heat until the granulated sugar is dissolved and the mixture comes to a full boil. Place a candy thermometer in the saucepan and let the mixture boil without stirring over high heat until the thermometer registers 240 degrees (the soft-ball stage).

Meanwhile, place the egg whites and the salt in the small bowl of an electric mixer. When the sugar syrup is almost ready, start to beat the whites at high speed and beat until they are very stiff.

When the sugar syrup is ready, with the beater still going at high speed, *very* gradually add the syrup to the whites. The syrup must be added in a thin, slow stream. After the syrup has all been added, beat in the vanilla and continue to beat for a few minutes more.

Then transfer the mixture to the large bowl of the electric mixer and continue to beat for several minutes until the mixture is cool and stiff. On lowest speed gradually add the sifted dry ingredients, scraping the bowl with a rubber spatula and beating as little as possible, *only* until incorporated. *Do not overbeat* or you will lose the air that has been beaten into the egg whites.

Place a plain tube with a ½-inch opening into a 15-inch pastry bag. Fold down about 4 inches of the top of the bag to form a deep cuff on the outside. Support the bag by placing it in a tall narrow glass or an empty jar so that it stands upright while you fill it. Use a rubber spatula to transfer all of the meringue to the bag. Lift up the cuff and twist the top closed.

Pressing from the top, force the batter through the bag to form the ladyfingers on the foil-lined sheets. Make the cookies 3 to 3½ inches long and ¾ inch wide.

Bake 30 to 35 minutes, reversing the sheets top to bottom and front to back once to insure even baking. Turn off the oven heat, open the oven door slightly (if necessary insert something to hold the door open 2 or 3 inches), and let the meringues stand until they are completely cool.

Slide the foil off the sheets. With your fingers gently peel the foil away from the cookies.

When you bite into one of these you will find it slightly hollow in the center—correct.

Chocolate Tartlets

60 TO 75 TINY
TARTLETS

These are tiny cookie cups with a baked-in chewy chocolate filling. To make these dainty French cookies it is necessary to use very small, shallow individual tartlet molds; they may be plain or fluted. Mine are French; they are assorted shapes and they vary in diameter from about 1 to 2 inches. There are Scandinavian ones, generally a little larger, made for Sandbakelser cookies—they may be used for these tartlets. Or you may use plain round, shallow French tartlet pans about 2 to 2½ inches in diameter and ½ inch deep. These little pans should be washed with only hot soapy water; anything rougher would cause the cookies to stick. Don't make these if you are in a hurry; they take time.

FILLING

4 ounces (generous ¾ cup) blanched almonds
6 ounces (1 cup) semisweet chocolate morsels
2 eggs
1 teaspoon instant coffee
¼ teaspoon almond extract
½ cup granulated sugar

In a blender or a nut grinder, grind together the almonds and the chocolate—these must be ground fine. (In a blender it will probably be best to do it in two batches, using half of the nuts and half of the chocolate in each batch.) Set aside.

In the small bowl of an electric mixer at high speed beat the eggs for about 5 minutes until very thick and pale in color. On low speed mix in the coffee, almond extract, and sugar, and then gradually beat in the ground almond-chocolate mixture. Transfer to a small, shallow bowl for ease in handling and set aside at room temperature.

PASTRY

6 ounces (1½ sticks) butter
Scant ¼ teaspoon salt

1 teaspoon vanilla extract
½ cup granulated sugar
2 cups sifted all-purpose flour

In the large bowl of an electric mixer (with clean beaters) cream the butter. Mix in the salt, vanilla, and sugar, and then gradually add the flour, scraping the bowl as necessary with a rubber spatula. The mixture will be crumbly. Turn it out onto a board or smooth work surface. Squeeze it between your hands until it holds together. Then, with the heel of your hand, break off small pieces of dough (about 2 tablespoonfuls at a time), pushing away from you on the work surface. Form the dough into a ball. If it is not completely smooth break it again.

Adjust a rack one-third up from the bottom of the oven and preheat to 350 degrees.

With your fingertips press a small amount of the dough into each tartlet mold (the molds do not have to be buttered). The pastry shell should be ¼ inch thick or a little less, and it should be level with the rim of the mold—use your fingertip to remove excess dough above the rim.

Place the molds on a cookie sheet or a jelly-roll pan. With a demitasse spoon or a small measuring spoon, place some of the filling in each shell. The filling may be mounded a bit above the edges but only a very little bit or it will run over. It is not necessary to smooth the filling, as it will run slightly and smooth itself as it bakes.

Bake for 20 minutes until the pastry is barely colored. Reverse the cookie sheet or jelly-roll pan front to back once to insure even browning. Do not overbake these or the filling will be dry instead of chewy.

Remove from the oven and let stand until just cool enough to handle. Then invert each mold into the palm of your hand and, with a fingernail of the other hand, gently release and remove the mold.

NOTE: If you do not have enough molds to bake these all at once the remaining pastry and filling may wait at room temperature.

Almond Tartlets

60 TO 70 TINY
TARTLETS

These fancy petit-four-type cookies are similar to Chocolate Tartlets, but these have an almond filling instead of chocolate and a different pastry. These are made in the same tartlet pans (see introduction to Chocolate Tartlets).

FILLING

5 ounces (1 cup) blanched almonds
2 eggs
½ teaspoon almond extract
½ cup granulated sugar

In a nut grinder, a blender, or a food processor, grind the almonds. They must be dry and powdery. If you use a blender the nuts might form oily lumps. If so, with your fingertips press the ground nuts through a large strainer set over a large bowl in order to aerate the nuts and break up any oily lumps. Any pieces too large to go through the strainer should be stirred into the strained nuts. Set aside.

In the small bowl of an electric mixer beat the eggs until foamy. Add the almond extract and then gradually add the sugar. Beat at high speed for about 7 minutes, until the mixture is almost white and forms ribbons when the beaters are raised. On low speed stir in the ground almonds. Set aside at room temperature.

PASTRY

½ pound (2 sticks) butter
⅛ teaspoon salt
1 teaspoon vanilla extract
½ cup granulated sugar
1 egg
2 cups sifted all-purpose flour

In the large bowl of an electric mixer cream the butter. Add the salt, vanilla, and sugar and beat well. Beat in the egg. On low speed add the flour, scraping the bowl with a rubber spatula and beating until the mixture is smooth and holds together.

Adjust a rack one-third up from the bottom of the oven and preheat to 350 degrees.

To line the molds with the dough (do not butter them), use a demitasse spoon or a small measuring spoon to place some of the dough in a mold. With the back of the spoon or with your fingertips spread the dough to make a layer ¼ to ⅓ inch thick. Don't worry about making the thickness exactly even but do make the top edge level with the top of the mold. Line all of the molds and place them on a cookie sheet or a jelly-roll pan.

Now, with a small spoon, put the filling into the lined molds, mounding it slightly higher than the rims. If the almonds in the filling have sunk to the bottom, stir lightly to mix before spooning into mold.

Bake for 20 to 25 minutes, until the crust is golden and the filling is well browned. Carefully reverse the position of the pan front to back once to insure even browning.

Remove from the oven and let stand for 5 minutes. Then, with your fingertips, carefully remove the cookies from the molds and place them on racks to finish cooling.

NOTE: If you do not have enough molds to bake these all at once, the remaining pastry and filling may wait at room temperature. The molds do not have to be washed and dried if they are to be re-used right away, but they must be cool.

VARIATIONS: Coarsely chop about ⅓ cup candied cherries or pineapple and place a few pieces in each pastry-lined form before adding the filling.

Place the racks of baked cookies over a large piece of wax paper. With your fingertips press confectioners sugar through a fine strainer held over the cookies to coat them generously.

Connecticut Date Slices

44 SLICES

A *prize-winning old New England recipe. These are moist, fruity, and sharply spiced.*

1 tablespoon instant coffee
½ cup boiling water
3 cups sifted all-purpose flour
1 teaspoon baking soda
½ teaspoon salt
1 teaspoon ground cloves
1 teaspoon cinnamon
½ teaspoon mustard powder
¼ pound (1 stick) butter
1 cup granulated sugar
½ cup molasses
1 egg
8 ounces (1 cup) pitted dates, coarsely cut
3 ounces (⅔ cup) raisins

Adjust two racks to divide the oven into thirds and preheat to 350 degrees. Line two 12-by-15½-inch cookie sheets with aluminum foil.

Dissolve the instant coffee in the boiling water and set aside.

Sift together the flour, baking soda, salt, cloves, cinnamon, and mustard and set aside. In the large bowl of an electric mixer cream the butter. Add the sugar and beat well. Beat in the molasses and then the egg and beat until smooth. Beat in the dates and raisins, then on lowest speed add the sifted dry ingredients in three additions with the prepared coffee in two additions, scraping the bowl as necessary with a rubber spatula and beating only until smooth after each addition.

Form two strips of the dough lengthwise on each foil-lined cookie sheet as follows: Use one-fourth of the dough, or about 1¼ cups, for each strip. Place heaping teaspoonfuls of the dough touching each other to form an even strip 14 inches long, 2 inches wide, and 1 inch deep. Leave 3 to 4 inches of space between the two strips. With a small metal spatula or a table knife smooth the strips slightly on the sides and top—they will flatten and spread a bit during baking.

Bake for 25 to 30 minutes, until the tops spring back when lightly pressed with a fingertip. Reverse the cookie sheets top to bottom and front to back to insure even browning.

While the cakes are baking prepare the following glaze.

GLAZE

*½ cup plus 2 tablespoons confectioners
  sugar
2 teaspoons soft butter
¼ teaspoon vanilla extract
2 tablespoons milk*

Mix all of the ingredients in a small bowl until completely smooth. The glaze should have the consistency of a medium-thick cream sauce; if necessary adjust it with a bit more milk or sugar. Cover the glaze airtight until you are ready to use it.

When the cakes are done slide the foil off the cookie sheets and let them stand for only a minute or so until they can be transferred (do not let them cool). Then, using a cookie sheet as a spatula, transfer the cakes to large racks. Using a pastry brush, immediately brush the glaze over the hot cakes.

If the cooling racks are not raised enough from the work surface, steam will form and cause the bottom of the cakes to be wet. Raise the racks by placing them over right-side-up cake pans or mixing bowls in order to leave room for air to circulate underneath. Let the cakes cool completely.

Transfer the cooled cakes to a cutting board. With a very sharp, thin knife cut the cakes at an angle into 1- to 1¼-inch slices.

Connecticut Strippers

These are soft, moist fruit-and-nut strips, traditionally a Christmas treat.

2 cups sifted all-purpose flour
½ teaspoon baking soda
½ teaspoon salt
1½ teaspoons cinnamon
½ teaspoon nutmeg
5⅓ ounces (10⅔ tablespoons) butter
1 teaspoon vanilla extract
1 cup dark or light brown sugar, firmly packed
1 egg plus 1 egg yolk (reserve the white for
    the topping)
3½ ounces (1 cup) walnuts, cut into
    medium-size pieces
7½ ounces (1½ cups) currants

Sift together the flour, baking soda, salt, cinnamon, and nutmeg and set aside. In the large bowl of an electric mixer cream the butter. Add the vanilla and sugar and beat to mix well. Add the whole egg and egg yolk and beat until smooth. On low speed add the sifted dry ingredients, scraping the bowl with a rubber spatula and beating only until incorporated. Mix in the nuts and currants.

Place the bowl of dough in the refrigerator for about half an hour or until it is firm enough to handle.

Adjust two racks to divide the oven into thirds and preheat to 400 degrees. Line two 12-by-15½-inch cookie sheets with aluminum foil.

Generously flour a large board or smooth work surface. Divide the dough into quarters and work with one piece at a time. Flour your hands, form the piece of dough into a ball, and turn it over several times on the board to flour it on all sides. Then, with your hands, form the dough into a roll 13 inches long and place it lengthwise on one of the lined cookie sheets. Repeat with the remaining pieces of dough, placing two rolls on each sheet about 4 inches apart.

With floured fingertips press each roll of dough to flatten it to ½- to ¾-inch depth.

Prepare the topping.

TOPPING

2 tablespoons granulated sugar
½ teaspoon cinnamon
⅓ cup walnuts, finely chopped (see page 13)
1 egg white (reserved from dough)

Stir the sugar and cinnamon together to mix thoroughly. Stir in the nuts. In a small bowl beat the egg white until it is foamy, not stiff. Use a pastry brush to brush some of the beaten white generously over one strip of the dough. Sprinkle with one-fourth of the topping. Repeat the process with the remaining three strips of dough.

Bake for 12 to 15 minutes, reversing the cookie sheets top to bottom and front to back as necessary to insure even browning. Bake until the tops of the strips spring back when lightly pressed with a fingertip.

Slide the foil off the cookie sheets and let the strips stand for about 10 minutes. Then, with a wide metal spatula, release but do not remove the strips from the foil. Let them stand until completely cool. Then use a cookie sheet as a spatula to transfer the strips to a large cutting board.

With a sharp knife cut the strips at an angle into 1- to 1¼-inch slices.

French Sugar Fans

These wafers may be served as plain sugar cookies, or place two of them, points down, at angles into a portion of ice cream. The dough must chill for at least an hour before baking.

36 FANS

2 cups sifted all-purpose flour
1½ teaspoons double-acting baking powder
¼ teaspoon salt
5⅓ ounces (10⅔ tablespoons) butter
½ teaspoon vanilla extract
¾ cup granulated sugar
1 egg
4 teaspoons milk
Finely grated rind of 1 lemon
Additional granulated sugar for sprinkling
over the cookies

Sift together the flour, baking powder, and salt and set aside. In the large bowl of an electric mixer cream the butter. Beat in the vanilla and sugar. Add the egg and then the milk and lemon rind and beat well. On low speed gradually add the sifted dry ingredients, scraping the bowl with a rubber spatula and beating until the dough holds together.

Tear off four pieces of wax paper. Place one-fourth of the dough on each piece of paper. Wrap the dough and flatten it slightly. Refrigerate (do not chill in the freezer) for at least one hour.

Adjust two racks to divide the oven into thirds and preheat to 375 degrees. Cut aluminum foil to fit cookie sheets.

Flour a pastry cloth and a rolling pin very well. Work with one piece of the dough at a time, keeping the rest refrigerated. Work quickly before the dough softens. Place it on the floured cloth and turn it over several times to flour both sides. With the floured rolling pin, roll the dough into a circle ⅛ inch thick and slightly larger than 8 inches in diameter (reflour the pin as necessary).

Now you will need something as a pattern for cutting an 8-inch circle of dough; use a flan ring, a canister cover, or a cake pan turned upside down. Place the pattern on the dough and cut around it with a plain or fluted pastry wheel (the fluted wheel will give a rippled, fanlike appearance). Or, in place of the pastry wheel, a small, sharp knife may be used to cut a plain edge.

With a long knife cut the circle into eight pie-shaped wedges. If the blade sticks to the dough, flour it as necessary.

With the back (dull side) of a knife or the edge of a metal spatula, mark each cookie with five or six lines that radiate from the point to the outside curve—the lines should be deep but not deep enough to cut through the dough. Flour the knife or spatula as necessary to keep it from sticking.

With a wide metal spatula transfer the fans to the cut aluminum foil, placing them 1 inch apart. Sprinkle the fans with granulated sugar. Slide a cookie sheet under the foil.

Bake for 7 to 10 minutes (depending on the thickness of the dough), reversing the sheets top to bottom and front to back as necessary to insure even cooking. The fans should bake only until they are slightly colored. They should not be brown, but if they are underbaked they will be too soft.

With a wide metal spatula transfer the fans to racks to cool.

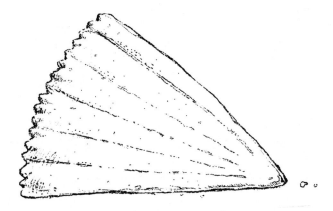

Swedish Fried Twists

30 VERY LARGE
TWISTS

*Most European countries have their own version of these sweet crackers.
And in China a similar recipe is called* Twisted Generals *(in honor of a
famous general who was crippled). In Poland they are called* Favorki *and
are traditionally made around Eastertime. In America they are known as*
Bow Ties, Knots, Christmas Crullers, *etc. They are light, dry, airy, and
extremely plain. These are generally served with coffee or wine, more
probably between meals than as an after-dinner sweet. You will need a
deep-frying thermometer and a pastry wheel.*

> Vegetable oil (for deep frying)
> 4 egg yolks (reserve 1 white to use later)
> ⅓ cup confectioners sugar
> 1 teaspoon ground cardamom
> Pinch of salt
> ¼ cup plus 1 tablespoon heavy cream
> 2 tablespoons cognac, brandy, or whiskey
> 1 egg white
> About 2¼ cups sifted all-purpose flour
> Additional confectioners sugar (for sprinkling
>   over the Fried Twists)

You will need a wide saucepan or a large, deep frying pan. Heat at least 2
inches of the oil in the pan over moderate heat. Insert a deep-frying thermometer and slowly bring the temperature to 365 degrees.

Meanwhile, prepare the dough. In the small bowl of an electric mixer
beat the egg yolks with the sugar, cardamom, and salt at high speed for
4 or 5 minutes until the mixture is very thick and light lemon-colored. On
low speed gradually add the cream and cognac, brandy, or whiskey, scraping the bowl with a rubber spatula and beating only until mixed.

Beat the egg white until it holds a firm shape and is stiff but not dry.
On low speed add the beaten white to the yolk mixture. Then, on low

speed, gradually add most of the flour, scraping the bowl with the spatula. When you have added enough flour to make a very thick mixture, remove the bowl from the mixer.

Spread the remaining flour out on a large board. Turn the dough out onto the flour. Using only as much flour as necessary to make a dough that is firm enough to knead, knead it on the floured board until it is very smooth and not sticky.

Cover the dough lightly with plastic wrap or with a kitchen towel and let stand for 15 minutes.

Then cut the dough in half. Work with one piece at a time. Set the other piece aside and cover it lightly.

On the floured board (no more flour than necessary), with a lightly floured rolling pin, roll the dough into an oblong ⅛ inch thick.

Using a ruler, and a plain or zigzag pastry wheel, cut the dough into strips 2 inches wide. Then cut across all the strips at once, so that each piece of dough is about 5 inches long, or a little less (see Note). Don't worry about any different-size pieces on the corners or ends—use them as they are.

Now, with the pastry wheel, cut a slit about 3 or 4 inches long length-wise down the middle of each piece of dough. Slip one end of the dough through the slit. (You may prepare them all before frying, or you may pull the end through each one just before you fry it.)

Adjust the heat as necessary to maintain the oil at 365 degrees. Fry only a few twists at a time; the number depends on the size of the pan—don't crowd them. Place a few of the twists in the oil, fry until golden brown on the bottoms, then with two flat wire whisks or slotted spoons or spatulas, turn them and fry until the cookies are golden brown on both sides. Drain on heavy brown paper.

When the twists are cool sprinkle the tops generously with confectioners sugar, pressing it with your fingertips through a strainer held over the twists.

Transfer them to a large platter or a deep bowl for serving.

NOTE: These directions are for very large twists. I do it that way because it is fun—and they look wild. But they may be made smaller, ¾ inch by 3 inches if you wish.

Basler
Brunsli

This is a classic Swiss recipe for unusual, mildly spiced macaroon-meringue bars. The cookies are baked about 5 hours after the meringue is mixed.

36 BARS

8 ounces (1⅔ cups) blanched almonds
1½ ounces (1½ squares) unsweetened chocolate
⅓ cup egg whites (2–3 eggs, depending on size)
Pinch of salt
1 cup granulated sugar
1 teaspoon cinnamon
¼ teaspoon powdered cloves
1 tablespoon kirsch
Additional granulated sugar for shaping the cookies

Line two 12-by-15½-inch cookie sheets with aluminum foil and set aside.

The almonds and chocolate must both be finely ground. It is best to use a food processor—or a nut grinder, the type that clamps onto the side of a table. (The ingredients go in the top, you turn a handle, and the ground ingredients come out the side—something like a meat grinder but not the same.) Or you may use a blender. But if you do the nuts may form oily lumps and if so they should be pressed with your fingertips through a large strainer set over a large bowl—to aerate them and break up the lumps. Any pieces that are too large to go through the strainer should be stirred back into the strained nuts. If chocolate is going to be ground in a blender it should first be chopped into coarse pieces. If you have a food processor you can grind both together.

In a large mixing bowl stir the ground almonds and chocolate to mix. Set aside.

In the small bowl of an electric mixer at moderate speed beat the egg whites with the salt until they become foamy and white. Beat in the sugar 1 tablespoon at a time, then the cinnamon, and cloves. Increase the speed to high and beat for 2 to 3 minutes until the mixture is stiff.

Remove the meringue from the mixer and fold in the kirsch. Then fold this into the almond mixture.

Spread about ⅓ cup of the additional sugar on a large board. It should cover a surface about 9 by 10 inches.

Place the meringue on the sugared surface. Sprinkle about 2 tablespoons of sugar over the top. With your fingertips pat the dough into an 8-by-9-inch rectangle ½ to ¾ inch thick. Use additional sugar if necessary to keep the dough from sticking to your fingers. Make the edges as even as possible. Let stand, uncovered, at room temperature for about an hour.

In order to cut neatly, mark the meringue with the tip of a small knife. Mark the 8-inch side into four 2-inch lengths and the 9-inch side into nine 1-inch lengths. Then use a long, thin, sharp knife to cut the meringue into 1-by-2-inch bars. If the meringue is sticky hold the knife under cold running water before making each cut—or coat the blade with sugar. Try both methods and see which works better for you.

With a wide metal spatula transfer the cookies to the prepared cookie sheets, placing the bars 1 inch apart. You may have to sugar or wet the spatula as you did the knife above.

Let the bars stand uncovered at room temperature for about 4 hours to dry out.

Adjust two racks to divide the oven into equal thirds and preheat to 350 degrees. Bake the cookies for 6 or 7 minutes, reversing the cookie sheets top to bottom and front to back once to insure even baking. Do not overbake—there should be a thin top and bottom crust but the middle must be soft. If you overbake the cookies they will lose their shape—the soft middle will run out on the sides.

With a wide metal spatula transfer the meringues to a rack to cool. When cool, these will be a light colored and crisp on the outside—dark, moist, and chewy on the inside.

Store airtight.

Hazelnut Rusks

This is an old German recipe. The rusks are hard, plain, dry, and crunchy.

ABOUT 78 RUSKS

3 cups sifted all-purpose flour
1 teaspoon double-acting baking powder
¼ teaspoon salt
3 extra-large or jumbo eggs
1¼ cups granulated sugar
½ teaspoon almond extract
12 ounces (2 generous cups) **blanched** hazelnuts (filberts), coarsely cut (see Note)

Adjust two racks to divide the oven into thirds and preheat to 350 degrees. Cut aluminum foil to fit two 12-by-15½-inch cookie sheets.

Sift together the flour, baking powder, and salt and set aside. In the small bowl of an electric mixer beat the eggs with the sugar at high speed for 12 to 15 minutes, until the mixture is almost white and forms a ribbon when the beaters are lifted. Beat in the almond extract.

Transfer the mixture to the large bowl of the electric mixer. On low speed add the dry ingredients, scraping the bowl with a rubber spatula and beating only until smooth. Fold in the nuts.

The dough will now be placed on the aluminum foil to form three strips, two on one piece of foil and one on the other. Place tablespoonfuls of the dough touching each other lengthwise on the foil. The strips should be 13 inches long, 2 to 3 inches wide, and about 1½ inches thick. The two strips that are both on one piece of foil should be about 3 inches apart. Place the dough carefully to make the strips rather even in shape but do not smooth over the tops or sides—they will run a bit in baking and will level themselves enough. Slide a cookie sheet under each piece of foil.

Bake the strips for 25 to 30 minutes, reversing them top to bottom and front to back to insure even browning. Bake until the strips are firm to the touch—they will remain pale in color. Remove the strips from the oven but do not turn off the heat.

Slide the foil off the cookie sheets. Let stand for 2 or 3 minutes. Place a folded towel or a pot holder in your left hand and invert a strip onto your hand. Peel away the foil and then turn the strip over and place it right side up on a cutting board. The strip will be hot and a little delicate so handle with care. Repeat with remaining strips. Let stand for a few minutes.

While strips are still slightly warm cut them with a finely serrated knife or a long, thin, very sharp slicing knife. Cut crosswise into ½-inch slices. These are best if they are no thicker.

Transfer the slices to the cookie sheets and place them upright with a bit of space between them.

Bake again at 350 degrees, reversing the position of the sheets again, for 10 minutes to dry the cookies. They will feel soft while hot but will become crisp when cool. If they are not crisp they should be baked longer—if they are thicker than ½ inch they might need a bit more baking —but do not overbake them or they will become too hard and dry.

When removed from the oven they may be left on the cookie sheets to cool.

NOTE: If blanched hazelnuts are not available buy the ones that have brown skins and blanch them yourself. To blanch hazelnuts: Spread the nuts in a single layer in a shallow pan. Bake at 350 degrees on the center rack for about 15 minutes or until the skins parch and begin to flake off. Then, working with a few at a time, place them on a coarse towel. Fold the towel over the nuts and rub vigorously. Most of the skin will come off. If a few little bits of skin remain on the nuts just leave them; it's O.K. Pick out the nuts and discard the skins.

Blanched almonds may be substituted for the hazelnuts but *do* try these sometime with hazelnuts—they're so good.

The nuts should be coarsely cut. For this recipe I find that chopping them on a board or in a bowl causes too many fine, small pieces. I prefer to cut them individually with a small paring knife, cutting each nut into halves or thirds.

Black-and-White Rusks

75 TO 80 RUSKS

This is German Mandelbrot or "Almond Bread," although it is not bread and there are no almonds in the recipe. The rusks are hard, plain, and dry.

3 cups sifted all-purpose flour
2 teaspoons double-acting baking powder
⅛ teaspoon baking soda (see Note)
¼ teaspoon salt
1 ounce (1 square) unsweetened chocolate
2 eggs
1 cup granulated sugar
1 teaspoon vanilla extract
¾ teaspoon almond extract
½ cup salad oil (not olive oil)
Finely grated rind of 1 large, deep-colored
    orange

Adjust two racks to divide the oven into thirds and preheat to 350 degrees. Line two cookie sheets with aluminum foil.

Sift together the flour, baking powder, baking soda, and salt and set aside. Melt the chocolate either in the top of a small double boiler or in a small, heat-proof cup set in shallow hot water over moderate heat, and then set the melted chocolate aside to cool.

In the large bowl of an electric mixer beat the eggs at high speed until foamy. Gradually add the sugar and continue to beat at high speed for a few minutes until pale in color. Beat in the vanilla and almond extracts. On low speed mix in one-third of the sifted dry ingredients, then all of the oil, and a second third of the dry ingredients. The mixture will be stiff; remove it from the mixer and use a wooden spatula to stir in the orange rind and the remaining third of the dry ingredients. Stir until thoroughly mixed.

Transfer ⅔ cup of the mixture to a mixing bowl and, with a wooden spatula, stir in the melted chocolate.

On a board, form the chocolate mixture with your hands into a thick roll 8 inches long. Cut the roll into quarters. On the board (it does not have to be floured), with your fingers, form each quarter into a thin roll 12 inches long. Set the chocolate rolls aside.

Now flour the board lightly (the white dough is a little sticky). Work with one-quarter (½ cup) of the white dough at a time. Flour your hands lightly and form the dough with your fingers into a roll 12 inches long. Then, on the floured board, using your fingers and the palms of your hands, flatten the dough until it is 2½ inches wide. Place one of the chocolate rolls lengthwise in the center of the white dough. With your fingers bring up both sides of the white dough to enclose the chocolate. Pinch the edges of the white dough together to seal.

Place the roll, seam down, lengthwise, on one of the foil-lined cookie sheets, allowing for two rolls on each sheet. Continue making the rolls, four altogether. With your hands, straighten them and shape them evenly.

Bake for 20 to 25 minutes, until lightly browned. Reverse the cookie sheets top to bottom and front to back once to insure even browning. Don't worry about the tops of the rolls cracking—that's O.K.

With a wide metal spatula transfer the baked rolls to a large cutting board. Do not turn off the oven.

Do not wait for the rolls to cool—slice the hot rolls at a sharp angle into ½-inch slices. (Try different knives to see which works best; I use a finely serrated knife.)

Return the slices, cut side down, to the foil-lined sheets. Then return the sheets to the 350-degree oven to bake the rusks until they are dry. Reverse the positions of the cookie sheets occasionally so that the cookies will dry evenly. Bake for about 15 minutes or until the rusks are only lightly colored—do not allow them to brown too much. They will become crisp as they cool.

Transfer the rusks to racks to cool.

NOTE: To measure ⅛ teaspoon, first measure ¼ teaspoon and then, with a small metal spatula or a table knife, cut away half and return to box.

Palm Island Brandy Snaps

40 COOKIES

These brittle ginger wafers are rolled, after baking, around the handle of a wooden spoon into a tube shape. The original recipe is from England. In old English books the directions are to fill the tubes with whipped cream (see directions below) and tie a thin satin ribbon around each tube. With the whipped-cream filling these cookies become an elegant dinner-party dessert. But, with or without the whipped cream and/or the ribbon, they are decorative cookies and fun to make. They are made without a mixer and are very easy although time-consuming since they are baked only five at a time.

½ cup sifted all-purpose flour
1½ teaspoons ginger
⅓ cup light molasses
¼ pound (1 stick) butter, cut into small bits
½ cup granulated sugar
1½ teaspoons brandy

Adjust a rack to the center of the oven and preheat to 325 degrees. Butter a 12-by-15½-inch cookie sheet.

Sift together the flour and ginger and set aside. Place the molasses, butter, and sugar in a heavy 2-quart saucepan over moderate heat. Stir until the butter is melted and the mixture is only warm, not hot. Remove from the heat. Add the sifted dry ingredients and stir well until completely smooth—if necessary, beat with a wire whisk. Stir in the brandy. Transfer the mixture to a small bowl for ease in handling. (The mixture will be thin; it will thicken slightly as it stands.)

Use 1 level teaspoonful of the mixture for each cookie. Place them on the buttered sheet, placing only 5 cookies on the sheet—these spread and they need plenty of room. Bake only one sheet at a time.

Bake for about 8 minutes or until lightly brown. Reverse the sheet front to back once during baking to insure even browning. (The baked cookies will have a mottled texture.)

Remove the sheets from the oven and let stand for 1½ to 2 minutes until a cookie can be removed without losing its shape. If the cookies have run together, use a small, sharp knife to cut them apart before removing them from the sheet.

Now work quickly before the cookies cool and harden. With a wide metal spatula loosen one side of a cookie and then, with your fingers, quickly but carefully peel the cookie away from the sheet and place it face down on a board or smooth work surface. Immediately place the handle of a wooden spoon (it must be round) at the closest edge of the cookie and roll the cookie loosely around the handle to form a tube. (If you roll the cookie too tightly around the spoon handle it will be difficult to slide it off.) Immediately slide the cookie off the handle, place it on the board or work surface to cool, and continue to shape the remaining cookies while they are warm. (If the tubes collapse and do not hold their round hollow shapes, they were removed from the cookie sheet too soon—they may be opened and rerolled while they are still warm. Or, if they have already become crisp, they may be replaced briefly in the oven to soften so they can be opened and rerolled. If the cookies cool and harden before they are rolled, replace them in the oven briefly only until they soften. If they are not completely crisp when cool, they were not baked long enough.)

It is not necessary to cool, wash or wipe, or rebutter the cookie sheet before placing another batch of cookies on it.

As soon as the cookies have cooled, store them airtight or they may become sticky.

NOTE: If you plan to serve these filled with whipped cream and would like a wider tube to make room for more cream, the cookies may be rolled around something about 1 inch in diameter. Metal tubes made for cannoli (Italian pastries) are about 1 inch in diameter and are generally available in specialty kitchen-equipment shops. Or you can use a piece of wooden doweling cut about 6 to 7 inches long.

DIRECTIONS FOR FILLING BRANDY SNAPS WITH WHIPPED CREAM

You will need a pastry bag (preferably a canvas bag with a waterproof or plastic coating on the inside) and a star-shaped tube with about a ½-inch opening, but that may vary depending on the size of the cookies. Insert the tube in the bag. Fold down the top of the bag to make a deep cuff on the outside of the bag. Set aside.

The bowl and beaters for whipping the cream should be chilled ahead of time. The amount of cream needed will depend on the size of the cookies. However, plan on about 2 cups of cream (before whipping) to fill one recipe of Brandy Snaps. To flavor 2 cups of whipping cream use ½ cup confectioners sugar and 2 teaspoons vanilla extract. Place the cream, sugar, and vanilla in the chilled bowl and, with the chilled beaters, whip the cream only until it holds a shape—if it is too stiff it will curdle as it is pressed through the pastry bag and tube.

Fill the pastry bag with the whipped cream and then unfold the cuff. Twist the top of the bag closed and press gently to force the cream to the opening of the tube.

Hold a Brandy Snap in one hand and with the other hand hold the pastry bag, inserting the tube a little way into the opening of the Brandy Snap. Press gently from the top of the pastry bag to fill one side of the cookie, forming a rosette at the opening. Then turn the cookie around and fill the other side, form a rosette, and place carefully on a tray. Continue filling the Brandy Snaps.

These may be refrigerated for a very short time (no more than 1 hour), but as the filled cookies stand in the refrigerator they will become less crisp. It is best to freeze them if they must stand for even a short time. And then serve them directly from the freezer. (The cookies may be made way ahead of time and stored airtight or frozen—if they are frozen they must not be exposed to the air until completely thawed. Then, if they are filled shortly before dinner and refrozen for only an hour or so, they will be at their best for serving.)

Chopped ginger, either the candied kind or the preserved, drained, is often added to the whipped cream—a few spoonfuls, to taste. But it must be chopped very fine or it will clog the pastry tube.

Marsh-mallows

1 POUND, 10 OUNCES
OF MARSHMALLOWS

These are candy—not cookies. But homemade marshmallows are so very popular and such fun to make that I want to share the recipe with you. You will need a candy thermometer and an electric mixer. And the cooked marshmallow mixture must stand for 8 to 12 hours (or a little longer if it is more convenient) before it is cut into individual pieces.

Vegetable shortening (such as Crisco), for
    preparing the pan
1 cup cold water
3 tablespoons (3 envelopes) unflavored
    gelatin
2 cups granulated sugar
¾ cup light corn syrup
¼ teaspoon salt
1½ teaspoons vanilla extract
Confectioners sugar (for coating the
    marshmallows)

Prepare a 9-by-13-by-2-inch pan as follows. Invert the pan. Cut a piece of aluminum foil long enough to cover the bottom and sides of the pan. Place the foil over the inverted pan and fold down the sides and corners just to shape. Remove the foil and turn the pan right side up. Place the foil in the pan and press it gently into place. With a pastry brush or crumpled wax paper coat the foil thoroughly but lightly with vegetable shortening. Set aside.

Place ½ cup of the cold water (reserve remaining ½ cup) in the large bowl of an electric mixer. Sprinkle the gelatin over the surface of the water and set aside.

Place the sugar, corn syrup, salt, and reserved ½ cup water in a heavy 1½- to 2-quart saucepan over moderately low heat. Stir until the sugar is dissolved and the mixture comes to a boil. Cover for 3 minutes to allow any sugar crystals on the sides of the saucepan to dissolve. Uncover, raise the heat to high, insert a candy thermometer, and let the syrup boil without stirring until the temperature reaches 240 degrees. Do not overcook. Remove from the heat.

Beating constantly at medium speed, pour the syrup slowly into the gelatin mixture. After all the syrup has been added, increase the speed to high and beat for 15 minutes until the mixture is lukewarm, snowy white, and the consistency of whipped marshmallow, adding the vanilla a few minutes before the end of the beating. (During the beating, occasionally scrape the bowl with a rubber spatula. The marshmallow will thicken and become sticky—if the mixture crawls up on the beaters as it thickens, carefully wipe it down with a rubber spatula.)

Pour the slightly warm and thick marshmallow mixture into the prepared pan and, with your forefinger, scrape all the mixture off the beaters. Smooth the top of the marshmallow.

Let stand uncovered at room temperature for 8 to 12 hours or a little longer if it is more convenient.

Then, sift or strain confectioners sugar generously onto a large cutting board to cover a surface larger than the 9-by-13-inch pan. Invert the marshmallow over the sugared surface. Remove the pan and peel off the foil. Strain confectioners sugar generously over the top of the marshmallow.

To cut the marshmallow into even 1-inch strips, use a ruler and toothpicks to mark it every 1 inch.

Prepare a long, heavy, sharp knife by brushing the blade lightly with vegetable shortening. Cutting down firmly with the full length of the blade, cut the marshmallow into 1-inch strips. (After cutting the first slice, just keep the blade sugared to keep it from sticking.)

Dip the cut sides of each strip into confectioners sugar to coat them thoroughly—you should have enough excess sugar on the board to do this.

Now cut each strip into 1-inch squares. (You may place three strips together and cut through them all at once.) Roll the marshmallows in the sugar to coat the remaining cut sides. Shake off excess sugar.

Store in a plastic box or any airtight container—or in a plastic bag like the commercial marshmallows.

NOTE: An interesting little aside about marshmallows. I gave this recipe to a friend who is a high-school home-economics teacher. She was ecstatic about it and taught it in all of her classes. She started each class by asking her students to write down the ingredients they thought were in marshmallows. No one knew. The guesses included egg whites, milk, cream, flour, cornstarch, and some said "marsh" or "mallow," which they thought was a natural substance that grows on trees.

But they soon found out, and my friend tells me that it is the single most popular recipe she has ever taught, and that now there are hundreds of girls in Miami Beach who make marshmallows regularly.

Cheese Pennies

55 TO 60 CRACKERS

This is not a cookie—it is a cheese cracker to serve with cocktails, or at the table with soup or salad. They are thin, light, crisp, and I make them quite sharp with cayenne. The procedure is the same as for making icebox cookies—the dough must be refrigerated for several hours or longer.

1 cup sifted all-purpose flour
½ teaspoon salt
⅛ to ½ teaspoon cayenne pepper (see Notes)
½ pound extra-sharp cheddar cheese
¼ pound (1 stick) butter
3 tablespoons sesame seeds (see Notes)

Sift together the flour, salt, and cayenne pepper and set aside.

Grate the cheese as fine as possible.

In the large bowl of an electric mixer cream the butter. Add the grated cheese and beat until thoroughly blended. On low speed gradually add the sifted dry ingredients and beat, scraping the bowl with a rubber spatula, until thoroughly incorporated.

Spread a bit of flour lightly on a board and turn the dough out onto the floured board. Flour your hands lightly. With your hands shape the dough as for icebox cookies into a round or square shape about 8 inches long and 1¾ to 2 inches in diameter.

Wrap the roll in plastic wrap or wax paper and place it in the refrigerator (not the freezer—if the dough is frozen it will be difficult to slice).

Let stand in the refrigerator for at least several hours, or several days if you wish.

Any time before baking the crackers, toast the sesame seeds as follows: Spread them in a small, shallow pan and place the pan in the middle of a preheated 350-degree oven. Shake the pan occasionally until the seeds have turned golden brown—it will take 15 to 20 minutes. Set aside to cool. (Toasting brings out the nutlike flavor of the seeds.)

When ready to bake the crackers, adjust two racks to divide the oven into thirds and preheat to 350 degrees.

Unwrap the roll of dough and place it on a cutting board. With a very sharp knife cut slices ⅛ to ¼ inch thick (I like these thin) and place them 1½ to 2 inches apart on unbuttered cookie sheets.

Sprinkle the tops of the slices generously with the toasted sesame seeds.

Bake for 12 to 15 minutes, until the pennies are lightly colored. Reverse the sheets top to bottom and front to back as necessary to insure even browning. They must bake long enough to be very crisp, but overbaking will burn the cheese and spoil the flavor.

These crackers must be removed from the sheets as soon as they are taken out of the oven. Use a wide metal spatula to loosen all the crackers from the sheet quickly and then transfer them to racks to cool.

Store airtight.

NOTES: I like these crackers sharp and spicy—I use ½ teaspoon cayenne. With ⅛ teaspoon they will have a good flavor but will be mild, ¼ teaspoon will make them warm, ½ teaspoon will make them hot, but for hot-hot, you may want to use even more. Be your own judge about how much to use.

There are white sesame seeds (hulled) and grayish-tan ones (unhulled) —use the white ones.

Index

Texas Cowboy Bars, 112–13
thermometer, oven, 9
Tijuana Fiesta Cookies, 68–9
timing, 15
Tropical Sour-Cream Cookies, 176–7
24-Karat Cookies, 40

Uppåkra Cookies, 186–7

Vanilla Butter Wafers, 70
vanilla sugar, 217
Viennese Almond Wafers, 170–1
Viennese Chocolate Cookies, 174–5
Viennese Chocolate-Walnut Bars, 84–5
Viennese Linzer Cookies, 116–18
Viennese Marzipan Bars, 120–2

wafers
    Arrowroot, from Bermuda, 184–5
    Date-Nut, 44–5
    Hot Butter, 181–2
    Lemon Walnut, 45–6
    Norman Rockwell's Oatmeal, 61–2
    Poppy-Seed, 67–8
    Praline, 46–7
    Santa Fe Chocolate, 20–1
    Swedish Rye, 157–8

Vanilla Butter, 70
Viennese Almond, 170–1
Whole-Wheat Honey, 160–1
walnut cookies
    Austrian Walnut Crescents, 228–9
    Butterscotch Walnut Bars, 104–5
    Chocolate Aggies, 213–14
    Chocolate Mint Sticks, 80–1
    "Chocolate Street" Cookies, 21–2
    Cream-Cheese Brownies, 76–8
    Florida Cream-Cheese Squares, 93–4
    Fudge Brownies, 78–9
    Hungarian Walnut Bars, 102–3
    Lemon Walnut Wafers, 45–6
    Norman Rockwell's Oatmeal Wafers,
        61–2
    Nut-Tree Walnut Jumbles, 49
    Oatmeal Icebox Cookies, 140–1
    Supremes, 86–7
    see also fruit-nut cookies; nut cookies
walnuts, as substitute for pecans, 11
Wedding Cakes, Polish, 118–20
wheat germ, untoasted, 158, 193
whole-wheat cookies
    Whole-Wheat and Honey Hermits,
        36–7
    Whole-Wheat Honey Wafers, 160–1
    Whole-Wheat Peanut-Butter Cookies,
        143–4
    Whole-Wheat Squares, 158–9
whole-wheat flour, straining, 37
Wienerstube Cookies, 128–9
Wild-Honey and Ginger Cookies, 161–2

A Note About the Author

Maida Heatter, author of Maida Heatter's Book of Great Desserts, is the daughter of Gabriel Heatter the radio commentator and has been cooking all her life. She studied fashion illustration at Pratt Institute and has done fashion illustrating and designing, made jewelry, and painted, but her first love has remained cooking. For eight years she prepared all the desserts for a popular Miami Beach restaurant once owned by her husband, Ralph Daniels, and has also taught cooking classes in her home and given demonstrations in department stores.

Ms. Heatter has one daughter, Toni Evins, a painter and illustrator, who did the drawings for Maida Heatter's Book of Great Desserts as well as those in the present volume.

A Note on the Type

The text of this book was set in Electra, a type face designed by William Addison Dwiggins for the Mergenthaler Linotype Company and first made available in 1935. Electra cannot be classified as either "modern" or "old-style." It is not based on any historical model, and hence does not echo any particular period or style of type design. It avoids the extreme contrast between thick and thin elements that marks most modern faces, and is without eccentricities that catch the eye and interfere with reading. In general, Electra is a simple, readable typeface that attempts to give a feeling of fluidity, power, and speed.

W. A. Dwiggins (1880–1956) began an association with the Mergenthaler Linotype Company in 1929 and over the next twenty-seven years designed a number of book types which include the Metro series, Electra, Caledonia, Eldorado, and Falcon.

Composed by American Book–Stratford Press, Saddle Brook, New Jersey. Printed and bound by The Haddon Craftsmen, Scranton, Pennsylvania. Typography and binding design by Virginia Tan.